SECRET REVOLUTION

MEMOIRS OF A SPY BOSS

Niël Barnard
as told to Tobie Wiese

Tafelberg

Tafelberg
An imprint of NB Publishers,
a division of Media24 Boeke (Pty) Ltd
40 Heerengracht, Cape Town
www.tafelberg.com
© Niël Barnard (2015)
Photo of Nelson Mandela on cover © Graeme Williams/ South Photographs / Africa
Media Online

Cover design: Michiel Botha
Book design: Cheymaxim
Translation: Bridget Theron
Editing: Angela Voges
Proofreading: Linde Dietrich
Index: George Claassen

Printed and bound by Paarl Media Paarl, 15 Jan van Riebeeck Drive,
Paarl, South Africa
First edition, first impression 2015
Second impression 2015

ISBN: 978-0-624-06617-0
Epub: 978-0-624-06618-7
Mobi: 978-0-624-06619-4

To the unknown intelligence men and women who dedicated their lives to their fellow man selflessly and without acknowledgement.

CONTENTS

FOREWORD

One of the most dramatic events of the late twentieth century was the intense struggle that raged for control of the South African state. Alongside the fall of the Berlin Wall it was the one event that captured the attention of people throughout the world.

PW Botha and Nelson Mandela were the leading actors in a titanic duel – the one in the most powerful position in the country and the other in jail. Botha and Mandela were both experienced politicians who, in their own ways, were prepared to put everything at stake for the cause for which each stood. What brought them together was the knowledge that in the long term no stability was possible in South Africa without the agreement of the other party.

The balance of power was difficult to gauge: the African National Congress (ANC) had the advantage of time, numbers and the unique leadership of Mandela; the National Party (NP) government had virtually all the instruments of power at its disposal, but it did not have legitimacy. Increasingly, uncertainty arose among NP leaders about whether they had the moral right to rule the country by excluding the majority of the population.

In 1979 Botha appointed Dr Niël Barnard, at the time a young Free State lecturer without any experience in the intelligence world, as head of the Department of National Security, later renamed the National Intelligence Service (NIS). This book tells the story of how Barnard and the people of NIS succeeded in providing a unique service to the South African state. In time, they made a crucial contribution by persuading the government to accept the idea of a negotiated settlement. We shall never know if Botha, had he retained his health, would have committed himself to negotiations with the ANC without any preconditions. Increasingly it appeared that the settlement process was the logical outcome of the discussions held with Mandela while he was in prison.

NIS gained its position of power by providing Botha with information and interpretations that were of far better quality than those collected by the police and the defence force. It was NIS and Barnard personally who, by the end of the 1980s, had made Botha realise that the oppression of black South Africans was indefensible in the long term and that Mandela would not accept a conditional release or the proverbial half-loaf as settlement.

This gripping book is not a conventional autobiography. It is Barnard's story as related to the top journalist Tobie Wiese. Wiese has the gift of immediately drawing the reader into the tale and holding the reader's attention throughout. In my view this works far better than an autobiography in which a ghost writer pays homage to the subject. Barnard and Wiese, with the support of Annie Olivier from Tafelberg Publishers, have succeeded in making the narrative come across as a discussion between old friends gathered around the campfire.

The book does not try to flatter Barnard, but brings an image to the fore of a man with a complex character: at times stubborn, short-tempered and anything but diplomatic, but also dedicated, responsible, involved, straight-talking and honourable. In the course of the book it becomes clear why Botha, who could not tolerate any evasive tricks or glib talk, began to listen to Barnard on the key decisions he had to make.

It was not only a matter of persuading Botha that the time of white supremacy was over. NIS also had to persuade the heads of several African states to put pressure on the ANC to abandon its futile plan to overthrow the government; spies from other countries who crossed the line had to be called to order or sent out of the country; and NIS had to interact with the intelligence services of other countries to keep in touch with the rapidly changing course of international politics.

But the most important task was to persuade Botha to meet Mandela and lay the foundation for formal negotiations. Simultaneously, Mandela had to be convinced to co-operate so that his eventual release and that of his closest comrades did not threaten state security.

Barnard and his colleagues could play their interpretative and espionage role to such good effect thanks to a wise decision by the government not to give the intelligence service any executive powers. In other words, there were no NIS operatives who, as was the case in the CIA, could eliminate enemies of the state. This meant that it was unnecessary for anyone from NIS to seek amnesty from the Truth and Reconciliation Commission (TRC). The book also corrects the crass misapprehension that plans to kill enemies of the state were discussed in meetings of the State Security Council, a statutory body. In fact, Barnard suggested that the Council's minutes be made public.

Most of the publications that have been written about the troubled 1980s are very disappointing. This is probably because the struggle for control of the state was not carried out in a conventional manner, but largely through the medium of propaganda. In this regard the ANC could rely on excellent advice from Moscow and could thereby steal a march on the government. Increasingly journalists, academics and other opinion-makers regarded the struggle as one in which the ANC enjoyed the moral high ground and the Botha government was the villain of the peace.

This book goes beyond the propaganda of the time and highlights the complexity of the political conflict in South Africa and the process followed to release Mandela.

Secret Revolution: Memoirs of a Spy Boss is a deeply human story. Like no other book this work evokes an understanding of how the main figures sometimes had to wrestle with impossible choices. It sketches a moving account of the discussions – there were just under 50 of them – that Barnard and the government team conducted with Mandela in jail. It throws light on Mandela as a person and on his political outlook at that time. The relationship that developed between Barnard and Mandela was of such a nature that Mandela later invited Barnard to walk out of prison with him.

But even more striking than the definitive image rendered of Mandela is the picture that is sketched of PW Botha as leader. These days he is unfairly portrayed as a churlish politician who rode roughshod over people and, because of his short-sightedness, bedevilled all chances of a political settlement. *Secret Revolution* makes it clear why it was necessary that a strong leader such as Botha was at the helm in the 1980s. Without the stable political platform that was in place in the late 1980s the political settlement that was eventually reached would have been practically impossible. Botha's leadership and the role of the security forces were crucial.

It was not just about Botha making it very clear to the ANC leaders that their organisation could never overthrow the state militarily, but also about the way in which he kept the security forces under control. The number of political deaths in South Africa as a proportion of the total population between 1980 and 1994 was the lowest of all the large ethnic struggles of the last half of the twentieth century. For this one should not only thank the top leadership of the ANC in exile, but also Botha and the heads of the security forces in particular. A glance at the devastation that government forces have recently wreaked in a country such as Syria illustrates this point poignantly.

Inevitably there were individual members of the security forces who were guilty of gross human rights violations. The TRC and the media made sure that no one could ever forget or ignore this, but along the way the bigger picture has been lost. It is necessary to point out that the security forces and Botha as head of state are the unsung heroes of the relatively peaceful demise of white minority rule. For this, the National Intelligence Service and Niël Barnard personally deserve recognition.

Secret Revolution is among the best books on the political conflict in the 1980s. The most prominent personalities are illuminated more accurately and in sharper focus in these pages than in any other book I have come across. It makes an extremely important contribution to a better understanding of one of the most troubled eras in South African history.

Hermann Giliomee
Stellenbosch

ONE DAY IN THE 1980s

It's sometime in 1986 and I am reporting to the president on the latest events and developments. Parts of the country are in flames and are rapidly becoming ungovernable.

PW is despondent, which is most unusual for him.

'Things are getting out of hand,' he says. 'Louis le Grange[1] says the police have everything under control but we all know this is not true. We are in deep trouble. I don't know what we should do.'

He sits quietly for a long time, staring out of the window.

'Doctor, you know what I think ...? I think we must be *hardegat*. If we go under, we go under *hardegat*.'

But that would not be necessary. There was another, far better option.

CHAPTER 2

'THE PRIME MINISTER WANTS TO SEE YOU'

On the steps of the Union Buildings a policeman barred my way. 'Who are you and what are you doing here?'

'My name is Barnard and I'm here for an appointment with the prime minister.' He gave me a strange look. 'I don't have a letter with me now, but I have to be here.'

At the western wing I climbed the stairs. It was October 1979, just three years after the bloody Soweto uprising, but there were no obvious security measures.

What I didn't want to show the policeman was that I found the situation almost as strange as he did. My only snippet of information was a communication – almost an order – from Kobie Coetsee, Deputy Minister of Defence and National Security, that PW Botha wanted to see me. That was all.

Could the request perhaps have something to do with the four months of academic research on nuclear strategy that I had just completed in America? Was I perhaps in trouble about that? Why, I wondered, had the briefcase with all my research findings and documents been lost mysteriously on the flight home, only to turn up innocently two weeks later in Bloemfontein?

A long, dark corridor with heavy wooden doors on either side stretched ahead of me. Underfoot was the typical civil service flooring of the time: brown linoleum carpets that were beginning to unravel here and there with all the foot traffic. As I walked I peered into a few open doors. Behind desks piled high with files were officials who appeared to be engrossed in their work.

In the reception area of the prime minister's office there was neither a middle-aged secretary with the aura of a strict headmistress nor an attractive young woman. Instead, there was a brisk and straight-backed man in a spotless white navy uniform: Commander Ters Ehlers. This struck me as rather strange, emitting as it did a decidedly military signal.

A short while later, when I was ushered into the prime minister's office, Botha rose and walked over to greet me with a friendly handshake. *Despite his public image as an unapproachable man, here, nevertheless, is Boer respectability and hospitality,* I thought to myself.

This was our first meeting. At that time, as in all the years thereafter, he was immaculately dressed.

Behind his desk were two imposing grey marble pillars. There were no papers or documents lying around. On the desk beside him was a framed photograph of the Botha couple and their five children. Against some of the walls were books arranged inneat rows.

The office was steeped in gravitas and orderly authority. This made an indelible impression on me. The four telephones on the desk struck me.

One of them was attached to an enormous device covered with knobs and cables. Although I knew very little about the workings of the espionage world, I knew from books and articles that on the desks of the presidents of America and the Soviet Union, for example, there was usually a red phone. If you had this number, you could reach the highest authority in the land.

I had also read about scrambling devices and had gathered that these phones were connected to one. Such a device ensured that nobody listening in on the line could follow what was being said. The listener would hear only a rustle, or nothing at all.

The conversation was short and to the point. 'I'll tell you what I want,' said Botha. 'There is a state department called National Security, the old Bureau for State Security. It does intelligence work. I want to appoint you as head of that department.

'There is no need to give me an answer now. If you accept, we will make the necessary arrangements for your transfer from the university. You will initially be appointed as the chief deputy secretary for a period of six months so you can settle in.

'I want your answer within a week. Remember, this is an absolutely confidential meeting.'

He also asked if I understood what was involved.

'Yes, sir,' I replied, not understanding very much at all – but what else could I say?

The conversation lasted for just over five minutes. Before I knew it I was out again, stunned and full of questions. It had all happened so quickly and was so unexpected that I had not even asked what the work entailed.

Back in my car, still dazed, I pulled off in the wrong gear and drove into the wall in front of me. I tried to console myself with the thought that I had only just acquired this second-hand Mercedes 230 and was not yet fully accustomed to its gears.

The visit to the Union Buildings was supposed to be a break in our family's journey: we were en route from Bloemfontein for a short holiday in the Kruger National Park. In Pretoria we stayed with my ex-student Daan Opperman and his wife Thea.

Back at the Oppermans I called my wife, Engela, to our room and told her about PW Botha's offer. She did not share my pent-up excitement. 'Where are they coming from with this? We are both far too young and inexperienced for something like this. I think you must say no.' Young we most certainly were – we were hardly 30 years of age at the time.

I phoned my father in whom I had the utmost trust, even though the matter was very sensitive. 'My child, I don't really know what to say. Give the matter some serious thought and do what you think is best. But don't let a good opportunity pass you by,' was his advice.

The next day I also went to visit Chris Swanepoel, who was with the SABC in Johannesburg. At the University of the Orange Free State he was a colleague and professor of music. We had met and become friends through the Afrikaner Broederbond[1] and the Ruiterwag,[2] of which I was a member, and I had a great deal of respect for his judgement.

He first poured us each a glass of wine and then asked me about the offer. I only had a few scanty details to share with him and also told him about Engela's objections. Eventually he said, 'Well, I know you and I think you must take this opportunity. But you go now and let me first talk to Engela.'

But he, too, failed to make any significant headway with Engela.

The next day, the Barnards – our boys Nico and Hannes were then five and three years old – made our way to the game reserve, where I struggled hard to fix my attention on the animals and birds and the boys' determined search for lion and elephant.

We had only been at the Satara rest camp for a day and a half when the police came to say there was a telephone call for me at the office.

'Dr Barnard, it's Ters Ehlers. The prime minister says you owe him an answer within two days, but it can't be delayed any longer. The press has ferreted out the story and you must let Mr Botha know almost immediately what your answer is.'

Amidst all the excitement and, admittedly, a tinge of anxiety,

I realised that whatever this offer might or might not entail, this urgent call from the highest political office in the country could only mean one thing: National Security was a place where important – possibly even destiny-defining – things happened. And here I was being handed the opportunity to make a contribution.

I phoned Chris Swanepoel and asked again for his opinion. He stood by his advice of a few days before. And Engela stood by hers, to put it euphemistically. 'It's a leap too far for us. I am frightened of this unknown situation. They are going to break you,' was her concern.

'But it's a wonderful opportunity to render a service to my fatherland,' I rebuked her. 'And as you well know, issues of security and wars and strategy are what keep my head busy.'

Then, as I often did in the years that followed when crucial decisions were involved, I followed my head and the feeling in the pit of my stomach. 'You may tell the prime minister that I accept the offer,' I informed Ehlers.

'Doctor, you must come immediately,' he said. 'Things are in turmoil.'

We packed up immediately and drove to Johannesburg. The atmosphere in the car was anything but cheerful.

The next day I was back at the Union Buildings in my suit and tie, making my way down the long passage with the brown linoleum carpet. It was the second of hundreds of visits I was destined to make in the years that followed. At the prime minister's office I duly signed a form accepting the appointment, still without any facts about what the post – its remuneration, advantages or dangers – entailed.

One could call it an act of faith.

'Thank you very much, I will talk to you later,' was PW Botha's clipped reaction.

That a youngster from academe who presumably knew nothing at all about espionage and such things had suddenly been made the country's new spy boss was a feast for the media. They set to work, speculating wildly about me with very few facts at their disposal.

'*Koppe skud oor ons James Bond*' (Heads shake over our James Bond) was *Rapport*'s huge front-page headline, while the *Rand Daily Mail* had supposedly discovered that the new spy boss was in favour of the atom bomb: 'New DONS chief backs the Bomb'.[3]

I tried to avoid the press – by no means one of my favourite institutions – for as long as possible. However, six months later, when I became head of the service on 1 June 1980, some of my senior colleagues did indeed persuade me to hold a press conference the following day. 'So they can see you don't come from Mars and the dust can settle,' they reasoned.

On my first day as head of National Security, my path crossed with that of the ANC, in a manner of speaking.

In the early hours of Sunday 1 June, limpet mines exploded at Sasol 1 in Sasolburg. Eight giant petrol tanks burned for days and caused damage to the value of about R66 million. From the point of view of the saboteurs the simultaneous attack on Sasol 2 at Secunda was less successful. A limpet mine also exploded there but did not cause a fire.

Oliver Tambo, at the time the president of the exiled ANC in Lusaka, claimed responsibility for the attacks. In the most dramatic way possible, these acts of sabotage confirmed my conviction that the ANC was South Africa's foremost enemy.

At the press conference the next day I had to answer questions about this attack, the ongoing school boycotts and other burning issues. Some of my remarks were presumably experienced by certain newspapers as *verlig* (politically enlightened); as a result I featured in a *Beeld* cartoon[4] with Naas Botha, who had just become captain of the Blue Bulls, as one of two 'new brooms' that were 'sweeping clean'. *Beeld* could not resist the fact that both of our initials were NB, cunningly adding that we were both '*Nog Bloedjonk*' (still youngbloods). For another newspaper, my greatest sins were my facial expression (apparently I did not smile) and the fact that I refused to speak English at the news conference.[5]

Perhaps my mother's remark to me in my childhood years that English was the 'language of the conqueror' had something to do with my refusal to speak it, but the real reason was that living in South West Africa (now Namibia) and also in the Free State I heard so little English that my pronunciation was poor – why would I go out of my way to make this painfully obvious to the world?

Although I disliked speaking to the media – later in my life, even more so – the press conference did help somewhat to clear the mist surrounding this seemingly mysterious being from the Free State.

I grew up in a home and environment in which the goal of making money was never spoken about. Both of my parents were teachers; in my family, serving others was a leading imperative, something to be done with pride.

Our descent and the family's history were also important frameworks for how we saw ourselves and our purpose in life. Our progenitor – I am the ninth generation after him – was Johannes Bernhardt, a soldier by profession who originated from Cologne in Germany and who, after a short period in England, made his home at the Cape. Here, he married a Dutch woman, Saartjie Strand, but a few local women apparently also played a role in his life.

My grandparents, like many other white people after the devastating drought of 1933/34, moved from Kenhardt and Carnarvon to South West Africa when my father – Nicolaas (Nico) Evehardus – was a young child. His father passed away on the journey and my dad practically grew up as an orphan with his mother, the granny I never knew.

We were often told of how difficult it was for them. It made a lasting impression on us as children that they had seen setbacks and difficult circumstances as challenges and were able to overcome them.

After matriculating in 1939 from Hoërskool Windhoek, my father studied simultaneously at the Bloemfontein Teachers' Training College and the Grey University College; within three years he had been awarded a teacher's diploma and a BA degree. Back in South West, he took a teaching post at a small settlement with the dismal name of Tranendal, on the outskirts of the Kalahari, not far from Keetmanshoop. There was no school building, just a few tents, but before long he and some of the local farmers had built two classrooms and the school had begun running a small farm with sheep and vegetables to provide the children with food.

In a neighbouring school at Gaidus, Magdalena Catharina (Daleen) Beukes[6] began her teaching career after receiving a qualification from the Teachers' College in Wellington. My father wasted no time in making her acquaintance, and in the wartime year of 1944 she became Mrs Barnard. She subsequently gave birth to four sons, of whom I was the second eldest.

We were fully aware that our parents had grown up in a pioneering environment; they were themselves pioneers who had elevated themselves and helped to tame a vast country. From them, I learnt that nothing significant can be achieved without a strong will and determination.

For the first three years of my life we lived in the small town of Otavi, north of Otjiwarongo. Another three years later my father, who was a natural leader, became headmaster of the primary school at Otjiwarongo at a young age. Later he was appointed as a school inspector; later still, as chief inspector of education in South West Africa.

It was very important to our parents' generation for their children to become well educated, even learned, so that – unlike their parents – they would not feel inferior to their English-speaking counterparts. At Kakamas, where my mother grew up, the people harboured bitter memories of the Anglo-Boer War. Their teachers taught, 'You do not speak English. It is the language of the conqueror.'

At Otjiwarongo my father often attended the regular small discussion groups that debated matters of a political-cultural nature. One such issue was transferring the church bank account from Standard Bank to Volkskas. According to my father, good Afrikaners had an obligation to bank at Volkskas. He was a member of the Broederbond but was a very balanced individual, also about being an Afrikaner. Nevertheless, there was no doubt about our identity. We were Afrikaners who set great store by values such as respect for authority, discipline, honesty, punctuality and good manners (particularly at the table). We imbibed a love of the Afrikaans language, and of Afrikaner culture and history with our mother's milk.

As a child one had to learn to be independent very early. Farm children were dropped off alone at the school hostel at the tender age of six because their parents lived on farms as far away as 400 km from Otjiwarongo.

At school and in the hostel, as in the home environment, there were standards; there was order, discipline: bells rang when it was time to rise and shine; more bells rang at mealtimes and when it was time to study; there were daily inspections of your shoes, your bedside cupboard and bed with its coir mattress; there were prayer meetings, Voortrekkers (an Afrikaner youth movement similar to the Boy Scouts and Girl Guides) and traditional folk games and dancing. We walked in single file to school, and for anything that looked the least bit like a serious transgression the cane was brought out.

All those who were in positions of authority were respected; their word was law. We knew exactly what was acceptable and what not.

For me, as was the case for most young boys at the time, guns and military things had a certain fascination. In cadets we learnt to drill with .303 rifles, marching in shoes we 'spit and polished' until they shone. In our imagination we were courageous soldiers who would, one day, go to fight in faraway wars.

Hunting and fishing were a natural part of every boy's upbringing. Boys didn't play the piano because that's what sissies did, but I did, indeed, learn to play the piano and chose tennis above rugby.

With rifles and hunting one went through certain phases, almost as in the church. You began with an airgun and spent days lying near water troughs shooting Namaqua sandgrouse. Then you progressed to a .22 and targeted larger birds – later, even small game. At the age of sixteen I shot my first kudu, then moved on to springbok, gemsbok (Cape oryx gazella), eland; years later, I shot two buffalo.

My compulsory military service was in the commando system[7] where I reached the rank of captain. In Bloemfontein I also joined the Citizen Force and regularly undertook periods of service in this capacity.

This meant that when I crossed swords with the heavyweights of the military shortly after my arrival at National Security, I had a reasonably good understanding of their way of thinking.

The inspirational idea that one could serve one's fellow citizens and one's country through education made teaching the obvious career for me. In 1968 I began my studies at the University of the Orange Free State (today the University of the Free State) with a merit bursary from the South West Africa administration. From an early age I had a keen interest in history and the world around me. However, my teaching bursary demanded that both of my major subjects had to be those taught in schools. Luckily my father was able to persuade the education department that I could take political science as a major along with history.

An honours degree and an MA[8] followed my BA degree; I completed my MA in 1972. By this time I was already a temporary lecturer in political science. I then embarked on a doctorate,[9] which I completed two and a half years later. I was a diligent student, but my life was not only about studying.

In the June holidays of my first year I went with my older brother, Leo, by train to Keetmanshoop. On the same train were Leo's roommate and his sister: an attractive, lively young teaching student by the name of Engela Brand. It was not long before we discovered that we had been in the same class in Standard 3 at Otjiwarongo before the Brands moved to Keetmanshoop.

On the train we began to make eyes at each other, during the holiday she cut my hair and, the next thing I knew, the die was cast. Right from the start I found Engela attractive on all levels. Like my mother, she is by nature a joyous and spontaneous person. She lives on the sunny side of life. Her mother was not an Italian for nothing!

At the end of our third year (1970) we became engaged at Hentiesbaai. Two years later, on 1 April 1972, our marriage was solemnised.

When I went to university I was fully prepared, like Engela, to pursue a career as a teacher when I finished my studies, but secretly I nurtured greater dreams. These were not yet crystallised but I hoped that one day I would be able to serve my country in a wider context.

Naturally, politics, which is closely linked to political science and history, also interested me, and on campus I became involved in student politics. I was elected to the student council but shortly afterwards began to lecture and could no longer serve officially on the council. During my student years it was at the back of my mind to become a politician, but academically I was making such rapid progress – at 27 I was promoted to professor – that an academic post also became a viable career option.

That is, until PW Botha's offer came completely out of the blue at 30 years of age and catapulted my life in a totally different direction.

After serving for a number of years at National Security and its successor, the National Intelligence Service (NIS), I was asked more than once to enter politics. The Bloemfontein West branch of the National Party asked me to make myself available for election against Kobie Coetsee; similarly, the Nationalists at Potchefstroom suggested that I stand in opposition to Louis le Grange.

But by that time I had already experienced the satisfaction of NIS's early successes and had also realised that a career in politics was not for me. Politics does not suit my personality. I am inclined to be on the dour side, am disinclined to kiss strangers' babies and have no desire to impress others. In addition, I have a strong streak of individualism – Engela has a less flattering word for this – that rebels against having to report regularly to others and trying to remain in their good books.

In the heady days after the prime minister's offer, I surmised that the intelligence service was a place where one could make a fundamental difference – perhaps even more so than in politics. This was exactly what happened.

Chapter 3

INITIATION AND DISILLUSIONMENT

The drab, grey Concilium building, with its obscure entrance next to the small Skinner Street post office in Pretoria, was not a particularly friendly structure. Its exterior was, however, a reasonably accurate indication of what went on inside; the spy world is indeed a harsh and unapproachable environment.

I entered the Concilium on Monday 3 December 1979 as chief deputy secretary at the Department of National Security (DONS), but everyone knew that if everything went according to plan, within six months I would become the new head of the department. This had been provided for in the prime minister's public announcement two weeks before.

As I walked along the passages and through countless security doors that day, office doors ahead and behind me opened and closed discreetly. I imagined I could hear whispers of sympathy (or was it surprise?).

Most of my colleagues believed – some probably hoped – that matters would not go according to plan. How could a *haas* (the nickname policemen at National Security gave to an academically minded person or someone they viewed as liberal)[1] – one scarcely dry behind the ears, at that – come and tell us old seasoned men how things should be done? An academic, on top of that! What could someone who sits in an ivory tower know about the tough life of spies on the ground?

My colleagues' conniving about my company car was a good illustration of their take on the situation. As an ordinary professor

I earned a relatively meagre salary in Bloemfontein, but here I was informed that one of my fringe benefits would be a swanky motor-car – a Mercedes-Benz 280SE, no less. So, one day the man from the transport section informed me: 'Doctor, we have received your car.'

I arrived to find a Mercedes 230, but I made no comment, having guessed what they had said to one another: 'This *manne-tjie* (little man) is not going to last very long. We mustn't give him too expensive a car, otherwise the state will lose too much.' But I would prove them wrong in the end – I worked and thrived at the National Intelligence Service for twelve years.

From my very first day I would walk into the offices of the department's employees across the country and ask them what their work involved. My aim was to ascertain what was happening at ground level and what was supposed to be happening. I found a significant number of proverbial racehorses who had the potential to win the Durban July but who were overweight, some never exercised and others had no suitable jockey in the saddle.

The intelligence service of any country should be an elite organisation but most of the personnel were unmotivated and inefficient; their work was of a low standard. Thus, although this was a group of very capable people (with the exception of some in the overseas offices), organisationally the place was in relative chaos and the personnel were poorly managed.

One reason for the low level of morale was the link between the department's predecessor, the Bureau for State Security (BOSS), and the information scandal (also called Muldergate). The head of BOSS – in effect, my predecessor, General 'Langhendrik' van den Bergh – was deeply involved in the scandal.[2] It had its origin in 1973 when the prime minister, Advocate John Vorster, accepted the suggestions made by Dr Connie Mulder, Minister of Information at the time, to use R64 million from the defence budget to launch a number of clandestine propaganda projects locally and overseas. Van den Bergh was one of Vorster's confidants; the scandal eventually claimed both of their heads, as well as Mulder's.

Another of the remnants of that time was the ongoing power struggle between the various departments that collected security information. And the walls have ears: everyone knew all too well that as a result of the scandal and the bureaucratic power struggle, National Security's continued existence in its form at the time was in jeopardy. As a result, I inherited quite a few challenges from Van den Bergh – as well as his peculiar desk. An extraordinary little steel weight and a concealed magnet had been installed beneath the desktop. When the general wanted to record a discussion, he apparently shifted the weight over the magnet, casually activating the tape recorder. In the adjoining room were massive tapes of all these discussions, still waiting to be transcribed.

I immediately had all of these things removed. After all, you can't work with people if you do not trust them.

Van den Bergh nevertheless commanded enormous loyalty, even if this was perhaps through fear. When I arrived at the department's offices in other centres, his portrait often stared down from the walls. I let them have their way because South Africa was not the Soviet Union where Leonid Brezhnev's photo would hang on the wall one day, only to be replaced by Yuri Andropov's the next.

Some of the general's former colleagues in the Bureau whom I encountered were exceptionally capable people, such as Mike Louw, Gert Rothmann, George Grewar and others; they have the sharpest brains that I have ever come across. No doubt some of them also said to themselves that this *haas* would not make the grade.

To a certain extent they had a point: my knowledge of intelligence services was, at that stage, most likely amateurish and academic in nature. But I did know enough to realise that the black telephone in the prime minister's office was our equivalent of the American president's red phone.

At least I was very much aware that I didn't know everything. During my first six months of 'initiation', therefore, I was very busy indeed with in-service training. This gave me the opportunity to identify the assets and liabilities at National Security so that I could determine where the trouble spots were, who were dragging their feet and how the organisation's potential could be extended and better utilised.

Thanks to my academic background I was acutely aware that South Africa, like any other country, needed a reliable intelligence capability to identify security threats timeously. On my arrival, the department's information reports were of a poor standard. There was also no comprehensive system of reporting.

I was thus immediately confronted by two challenges. The department had to be organisationally overhauled and better managed so that it could deliver a better intelligence product. In order to do this, the personnel had to be motivated and proud of their work. They had to have confidence in the new captain of the ship. This would not happen on its own; the captain would have to evoke and inspire confidence.

Only if these things happened would we meet the other challenge: to fend off the attack against the department that came, ironically enough, from colleagues in the intelligence community who should have been our allies.

In the process I had to make a few difficult decisions and even had to replace certain personnel in key positions. One of these was the important post of deputy secretary. I would be out of the city – and the country – on a regular basis. At these times, in terms of the law, the deputy secretary had to act as head of the service.

The obvious claimant was Gert Rothmann, a brilliant but difficult man and an individualist. He deserved the promotion, but it was important that the iron grip that the operational policemen had on the service be broken.

I agonised a great deal before making the decision to pass him over. In the end this proved to be a temporary arrangement: a few years later, Rothmann received the promotion he deserved.

Cor Bekker, who also came from Van den Bergh's days but not from the police force, was appointed as the new deputy secretary – a calculated slap in the face of the strong-arm tactics of the old guard. It was a clear signal to everyone that the era of 'blood and thunder' was over; instead of our fists, we had to start using our heads.

What softened the blow somewhat was that Bekker was not the next best candidate. Far from it. He was a lecturer at the Heidelberg Teachers' Training College and when the Bureau was looking for a researcher, a senior member persuaded Van den Bergh to appoint Bekker. He had thus also come in from the outside as a *haas*.

Bekker is a man with gravitas and a strong personality. His appearance and bearing are those of a classic jovial and somewhat robust farmer, but don't let that mislead you. He is a progressive thinker who, as time went by, came to play a significant role in making me think along the lines of a new and strategic solution for the country's political problems.

A few things counted in my favour in the process of whipping the department into shape. I was highly motivated. My knowledge of political science also made me realise that at this time in particular the department could play a critical role in the country's history. I enjoy being near the fire, there where things are happening, and having the opportunity to make a positive contribution. Working behind the scenes with as much freedom as possible and making a difference there has always been more important to me than sitting at the front of the stage but having achieved nothing significant on leaving that stage.

Furthermore, I have a natural ability to manage an organisation and to take the lead. Even if I say so myself, I am a bloody good chairperson. I make decisions, timely decisions, see to it that they are carried out, and I function well under pressure.

An advantage that I had over many of my new colleagues was that policemen don't like to write. They want to run around outside, catching crooks and criminals and sorting them out. They don't like to evaluate events and information and compile reports about such matters – that's for pen-pushers. My academic propensity for analysing things, viewing them from all sides and putting the result down in writing, gave me a distinct advantage.

The tough but beautiful nature of the place of my birth taught me an important lesson that has stayed with me all my life: if you give up and lie down, you are dead. So, from early on, I imbibed a large dose of determination. The flipside of this is that I have very little sympathy for people who give up too easily.

Popularity has never been important to me. I abhor having to sit and listen to people who spew out rubbish, especially when they think they have discovered eternal truths which the whole world then has to hear about. As Engela readily confirms, I suffer from an unhealthy dose of stubbornness. If I believe I have a good point to make on a matter of importance, I refuse to be derailed by anyone.

In short, the work and the unique circumstances of the intelligence service fitted my personality like a glove.

Throughout the years I have been asked many times: 'Why did

PW Botha appoint you, a young academic with no experience of bureaucratic management, in such a sensitive post? Public administration was not even your field of study.'

My honest answer: I don't know. I never asked him.

Of course, I had my suspicions. PW was close friends with Alwyn Schlebusch, the Free State leader of the National Party. He was one of very few members of the Cabinet who had the courage to stand up to Botha when he felt it was necessary. In the election for the premier's position in 1978, Schlebusch made sure that the decisive Free State vote went in favour of PW (and not to Dr Connie Mulder, the Transvaal NP leader). Perhaps afterwards PW felt he owed the Free State something.

Schlebusch and I became acquainted when I was the resident lecturer in the Karee hostel at what was then the University of the Orange Free State. He was concerned about his son who was in one of the other hostels and asked me to keep an eye on him.

Another consideration for Botha, possibly the most likely, was the unfortunate recent history of the security services. He and General Van den Bergh had no time for each other.

Not only did Botha – who had committed himself from the first day of his premiership to clean administration – want to erase the legacy of the information scandal, he possibly also wanted to clip the wings of the intelligence service to prevent further wrangling.

So, he initially acted from the viewpoint that the new service should fulfil a downscaled, research-oriented role that would include the interpretation of security information. It would make sense to appoint an academic as the head of such a department. The operational acquisition of information – in other words, carrying out covert spying – was the exclusive function of Military

Intelligence. He believed the old feud between the civil national intelligence service and the South African Defence Force over their respective territories would thereby also be resolved.

PW more than likely realised how stubborn and difficult the old guard of former policemen, whose careers would be threatened by this plan, would be. He probably said to himself: 'Let's do this in phases. And why should I have to do it? Let's use Barnard to neutralise this thing.'

But as is often the case in history, irony had the final say – the opposite of what Botha foresaw came to pass.

The wrangling to demarcate the various domains of South Africa's intelligence services and to synchronise their activities had been a long haul.

From 1963, the need for a central intelligence organisation in South Africa came increasingly to the fore. As far back as 1947, the South African Police (SAP) sent a delegation to Britain to study the Special Branch in London. The outcome was the founding of the security branch of the SAP whose main task was to collect and process information.

In the 1960s, the prime minister at the time, John Vorster, formed a Cabinet committee for defence, with himself as chairperson.[3] This committee decided that a central intelligence organisation should be set up and tasked with collecting information for the police and the military. It was also decided that General Van den Bergh, who was on the point of being named as the new Commissioner of Police, would become the first head of this new intelligence service and would report directly to the prime minister.

On 1 May 1969, the new Bureau for State Security began to function. South Africa had acquired its own central and civil intelligence service. The key concepts – 'central' (or national) and 'civil' – were of primary importance because they were based on the following points of departure: the threat to the state was not only domestic and military in nature; it was also from outside the country and non-military in nature. Furthermore, the 'central' character of the service implied that the overarching threat against the state had to be investigated in its totality.

What was not said was equally important: the service had no executive power and did not carry out any operations.

In terms of a government notice it was laid down that the functions of the new Bureau would be to 'investigate all matters affecting the security of the state, to correlate and evaluate all information collected and to inform and advise the government thereon ...'[4]

PW Botha (Minister of Defence at the time) was not in favour of the defence force relying on the Bureau for its information requirements, however. This presumably had a great deal to do with Botha's lack of confidence in Van den Bergh and the way he treated him.[5] For Botha and the senior leadership of the defence force, Van den Bergh was a fly in the ointment, but they had to put up with him because he was the prime minister's anointed one.

Problems between the Bureau for State Security and the rest of the intelligence community worsened quickly. Indeed, the acrimony between the Bureau, the defence force's Directorate of Military Intelligence (MI), the police service's security branch and, on occasion, the Department of Foreign Affairs, sometimes reached epic proportions.

When Botha became prime minister in 1978, he forced the Bureau and MI to work together by, among other things, placing them in the same office block – the Alphen building, next to the Concilium. He thought that if he scaled down the responsibilities of the Bureau enough and transformed it into a research institute with very little clout, the power struggle would become a thing of the past.

His plan had roughly the opposite effect. General Fritz Loots, a capable soldier for whom Botha had a high regard, was at this stage the head of MI, but Van den Bergh treated him like an upstart. They did not greet each other and even refused to use the same lift.

Nor did it end there. At night MI planted monitoring devices in Van den Bergh's office to find out what he was up to and, in turn, Bureau people spied on MI to check whether they were entering all their information on the central database!

Their childish behaviour was laughable but for those involved it was deadly serious, because behind it lay the question: Who controls the information the prime minister receives? And who, then, holds the power?

In an attempt to rescue the situation, Vorster appointed HJJ Potgieter, a prominent appeal judge, as head of a commission with wide-ranging instructions to advise whether the security structures in South Africa were functioning effectively; and to make recommendations for improvement. Judge Potgieter made important recommendations that led, among other things, to the establishment of the State Security Council (SSC). Key issues, such as who was charged with covertly collecting information inside the country and who was responsible for doing so outside South Africa's borders, were also decided.

The commission was strongly in favour of the centralisation of intelligence and provided good insight into the nature and potency of such information. Among other points he made, the judge said (translated): 'I do not wish to dismiss the possibility that a single body that is charged with maintaining state security from the information point of view may in itself pose a threat to state security.' The commission felt that constitutional remedies should be sufficient to prevent the misuse of intelligence.

After my appointment it became clear to me that the name 'National Security' was not a true reflection of the department's terrain and responsibilities. It was, after all, an intelligence or espionage service and did not provide security in the ordinary sense of the word. We did not carry weapons, wear uniforms or make war, and were not out to catch criminals.

The security we strove for was security made possible through accessing information, insight and knowledge. *Scientia Munit* (knowledge protects) was the old Bureau's motto on its heraldic coat of arms. For everyday use I popularised my own version: 'Those who know, win'.

Until about the time of World War II (1939-1945), gathering intelligence was regarded as a wartime activity; intelligence was essentially military information that was necessary to wage war. But after WWII the realisation dawned that the security threat against the state was not exclusively military in nature. The notion of a 'national' or 'civil' service came to the fore, an overarching service that studied all aspects and tried to prevent developments that threatened the security of the state. This in turn gave rise to the concept of 'total onslaught'. However, due to tradition and the unique role played by the military in defence of the state, most countries have retained the practice of having a separate military intelligence facility.

In South Africa's case, which differs sharply from, for example, the American set-up, the ('civil/national') intelligence service has no power of execution; it may not take action based on the information it accumulates and processes. I believe very strongly in this principle and have adhered to it throughout my career. We did not act like the CIA, storming into distant countries with Special Forces members, shooting people and trying to set up a new dispensation.

Taking everything into account, and after many debates, we settled on the name National Intelligence Service (NIS) because it was the most accurate reflection of the essence and aspirations of the department.

Engela tells the priceless story of how one day at the pharmacy, the shop assistant insisted that she provide information on the medical fund to which the Barnards belonged and where her husband was employed.

'At National Intelligence,' whispered Engela discreetly.

'Oh, wonderful!' came the answer.

'We have been looking so long for a place where we could have the children's IQ tested.'

The report of the Potgieter Commission and the legislation it inspired did not, however, bring an end to the squabbles and destructive competition in the intelligence community.

On the same day that I began my service, the Coetsee Commission met for the last time. Kobie Coetsee, at the time the Deputy Minister of Defence and National Security, had been appointed by the prime minister as chairperson of a commission to investigate, yet again, the intelligence framework in South Africa and to delineate the fields of the various roleplayers.[6]

The principle of a central intelligence service was approved but, despite a great deal of intense debate, no agreement could be reached on the responsibilities of each roleplayer.

In the years that followed, on many occasions I became aware that officials' apparent stubbornness in bureaucratic infighting was often the result of ministers who put the fear of death into them if they made any concessions. In particular, Lieutenant General PW van der Westhuizen of Military Intelligence and Major General Johann Coetzee of the police secretly tried their best to wring National Security's neck. Apparently they hoped this would extend the powers of the military and the police.

The Coetsee Commission was unable to reach consensus on the core issue of demarcating the intelligence terrain and, without formally disbanding, it simply ceased to function. It did, however, make one significant recommendation: that in the light of the need for timely and uninterrupted information the prime minister should be provided with a daily information report (*informasie-rapport* or 'Inforap'). All the intelligence parties were required to contribute to this report.

This was certainly a useful and practical suggestion but, in the climate of disunity and ill-feeling, was it attainable?

In the interests of the country, the critical question – which intelligence tasks should be entrusted to whom? – had to be answered as quickly as possible.

Furthermore, it was not PW Botha's management style to let a wound fester. His order to us in the second half of 1980 was, more or less, 'I am sick and tired of your squabbling. The country cannot afford to let this continue. Get together somewhere and sort the matter out. And don't come back until you have drawn up a plan that you are all reasonably happy with.'[7]

An ideological–strategic confrontation 'to the death' among the country's spies was unavoidable.

CHAPTER 4

THE BATTLE OF SIMON'S TOWN

With exemplary hospitality I was offered the main bedroom in the South African Navy's imposing Admiralty House in Simon's Town. The place had an old-world atmosphere that reminded one of the days of Lord Nelson and the Battle of Trafalgar in 1805. The heavy carpets, the oil paintings of bygone naval battles and heroes and the dark wood panelling somehow seemed to say, 'Look at everything that has gone before you. You are by no means the first to sail on these waters.'

I accepted the offer of the elegant bedroom graciously, but was not so naïve as to think that this hospitality was without significance. The room was no doubt fitted out from top to bottom with monitoring devices.

Yes – we all shared a common goal: to serve our country by collecting reliable information.

But no – there was not any consensus yet as to how this should be done, which of us was best equipped to do what, and how the collected information should be interpreted.

The 'us' were the top people of four contending state departments: the National Intelligence Service (NIS); the South African Defence Force (specifically its Military Intelligence division); the South African Police (more particularly its security branch); and, to a lesser extent, the Department of Foreign Affairs.[1]

Especially for us from NIS and for the men of MI, there was an enormous amount at stake. That was why the generals and brigadiers tried to listen in to what was being discussed in my room, but we were no fools and held our deliberations under the trees, beside the sea.

There was a great deal more at stake than the matter of who could collect the information that the state required most efficiently. The critical and complex question was: What did that information *mean*? How it should be interpreted was closely connected to ideological–strategic considerations, about which there was no agreement. The military representatives were convinced that they had the final answers to these questions and that, for this reason, they should have the last word.

For me, virtually everything was at stake. In any event, that is how I experienced the 'Battle of Simon's Town'. Needless to say, my colleagues watched me closely to see if I was able to stand firm and hold my own when the proverbial pirates divided the booty.

What I realised without a shadow of doubt was that if NIS was emasculated here, it would be the end of my short-lived career in the service of the state. Our ideal was to be the country's national intelligence service, not merely a research institute that could not rely on its own information. 'If you lose this fight, everyone will say you couldn't make the grade,' I said to myself. For this reason it became, in a manner of speaking, a matter of life and death for me.

At the back of my mind was also the firm conviction that I could not rely on anyone for political support or protection. Although the prime minister had appointed me, and although he was a very loyal person, he wouldn't mind one jot if NIS was downscaled to an insignificant little group of analysts. Indeed, he would probably quite enjoy it because then the legacy of his old enemy, Hendrik van den Bergh, would fade and the turf war with the defence force and the police would end.

A small advantage we had over our colleagues (in the broadest sense of the word) was that I was the chairperson of the deliberations: in terms of rank, I was the most senior official. The chairmanship was the one thing that was not open to debate. This meant that our department provided the secretariat and saw to it that all the proceedings were accurately minuted.

If I may put modesty aside: I have the ability to gauge people's train of thought very quickly and am often able to put this into words better than they are able to themselves. In Simon's Town this helped us to reach clarity fairly quickly on the standpoint of the various parties.

With me were André Knoetze, head of NIS's administration, and Dr Cobus Scholtz of our legal department, who was the secretary for the Simon's Town consultations. I would have liked to have had the extremely capable Gert Rothmann with us, but he is a man who speaks out quickly and does not mince his words; his presence would probably have fuelled the fire.

In the South African Defence Force's (SADF) corner was Lieutenant General PW van der Westhuizen, head of MI, an unimpressive individual who was described by Chester Crocker, America's Assistant Secretary of State for African Affairs, as PW Botha's 'rat catcher'.[2] As far as national strategic insight was concerned, Van der Westhuizen had very little to speak of; furthermore, he often failed to keep his word. We gave him the nickname *Vuil Uil* ('rascal', loosely translated). Nevertheless, the SADF had a formidable negotiating team, which meant that we had to rise before cockcrow to prepare for each day's discussions.

In the South African Police's (SAP) corner was Major General Johann Coetzee, head of the security branch, a sharp-witted but slippery character with one brown eye and one blue eye, which for me was symbolic of his dealings. He was obsessed with appearing scholarly and constantly used Latin quotations. He aspired, at all costs, to become the Commissioner of Police, which did, indeed, happen later, but his ultimate dream, of which he made no secret, was to become Minister of Police. Unlike Van der Westhuizen, Coetzee did not have capable aides in his corner at Simon's Town.

The presence of the Department of Foreign Affairs was primarily symbolic. The shrewd Pik Botha was too opportunist to be drawn into the power struggle in the intelligence community; as for Dr Brand Fourie, director-general of the department, he was too much of a gentleman to become involved in such matters.[3]

The SADF's good-natured but capable Lieutenant General André van Deventer, who had been seconded to the office of the prime minister, was also there. He was obviously PW Botha's spy at Simon's Town.

By the 1980s, two clearly distinguishable schools of thought concerning the security and political situation in the country had crystallised. This polarisation was also evident at Simon's Town.

On the one side was the group to which the SADF and the police gravitated. This group believed strongly that the country's only problem was the influence of communists, embodied by the Soviet Union. Members of this group saw an ominous threat in Russian support to independent African states in which Marxist governments had come to power. The SADF and police believed that the communists' ultimate goal was to take over South Africa.

Their answer to this threat was a long-term military strategy in which South Africa would create a buffer zone on its northern border of states under its control, in which friendly governments would be placed and assisted. With this in mind, South Africa would support resistance movements such as Unita in Angola, Renamo in Mozambique and, from time to time, certain rebellious groups in Zambia and Zimbabwe.

Brigadier John Huyser, head of staff planning in the SADF,

propounded this strategy, which became the military establishment's standard response to the political and revolutionary onslaught against the country. According to this doctrine South Africa did not need to engage in a military struggle on its own territory, but would do so in the so-called buffer zones on our borders.[4] Huyser went so far as to include Zimbabwe and Zambia in this plan: I attended lectures in which he explained that even Tanzania should come under South Africa's control – indeed, the entire African continent south of the equator.

In this way Huyser's visions became part of the SADF's *voorste verdedigingstrategie* (forward defence strategy). In Simon's Town we were lectured on this ad nauseam, but unconvincingly.

There was another, more sinister, element to the SADF's strategy. Because of the arms boycott against South Africa, the country developed its own massive weapons industry with the help of Armscor. Over time it became necessary to feed exaggerated information about the military threat from neighbouring states to the political leadership in order to justify Armscor's ambitious programme of weaponry development. If necessary, information had to be fabricated to help 'friendly' rebel groups (such as Renamo and Unita) to carry out revolutionary 'liberation wars' in nearby states.

The other school of thought, in which NIS took the leading role, was that the shadow-boxing in the country's neighbouring states was simply a bluff. In reality, it was a military answer to a political problem.[5]

At NIS we were convinced that the SADF's strategy was not based on sound information. The reliable and objectively judged information we had at our disposal told us that South Africa's survival was not primarily linked to wars against communists on the country's borders. Instead, it was first and foremost concerned with having to find an answer to the country's internal political problems. The bald fact was that at the time, the government's reaction to the onslaught against the country was unacceptable to the majority of South Africans, and we were never going to persuade the black majority of the validity of this particular answer.

To be completely honest, at the time of the Battle of Simon's Town this conviction was still in its embryonic stage, as far as both my own awareness and that of NIS were concerned. Among us there was not yet general consensus about this, but one thing was certain: to find the most appropriate answer to the country's political problems, the best possible information was vitally important.

And who was going to collect and interpret this crucial information, which would most probably determine the political course of the country?

This was the driving force behind the intense war of words that was waged in the five days at Simon's Town. The reason for this was simple: knowledge is power and power is the oxygen of politics, and politics is the vehicle through which a country determines its future.

For hour after hour, the weighty arguments that had been used over the previous months on various platforms were reiterated. Van der Westhuizen of MI and Coetzee of the police were obviously hand in glove. In what they thought was a subtle manner they tried their utmost to bring NIS down.

As far as institutional memory was concerned, NIS had nothing to fall back on. In the days of our predecessor, the Bureau for State Security, a police culture had clearly prevailed, which meant the first impulse was to beat problems into submission. Wherever there were rumblings of war, General Van den Bergh was inevitably nearby. I spoke to him a few times and it was clear that talks and negotiations between opposing parties did not interest him very much.

However, he did promote John Vorster's attempts at détente with other African states.

Meanwhile, we knew that Simon's Town would determine NIS's fate.

If we lost the function of collecting information outside the country – which is what the SADF wanted – the SADF would only relay the kind of information that suited its agenda to the politicians. If we were forced to forgo the collection of information inside the country – which is what the police hoped for – this would also portend disaster, the police's idea of addressing a problem being to shoot and bludgeon whatever stood in their way.

But at the same time, it occurred to me that it was unrealistic to expect that we would get our own way in every respect.

Our only firm footing was the Potgieter Report, which had recommended the establishment of a central and national intelligence service. Because Judge Potgieter had recognised the danger associated with a single intelligence institution, Act No. 64 of 1972 – passed as a result of his report – made provision for this possibility in a controversial paragraph which read that Military Intelligence could collect information 'with the knowledge and consent' of the Bureau for State Security.

For the SADF this was like a red rag to a bull. By law, they had to ask our approval to operate outside the country's borders and had to inform us about what they were doing there. But, of course, legislation can be amended, and Magnus Malan, the Minister of Defence, had great influence with PW Botha. Everyone knew this.

I knew in my heart of hearts that if we were to have any kind of co-operation, we would have to forget about this particular stipulation in the law. It was out of the question that the hard-boiled staffers of MI were going to accept that clause.

One of the reasons why my later negotiations with Nelson Mandela and with others were relatively successful was because intelligence work had perhaps made it easier for me to put myself in the shoes of my opponent. I always ask myself: 'If I were that man or that woman, what would I have done?' Even if I am only fifty per cent correct in my assessment, I am able to plan a counter-move. Somewhere in the middle we will have to findone another.

With this in mind, we made two critical concessions at Simon's Town. First, I told the SADF: You don't have to have our 'knowledge and consent' for intelligence work in other countries. You can collect what is called 'conventional military information'.

I explained this to them more or less as follows: 'It is a weakness in the Potgieter Report to have recommended that the National Intelligence Service should provide information to the military about the enemy's activities outside South Africa's borders. On occasion, operations by your Special Forces go wrong and innocent women and children are killed. On top of that NIS would then be accused of providing inaccurate information. This being so, we gladly hand over this duty to you.'

Van der Westhuizen and his military die-hards found this acceptable.

The other issue was that the police wanted to keep us out of the domestic intelligence field because in their view we were softies who were looking for a political solution for the total onslaught. But realistically speaking, how could we – who had offices and personnel in Pretoria, Cape Town, Port Elizabeth, East London, Kimberley, Bloemfontein, Durban, Richards Bay, Johannesburg and Pietersburg – now be told to stay out of local issues? This was unthinkable.

We therefore made a concession to the police: 'We understand the close connection between internal and external threats. The

ANC does not make any distinction between the two. Information on the one is directly linked to information on the other. Similarly, we cannot separate the two.

'We suggest that you handle domestic security information. Within our borders we will collect *staatkundige inligting* (information concerning governance)'.

Coetzee said that he understood the difference and agreed. (We did not point out that the meaning of the term '*staatkundig*', is as wide as the grace of God. And what exactly is 'conventional military information'? Sometimes there are a few advantages to being a *haas*!)

Gradually, as far as all the important issues were concerned, reason began to triumph over emotion. From the thousands of words and reams of paper, in time a fundamental agreement came to the fore. It diverged in certain respects from the Potgieter Report and its accompanying legislation, but it placed South Africa on a new intelligence path. The key aspects were as follows:

• The provision of intelligence products would be the joint responsibility of all the intelligence institutions. It would be co-ordinated by the security planning branch, which fell under the office of the prime minister.
• The overt (open) acquisition of security information would be the separate responsibility of each intelligence institution, but attempts would be made to avoid duplication and unnecessary expenditure.
• The National Intelligence Service (NIS) accepted primary responsibility for the covert (secret) acquisition of 'govermental' information inside the country.
• The NIS also accepted primary responsibility for the covert collection of non-military security information outside the borders of South Africa.

- The security branch of the SAP would be responsible for the covert acquisition of non-govermental (*niestaatkundige*) security information inside the country.
- The SADF, through Military Intelligence (MI), would be primarily responsible for the covert collection of military information inside the country as well as beyond South Africa's borders.
- Foreign Affairs would only deal with overt diplomatic information which would be coordinated with the activities of the intelligence community.
- A co-ordinating body for the management of security information had to be set up. This soon became known as the Co-ordinating Intelligence Committee (CIC, or 'KIK' in Afrikaans) which operated under me as chairperson, and played a useful role in co-ordinating information from the various intelligence arms.[6]

This agreement meant nobody left Simon's Town empty-handed. The SADF and police had not succeeded in turning the NIS into a mere research institute, but to their great joy we had conceded that our function as the dominant national intelligence service had been watered down. However, this was certainly not what happened in practice.

Most countries do not have a single service that carries out both domestic and foreign intelligence work. Western states usually have a foreign service, such as the American CIA, the British MI6 and the German Bundesnachrichtendienst (BND), that spies on potential foreign enemies. The task of domestic counter-espionage services such as the American FBI, the British MI5 and the German Bundesamt Für Verfassungsschutz (BFV) is to curb spying by other countries on their own soil and to counter local groups that act unconstitutionally. This approach is based on the false assumption that enemies of the state are always based outside a country's borders.

However, because South Africa's security threats came from within the country as well as beyond its borders, an organisational separation of these services would have catastrophic consequences. In such circumstances espionage had to be managed from one central point. In any event, no spy would be prepared to hand over the details of sources – who have often been cultivated and fostered over a lifetime – on a tray to competing colleagues at the country's borders.

Simon's Town was a landmark for me, and not only because the onslaught against NIS had been averted. Far more important was the fact that from then onwards NIS had the opportunity, through the quality of its people and their work, to prove itself and show its mettle.

What stood me in good stead there was my being a good listener – perhaps precisely because this was not always apparent – and the faculty of strategic judgement. Although I had only been at NIS for a few months, I realised that even in the world of spying negativity would bring only limited success. We already had a positive vision: for the immediate future to ensure the survival of the service and then to have a two- or three-year period in the medium term during which the service would be re-organised and fine-tuned.

From the elegant comfort of Admiralty House in Simon's Town we returned to the grey corridors of the Concilium building in Pretoria. I delivered a report to my colleagues on what had happened in the Cape. The three of us were well satisfied with what we had achieved there, but were greeted coldly by the old diehard policemen. I explained how things had developed, that if we had maintained a hardball attitude we might well have lost the battle, and how we had ensured the provisional survival of the service.

However, as with the Israelites of old, there was a murmuring among the crowd because I had compromised on the 'knowledge and consent' stipulation in the law. We should have wiped the floor with the military and police immediately, they said.

'Look, I can understand that some of you may think the concession is unacceptable, but I don't give a fig. What you presumably don't realise is that we are in a struggle for survival. This was the best we could do for now,' I told them.

'This agreement on paper doesn't really mean a great deal and it is not included in any law. The question is this: Can we provide the prime minister with better information than they (the military and police) do? And anyway, I don't really care if you collect so-called *niestaatkundige inligting* (non-governmental information) inside the country. If it's better than what the police provide, nobody is going to ask whether we have collected it in terms of the Simon's Town agreement.

'The question is: Who will put the best information on the table? This is our challenge. This will ensure our survival.'

The agreement at Simon's Town did not mark the beginning of a thousand-year truce in the intelligence community. Nobody really expected that it would. Nevertheless, the way some individuals tried to distort the terms of the agreement amazed me.

A few days after the deliberations when our little team, feeling relatively pleased with ourselves, arrived at the prime minister's office in Cape Town, a most unpleasant surprise awaited us.

Van der Westhuizen, the very same *Vuil Uil*, nonchalantly handed out a document of a page and a half in which he systematically negated the agreement that had been reached over the five days in Simon's Town and placed the same old SADF viewpoints on the table once again.[7] As if no agreement had been reached! Not a word was mentioned of the delineation of NIS's working terrain as had been agreed upon.

'NIS (will) be responsible for political information,' it read – a category that had never, at any stage, been discussed.

Botha and Ministers Magnus Malan (Defence), Pik Botha (Foreign Affairs) and Louis le Grange (Law and Order) listened attentively to Van der Westhuizen. In fact, the document said the following: 'This new division of functions implies that the national information service (sic) cannot continue to exist in its present form; in essence it will not be a national information service.'

My anger almost boiled over at this dishonourable and untruthful action by the head of Military Intelligence but I managed to control my temper. Happily, this underhand manoeuvre failed when Botha later decided that the actual and well-documented Simon's Town agreement had to be implemented.

I suspect that Botha understood the dilemma all too well, as is expressed in the phrase: Who will guard the guardians? Or, put differently: Who will keep a watchful eye on the spies?

While he was fed up with the infighting between the various intelligence roleplayers, Botha realised that a healthy measure of overlap had certain advantages. In this way a situation whereby one institution distorted, exaggerated or withheld information could be prevented. Needless to say, after this incident Van der Westhuizen's word was never trusted again in any negotiations. Magnus Malan could also not be completely exonerated for this attempted disregard of the Simon's Town agreement.

Van der Westhuizen did not, however, stop with his tricks. Five months after the Battle of Simon's Town, in June 1981, MI tabled a document entitled (translated) 'Functional Division of Responsibilities of the Intelligence Community' at the co-ordinating committee. A further attempt was made to undermine the role of NIS, this time by claiming that all of the intelligence institutions would be placed on an equal footing.

The SADF simply would not accept that their escapades in Africa could be trumped by other organisations supplying better information. They still clung to the delirious dream that South Africa's problems were caused exclusively by the actions of communists in our neighbouring states. While this was indeed an issue, it was by no means the core of the problem.

On 22 June 1981 Van der Westhuizen and MI were foiled again when the prime minister and the relevant ministers finally accepted the Simon's Town recommendations. The time for talking was over; the same applied to us at National Intelligence.

CHAPTER 5

OPERATION CLEAN UP

With Simon's Town and the post-mortem that followed it behind us, we at NIS set to work with a sometimes unfettered enthusiasm and fervour. This was no less than was required, because there were mountains to move.

We created a regular, effective and streamlined management mechanism to organise the service. Weekly and monthly programmes with specific, measurable targets were set; each morning the management team met and the research people gave a report on the past 24 hours' events and the information they had collected about them. There would be a discussion after which it was decided who would do what, what the timeframe would be, and so on. This happened every day of the week and was a totally new experience for the staff.

Once a week I met with the four chief directors. Sensitive projects, including financial and staff affairs, were discussed.

A matter which immediately received urgent attention was the upgrading of the information reports which, upon my arrival, with all due respect, were an inferior product. Despite the recommendations of the Coetsee Commission there was still no proper system of reporting.

This was apparently because exciting operational work – that is, espionage – was still the focus; the policemen who were largely the founding members of the intelligence service considered the analysis of information and the writing of reports as work for pen-pushers.

Research and the evaluation of security information remains, unfortunately, the Cinderella of careers in the intelligence profession. Evidently it is not imbued with the same romanticism and does not provide the surge of adrenalin experienced when attending secret meetings, pursuing foreign spies or planting monitoring devices. And yet reliably interpreted information is the basic aim of allespionage activity.

I took the view that any secret service worth its salt should deliver intelligence reports almost daily. 'It is of no use that you tell me about the wonderful sources you have recruited and the valuable information you have intercepted. It must be put down on paper (in those days) so that we are able to pass it on to someone,' I said repeatedly.

Their response was to refer me to the so-called National Intelligence Assessment. It ran to hundreds of pages and appeared once a year!

By the end of the 1970s it was the department's *only* information piece: a comprehensive evaluation of the governmental and political realities of the state, with predictions about future developments. It sometimes ran to as many as four volumes. According to one account, a certain year's volumes were later found in the cellar of the HF Verwoerd building in Cape Town – still unopened. On another occasion the annual review was discovered months after it had been despatched to Cape Town, in a storeroom at the airport, also untouched.

My implacable rule was that this review – for any intelligence service the standard bearer of its research ability – would, in future, be no longer than 120 pages. Soon it appeared twice a year; it had to be as fresh and relevantas possible.

Good intelligence services throughout the world receive a massive stream of information minute to minute, hour to hour, day in and day out. What will perhaps surprise many people is that

80 per cent of this information comes from open sources such as the news media, social media and the internet, and is available to everyone. The remaining 20 per cent comes from covert sources and is sometimes collected under life-threatening circumstances. This is the critical information that constitutes the missing pieces of the jigsaw puzzle.[1]

This, then, is also – in the intelligence context – the difference between an academic and an intelligence researcher, for example. The latter has at his or her disposal the secret information that complements the open, publicly available information, and which frequently also contradicts the publicly available information or places it in an entirely different light. This gives the researcher the opportunity to form a more complete, accurate and truthful rendition, or to come as close to this as humanly possible.

Added to this, the researcher must have the ability to think strategically and to gain a 360-degree view of an issue, institution or individual. What crosses his or her desk is all of the wheat – the grains of truth and insight must still be separated from the chaff by skilled, experienced people using appropriate methods. For intelligence services, only then does information become intelligence.

Interpreted security information must meet a number of critical criteria including, among others: it must be as close as possible to the truth; it must be timely; it must be formulated and communicated concisely and comprehensively; and it must be objective and truthful without pandering to the recipient's political sentiments. Those working in the intelligence service must have the courage of their convictions to communicate their conclusions without fear or favour.

No head of state or government should have to base decisions on raw, unevaluated information. For this reason the timely, impartial and, most importantly, skilled assessment of information is imperative.

With this in mind, NIS developed a new product, at which Mike Louw proved masterful. The *Nasionale Intelligensieflitse en -sketse* (NIFS, news flashes and sketches on national intelligence) provided brief daily reports and in-depth analysis of the most recent security information. With that we were immediately in the loop. Suddenly everyone at NIS understood that the litmus test for an intelligence service was what it produced on a daily basis in the form of security information for decision-making.

The items of intelligence news and sketches were in the first place for the attention of the head of state; I reported directly to him and the service was accountable to him. In time we also compiled information reports for the attention of specific ministers and departments on developments and facts we felt they should know about.

Fresh, up-to-date security information that leads to timely decisions calls for open and effective channels of communication between an intelligence service and the political decision-makers. Clogged liaison channels and offhand, nonchalant decision-makers are a nightmare. It is not for nothing that so-called hotlines and special telephones grace the desks of heads of state. As long as they are manned and answered!

A challenge for intelligence services worldwide is to ensure that political decision-makers actually read – and preferably study – the information on which millions has been spent and which has often been procured at great risk. It is said that precisely for this reason the American CIA included snippets of news of a sexual nature in its reports to President Lyndon Johnson.

At NIS we were less banal. A ruse we came up with was to send unprocessed telephone reports and intercepted, transcribed conversations to the prime minister, and sometimes also to individual ministers. Coming straight from the horse's mouth, these were read with great interest. I am told that PW sometimes even interrupted meetings to read these reports.

The fact that people world wide were becoming increasingly visually literate also did not escape our attention. By the end of the 1980s we began recording our information on video tapes accompanied by appropriate visual material, and these tapes were then used at information sessions. For this purpose special staff, usually attractive women, were selected and trained as information readers.

Later we also devised the trick of creating reports exclusively for a specific recipient who had asked for information about particular organisations or individuals or who, in our view, needed to be made aware of this information. This was always highly sensitive information from covert sources. Its incorrect use could lead to the source's cover being blown. Therefore the gravity of the matter always had to be communicated. Such documents were trimmed in red and there was an instruction that they had to be shredded after use.

However, sometimes we had the ridiculous and disconcerting situation where certain ministers used their secretarial staff to highlight parts of these reports for their attention – those parts the secretaries deemed important!

Over the years we established that personal information sessions were still the best way to relay information. These took place formally during meetings or individually during personal encounters. In this manner the particular information requirements of the various ministers could be gauged more effectively.

The universal problem in this regard is that politicians are loath to listen. They would far rather talk. Often one had to muster up the grace to listen with tact and patience while ministers tried to impress world-class experts with their superficial knowledge about a particular issue.

A practice in which I believed strongly was that the person who was the most knowledgeable about a particular matter should be the one to write or inform others about it. From the outset I made it clear that although I was the head of the service I was, for example, not going to be responsible for all presentations to the State Security Council.

'We use the man who knows the most, even is he is a junior,' I informed my colleagues. Naturally, I was always there to extend a helping hand because my colleagues were sought-after targets for ministers who may have had their knives into us. (We'd made peace at Simon's Town, not fallen in love!)

Through this high-level exposure we contributed to the development of a corps of capable people. For them, particularly the younger ones, it was extremely satisfying that some of their work and expertise was recognised at the highest level of government.

Good researchers are an indispensable asset for any intelligence service. At NIS we also did everything possible to identify the researchers' abilities and to improve their level of knowledge and skills. In the eyes of the operational spies I committed sacrilege when, after some time, I placed researchers in offices outside the country such as New York, Washington, London, Dublin, Paris, Munich, Rome, Vienna and Harare. In this way, an initial interpretative filter was built into the system that could separate the wheat from the chaff at the early stage, making the final interpretation at head office so much easier.

This meant that researchers could emerge from their caves and develop what the Germans call a *Fingerspitzengefühl* by experiencing their theatre of responsibilities with their own eyes and ears. Of course, they also experienced first-hand that there is a far greater world out there. Apart from the knowledge they gained in this way, they also gained the self-confidence they needed to talk with authority when they were confronted by the politicians' know-it-all attitude ('When I was last there ...').

In the process of making the NIS the state's leading intelligence partner, the service produced many legends. These were exceptionally gifted men and women who did not hesitate – politely but with conviction – to indicate to me, or members of the Cabinet, our flawed reasoning or misinterpretation of information.

Even the formidable Dr Gerrit Viljoen, while serving as administrator general of South West Africa, bumped heads with a young but talented researcher whose strategic analysis of Swapo did not agree with Viljoen's. However, the researcher fearlessly adhered to the facts and his interpretation of them, to the extent that Viljoen later complained informally that 'that young fellow is far too full of himself'.

Like all scientists, researchers in the world of espionage must have an open and honourable intellectual disposition. He or she must be open enough to be convinced by new facts, for example that radical adaptations in a country's political dispensation have become necessary, and must allow himself or herself to be led by sober truth and not by hot-blooded arguments. The fact is that the interpreted truth about security information can never be reconciled with party politics and ideological crusades when the facts are forced into preconceived frameworks.[2]

Intelligence services that strive for popularity with their political bosses do the state a major disservice. To go to all the trouble and expense to glean the necessary information, to interpret it as accurately as possible but then withhold its full implications from those in power or water it down so it becomes insignificant is plain stupid.

When the emperor wears no clothes, he should know it. After all, this is in his – and even more importantly, the country's – best interest. It was sometimes my duty to bring home this uncomfortable truth.

Intelligence research must also, of course, predict the prospects for the future security of the state as accurately as possible. This is often necessarily speculative and risky. However, it is far better to make a decision now about an urgent matter, even if it is only 60 per cent correct but it can avert or prevent a security threat, than to make a call tomorrow that is 100 per cent correct but comes too late for one to do anything about the situation.

One safeguard against the risks inherent in predictions – one which is unfortunately used too seldom – is penetrating interaction with other knowledgeable people and academics. Differences of opinion ought to be debated in detail and if strong disparity remains, decision-makers should be given the advantage of hearing opposing viewpoints. Sadly, this worthwhile practice is never popular with politicians.

It is known that certain intelligence services such as the CIA make use of so-called A-team and B-team researchers. The instruction to the A team is the customary 'make the best possible analysis using the information and insights at your disposal'.

The instruction to the B team is to shoot the A team's interpretation to shreds on the basis of good information while maintaining their integrity. The point is that within an intelligence service there must be the opportunity and ability to test and debate various interpretations. The reasoning behind this is that the best researchers, indeed even an entire intelligence service, may develop tunnel vision on a set of circumstances.

Were tunnel vision and similar tendencies perhaps one of the causes of the catastrophic American invasion of Iraq in 2003? Or was the Bush administration sold down the river by the meagre information and vacillating interpretations of its intelligence agencies? The Americans are still arguing about what really happened.[3] It is thus imperative to devise all kinds of ways to wrench oneself and one's researchers out of their comfort zone.

Espionage is an exceptional and unique profession. Needless to say, it has its own training requirements. Because of the exclusive nature of espionage and the necessity of maintaining secrecy, one cannot simply contract a team of professional consultants to train intelligence workers. Spies have to be trained by spies.

Operational trade secrets, in particular, can only be taught to new recruits by experienced old hands and this training happens not in lecture halls but in the numerous operational theatres of the profession – which are often on the other side of the railway tracks. These theatres extend from the White House to President Kenneth Kaunda's private game park in the Luangwa National Park in Zambia, from the Pigalle in Paris to the Copacabana in Rio de Janeiro and to small hamlets in Africa.

In October 1985 a world-class establishment – the National Intelligence Academy (NIA) – was opened at the service's 'farm' called Rietvlei, outside Pretoria. Here top-level training was provided and courses were offered to friendly intelligence services from African countries. Also, no one was appointed at NIS without undergoing a full range of psychological tests.

One day PW Botha asked me whether his daughter Rozanne could come to work for us. 'That's fine,' I replied, 'but nobody gets a job at NIS without first undergoing psychological tests.'

Although she was the prime minister's daughter, as far as I was concerned she had to be treated in exactly the same way as all the other applicants.

However, that was the last we heard of it. We never received an application from her.

From the outset I realised that a technological renewal of NIS's capacity was needed. The very latest computer technology was acquired and the technology department upgraded to a fully fledged chief directorate on the same level as other chief directorates: collection, research and administration. André Knoetze became the first chief director and did trailblazing work. The outstanding George Grewar succeeded him and, in time, took our technological capacity to an even higher level.

At Rietvlei they developed a unique interception capability known as Valkoog ('hawk's eye'), which made it possible for us to intercept satellite communication throughout the world – even though our focus was on Africa. This meant that when Thabo Mbeki contacted the ANC headquarters in Lusaka from London, we intercepted the conversations since they usually contained valuable information. However, because the interceptions provided unwieldy volumes of information, other aids also had to be used, such as voice and number recognition devices and the occurrence of selected key words.

The coming of the internet and super-intelligence technology offered espionage services exciting possibilities about which they had previously only dreamt. Interpreted information could now be provided immediately to the prime minister, members of the Cabinet or State Security Council. When I first arrived at NIS, the technology department's main task was monitoring telephones and intercepting post, especially letters. Today, the focus is on intercepting e-mail, which is far quicker and easier.

NIS also saw to its own cryptology: protecting its own communication systems and breaking into or disrupting those of its intelligence targets (in our words, the enemy). As early as 1981, a section at NIS was charged with the study of crypto-analysis. Staff in this department used a powerful computer that was responsible for deciphering and breaking into the ANC's communication networks. The system of secret codes used by well-known anti-apartheid figure Bram Fischer and navy spy Dieter Gerhardt was deciphered by NIS and our predecessors; this made a critical contribution to convicting both of these men.

NIS's counter-espionage department was also extended, which was responsible for much excitement and many significant achievements. South Africa's strategic importance and its key role in Africa led to a comprehensive espionage assault – ideological enemies such as the Russian KGB and the Stasi of East Germany, but also the Americans, British, Germans and French, were very active in political espionage.

The Americans, in particular, launched a large-scale attempt to find out more about South Africa's nuclear weapons capability.[4] It was most likely the Americans who had intercepted my briefcase of documents in 1979 on my way back to Bloemfontein after my research on nuclear armaments strategy in Washington.

NIS also played a leading role in extending the defensive side of counter-espionage – implementing security measures and protecting the state's security interests. It remains an ongoing struggle to safeguard the state's confidential information, especially because no value can be placed on its importance.

To sensitise people about this, sometimes our Takkraal team (a *takkraal* is a *zareba* or protective enclosure made of thorny branches or bushes) visited the offices of ministers and senior officials to photograph sensitive documents containing extremely important information that had carelessly been left lying around. A paradise for foreign spies! Our 'raids' did not make NIS very popular but they did make people more aware of the need for security in the public service.

NIS also took on the responsibility of protecting South Africa's VIPs in foreign countries. A dedicated corps was established specifically for this purpose, receiving advanced training from Mossad, the Israeli secret service, and Germany's GSG (a counter-terrorism and special operations unit). This unit was given the appropriate code name of Takkraal, harking back to early pioneer history when herds of livestock had to be protected at night from predators. Takkraal was one of NIS's few public showcases, but its professional conduct (for example, during PW Botha's European visit in 1984 and FW de Klerk's visit to America in September 1990) earned it wide recognition.

After Simon's Town, we immediately attended to the weal and woe of our employees and did all we could to make their daily lives as pleasant as possible.[5] Spies and their families often lead a lonely life. Espionage is not a career for social butterflies who like to be the centre of attention. Obviously one avoids people who ask probing questions one cannot answer truthfully, and places where – perhaps because of what people *presume* one does – one is looked at askance. This could lead to employees and their families becoming socially isolated.

Through Engela's contact with the wives of some of my colleagues, and her own experience, she made me realise that we were all family. Although I am not by nature a warm, outgoing person, I made a point of socialising with everyone – members of staff and their families – on a regular basis. With her exceptional people skills, Engela continually came up with ideas about how we could create cohesion outside the work environment.

Because the spouses (mostly women in the NIS of those years) played a very important role in our success, on occasion I allowed the women to travel overseas with their husbands so they could also experience and talk about the wider world out there. In this way, the wives became allies who understood the unique circumstances of the profession, which in turn made them willing to walk the extra mile in the interest of the country. With hindsight, it was perhaps my biggest mistake not to have realised sooner the unique contribution women could make in NIS.

In the meantime, while the stern Concilium got a friendlier face on the inside, strict rules still applied to everyone. Employees' office doors had to be locked when they left and no papers could be left out. At night, members of Takkraal moved through the building. Heaven help you if you had left a single sheet of paper on your desk!

Why was this necessary in already well-protected surroundings? For the simple reason that one of your colleagues could be a spy for the KGB, the CIA, or whichever other agency. That was how suspicious and, alas, cynical one had to be.

Considering that NIS was a state department, I followed a very liberal personnel policy. It was not important in my eyes for staff to spend a full eight hours a day in their offices. We put in so many hours of overtime that I saw no reason why people should twiddle their thumbs at the office if they had nothing to do. In those years, we worked straight through many weekends.

We also often worked through the night, but I seldom took work home. It was not unusual to go home in the early hours of the morning, have a shower, shave and enjoy a quick cup of coffee with Engela before I returned to the office. She basically raised our children on her own.

When the discussions with Nelson Mandela began in May 1988, I frequently arrived at the office at ten o' clock in the evening.

We then worked until two or three the following morning, formulating documents and so forth. The rhythm of our work was determined by the demands of the moment. Crises – and there were many – cared little about whether it was convenient for us to deal with them.

Because NIS took on numerous new challenges and fields of endeavour, the personnel had to be enlarged accordingly. In the twelve years until I vacated my post in 1992, numbers increased threefold to just under 4 000.

Before long, an efficient administration was established; the personnel were united in pursuit of a common goal and their talents were identified and unlocked. NIS was on a steady course and began firing on all of its cylinders. It had become an admirable organisation that did not require many motivational speeches; its people were self-motivated.

Within four or five years, NIS succeeded in showing the president that our information was better than that of other state institutions that also collected security information. We did not make this claim, nor was it necessary to do so. PW Botha noticed it immediately.

On what grounds could we claim that our information was better?

NIS's processing of information and its interpretation thereof with regard to the present, as well as the future, was simply superior to that of our colleagues in other state departments. Our information products were better because they were more accurate and dependable and, thus, more useful. My trust in theoretical analysis and intellectual insight was vindicated.

What is the best barometer of the trust placed in an intelligence service?

The answer lies is a counter-question: Who is called first when things go pear-shaped – such as on the night of 19 October 1986, when the plane of President Samora Machel of Mozambique crashed in South Africa two years after he had signed the Nkomati Accord?

When the head of state has to manage a crisis like this, he consults the person who he knows can think independently – the person who will be able to get him out of trouble. And believe me, politicians are often in a tight spot – when they have to get out of it, they instinctively know it's not the best time to listen to cheerleaders.

Another factor was that my colleagues and I could get to the crux of a matter succinctly. More than once Botha said in public: 'The one thing about Barnard that always impresses me is that he can say in three minutes what most of my colleagues take two hours to tell me.'

To give a practical example of how quickly and effectively NIS could work with Botha's help: an NIS director (call him X) suffered a fatal heart attack one night. He occupied a very important position and urgent decisions had to be made. The next morning I called together a small group of people whose opinions I valued and asked them who should succeed X. I listened to everyone's input and we debated the issue.

When the group had left, I decided it should be A. The chief director of personnel services prepared a letter of appointment the prime minister had to sign. I knew the Cabinet was sitting that morning but nevertheless phoned Ters Ehlers and said I had to speak urgently with the president (whose title was prime minister until 1984). Ehlers phoned me back: Botha could see me at the Union Buildings during the lunch break. When I got there, I explained what had happened and why it was urgent that the matter be resolved.

All Botha asked was: 'Where must I sign?'

I drove back and called A in; he accepted the appointment and signed the forms. At four o' clock that same afternoon everyone assembled on the eleventh floor and I informed them that A was the new director. We drank a quick toast to him (and to X, who was buried a few days later).

In 1987, with the help of a doer such as PW Botha, we were able to appoint a successor to replace a senior colleague within eighteen hours of his death. In 2014, after twenty years at the helm of the government, the ANC is still struggling to fill senior posts in the State Security Agency (SSA).

CHAPTER 6

THE ART OF ESPIONAGE

By a clever reading one can trace spying back to a divine instruction in biblical times.

In the book of Numbers[1] it is told how some 1 400 years before Christ, God instructed Moses to go into the promised land of Canaan to spy out the country prior to launching an attack. In reaction, Moses sent twelve scouts to determine Canaan's agricultural potential, to see who lived there, if they were strong or weak, few or many, and if their cities could easily be taken.

The twelve returned laden with fruit as proof of the fertility of the land and with majority and minority reports on whether an attack on the country was viable. Only one of the Israelites, Caleb, was confident that an invasion of Canaan would meet with success. Already there were divergent interpretations of the information that had been collected!

Without espionage – probably the second oldest profession after prostitution – no state can survive. Information provides knowledge which, in turn, renders foreknowledge. This puts a head of state in a position, in the widest sense of the word, to make decisions to ensure his country survives and succeeds. For any state, knowledge is therefore crucial for ensuring its sovereignty.

My colleague Mike Louw was fond of saying at instruction sessions that 'intelligence is truth well and timely told'. The core function of intelligence work is simply the collection and interpretation of information.

In accordance with legislation, state intelligence services are often permitted extraordinary freedom to collect information. This leads to many moral dilemmas. If the independence of the state is at risk, from priests to prostitutes can be roped in. And one is often amazed by how the holy and profane alike succumb to Mammon. The secretary who shares the president's four-poster bed can – if she so wishes and if it is to her advantage – gain access to secret Cabinet minutes.

Through the ages human spies have been decisive sources of information. In practice this often comes down to exploiting human frailty to acquire information. Money, power, prestige, sex, bribery, drugs, skeletons in the cupboard, and all the other weaknesses that human nature has on offer are exploited every day to collect information for the sake of the security of the state.

Ironically enough, the emphasis on human rights in a century in which demands are continually made for everything to be publicly known has made sources of information less accessible. In most societies, the state is no longer held in the highest esteem.

Technological methods have become an indispensable part of collecting information – this includes computers, cellphones, satellite communication, monitoring devices and other forms of communication interception, as well as the measuring of electromagnetic and acoustic radiation. However, technology has its limitations: it cannot (as yet) get inside a person's head to find out what information is hidden there – and it is often precisely here that the deepest, most significant secrets lie.

As the Chinese military philosopher Sun Tzu (544–496 BC) said: 'All men can see these tactics whereby I conquer, but what none can see is the strategy out of which victory is evolved.'[2]

Soon after my arrival at the old Department of National Security at the end of 1979, Alec van Wyk, then head of the department, accompanied me on an overseas tour to introduce me to our personnel abroad and my counterparts in other intelligence services, and to give me some insight into the art of liaison between spies.

In Germany Klaus Kinkel, head of the Bundesnachrichtendienst (BND), received us very cordially at Pullach, the headquarters of the German espionage service near Munich.[3]

By 1980 it could no longer have been easy for the Germans to liaise openly with South Africa. The good-natured but sometimes heated debate on the political situation in southern Africa that evening in Kinkel's private residence over a very enjoyable dinner did, at least, contribute to a better understanding of each other's position. The most important point of dispute was the country of my birth, South West Africa. In Kinkel's mind, it was still part of a bygone German colonial empire and, according to him, was being used illegally by South Africa to destabilise Angola through military incursions.

The debate soon brought home to me one of the dilemmas of 'spy diplomacy'. Important parts of Kinkel's viewpoint were correct, but surely one is obliged to defend the official policy of one's country? Or should intelligence services tell one another the truth as each sees it, and admit to their own errant ways?

Although that evening I defended the government's policy unreservedly, I quickly realised that the answer to the last question is, in fact, yes. As a state department it is, indeed, one of our unique and cardinal responsibilities. A lack of insight and experience, coupled with youthful exuberance, must serve as an excuse for my mistake at Pullach.

Our next destination was Paris, where we were the guests of the legendary French intelligence chief Alexandre de Marenches. At a splendid lunch in his office he thought it appropriate to provide this rookie with an important lesson in espionage: 'The truth is not what it seems to be.'[4]

During the meal I noticed that the French discreetly served a wine of the year of my birth – 1949. Coincidence? I doubt it. It was probably to remind me that there are older civilisations – and thus more experienced intelligence services – than the one on the southern tip of Africa.

In America, Stansfield Turner was the head of the CIA at the time and after the presidential election a fierce dispute arose over the retention of his post. Under these circumstances South Africa was certainly not one of his priorities, and our visit to the CIA headquarters in Langley, Virginia, was tentative and superficial.

Intelligence services have among the most widespread and sensitive channels of communication in the world. Their mutual relationships are a science in itself and constitute one of the pillars of a successful espionage service. As my counterpart in Singapore, Eddie Teo, put it: 'Intelligence liaison is valuable because it can be conducted quietly and is not subject to the whimsical dictates of diplomatic posturing.'[5]

Mastering this art demands great talent; lack of depth and experience can quickly lead to isolation, because spies do not keep friends who are not worth their while. The aim of interaction between intelligence services is the exchange of information which is mutually useful. This is mainly information about threats against their respective states which services can supply to each other. The terrains of interaction are specified precisely by each liaison service and are based on the precondition that they will not be to the detriment of their respective interests.

It stands to reason that services will not use very expensive covert methods of collecting information if it is not primarily in their own interest to do so. On the other hand, it usually also depends on the quid pro quo that a service receives for the information it has delivered; it may be worth the trouble to help another service because the return is high. This return may not be immediate or equivalent.

When the KGB spy Major Alexei Kozlof was captured, we had the opportunity to repay our debt of honour to the Germans, particularly for their help with training. Kozlof was arrested in January 1981 after having entered South Africa earlier under the name of Svenson with false Swedish and West German passports. He was returned to the Russians as part of an exchange deal that included eleven West German spies of the BND as well as Sapper Johan van der Mescht, who had been captured by Swapo in February 1978.

This South African gesture to the West Germans laid the foundation for future assistance, especially of a technical nature.

The focus of liaison between services falls on threats and target areas where one's own access is limited. During my time there, NIS provided high-quality information about southern Africa to numerous intelligence services in Europe, the USA, Latin America, the Middle and Far East and North Africa.

In exchange, we received information about the activities of our intelligence targets (primarily the ANC) in those parts of the world. Because the political sympathies of a number of the governments lay with the ANC, the information about this organisation which came through official channels was often very limited. This did not mean, however, that information about which the political masters had no knowledge was not frequently transferred to us surreptitiously.

Agreements about the relationships between intelligence services were sometimes very complex and differed from case to case. Normally, with the knowledge and permission of both countries, official representatives were placed under diplomatic cover in each other's embassies or consulates. They served as official liaison channels.

The rule was that the diplomatic corps of both countries should know about such an arrangement and endorse it. However, it goes without saying that this was not always done, which is why the relationship between spies and diplomats is seldom cordial.

In countries where no diplomatic relations exist, spies follow unique and distinctive liaison channels and structures. In the late 1970s and the 1980s, when NIS placed various agents in African states with the approval of the political heads of state, most of these agents operated under the cover of private business concerns. The main issue was that the cover should be credible and easy to explain by the host country. It is a core principle of the operational intelligence world that agents should never be noticeably different. It requires a great deal of resourcefulness and considerable ingenuity to create such a cover and to live in accordance with it from Togo to Malawi and from Zambia to Egypt.

For NIS, too, it was often a challenge to find the right people to be our agents in unusual and trying living conditions. There are not many shopping malls or amusement parks elsewhere in Africa.

With the current reign of terror against Western countries in particular, it is, for example, crucial that spies are able to operate unnoticed and effectively in foreign countries. They must be able to merge with the local people who live in the clay huts of Afghanistan, in remote hamlets of Africa or the dreadful slums of Calcutta, Mexico City and Lagos.

Another remark of the wise Sun Tzu is relevant here: 'As living spies we must recruit men who are intelligent but appear to be stupid; who seem to be dull but are strong in heart; men who are agile, vigorous, hardy and brave; well-versed in lowly matters and able to endure hunger, cold, filth and humiliation.'[6]

It is only in this way that spies will get access to the true aims and aspirations of the people and be able to build reliable intelligence networks. Without this, countries will lose the struggle to acquire meaningful and truthful information – the very basis of sound strategic decision-making. I often wonder how many people are still this self-sacrificing.

Liaison between intelligence services regularly takes place on an ad hoc basis. Permanent representation is certainly not a prerequisite. Through the years NIS built up hundreds of liaison relationships. Some were on a one-off basis. Others were longer lasting. On more than once occasion members of NIS, myself included, had to sit for many hours in the State House in Entebbe with its neglected, sagging furniture while waiting for an audience with President Yoweri Museveni of Uganda.

In this interaction, too, the access to intelligence services was not determined by ideological preferences and alliances, but by how good the intelligence service was: the value and reliability of its information. Services that were acutely aware of what was happening and were known to maintain confidentiality were sought-after liaison partners. It was often interesting to find out what the information you had was worth to the heads of state who needed it. At times, some countries' services did indeed have access to information but were too wary of handing it over to their political masters. It was often easier to chop off the messenger's head than to do something about his message!

The mutual understanding is that interaction takes place between professional counterparts. This means national services interact with national services, military services with military services, police services with police services, and diplomats with diplomats.

However, for the most part, one finds that liberal transgression of these rules take place by all participants.

The question is not which other spies or sources you may speak to. The fact is all kinds of spies are as keen as mustard to speak to you should you have certain information that will make the liaison imperative for them.

In the interaction between spies, however, it is taboo to plough with someone else's heifer. This means that you may not offer information you have received from another intelligence service and claim that it is your own. You would be surprised how easily you get caught out. Nothing forbids spies from using their ferreting-out techniques on other spies!

In addition, one learns very quickly who is capable of doing what. For example, when Ciskei president Lennox Sebe's notorious 'Elite Squad' began to provide important information on the CIA, it was taken with more than the usual pinch of salt.

Good spies do not work in clearly delineated compartments. How stupid it would be, for example, if NIS's representative in Zambia, during a discussion with the Zambian head of intelligence on political developments in South Africa, did not take careful note of what this person said about the numerical strength and available arms in ANC camps in Zambia. It could be our defence force generals had no liaison with their counterparts in Zambia.

Or, possibly, there was official liaison, but the head of military intelligence refused to have any contact with his South African counterpart on account of a personal aversion to him. Perhaps they did meet but, due to a lack of trust, vital information was not communicated. In such an atmosphere it is difficult to gauge what your counterpart knows and what he or she doesn't know.

When intelligence services liaise with each other, good

interpersonal relationships are crucial. Through the years NIS produced masters in the art of cultivating cordial, pleasant relations with a totally diverse range of people. Often the calibre of the relationship was based on a close knowledge of the fellow spy's strong points and weaknesses.

This is when 'cultural weapons' such as good Cape wine, matured Scotch whisky and Uganda's notorious gin (with its alcohol content of 80%!) come in handy. An oversupply of German beer has caused many a spy's vigilance to falter in the wee hours.

Who can gauge the value of Cor Bekker's jovial thump on the shoulder of his Japanese counterpart sending him tumbling to the floor of his house in Tokyo when the two men discovered they had both just become grandfathers? The slightly built Japanese luckily laughed it off and, before our visit to Japan came to an end, the two exchanged dear little outfits for their respective grandchildren.

Or what is the value in intelligence terms of the shenanigans of two NIS men who were on the banks of the Zambezi showing off in front of their Zambian colleagues by cutting off the tops of champagne bottles in the French tradition – not with swords but with penknives? No doubt, under the star-studded African sky that night NIS acquired information that would otherwise never have been remotely accessible.

THE BRITISH

Over the centuries the British have developed one of the world's best intelligence services. The famed MI6 – these days the Secret Intelligence Service (SIS) – has, in many ways, set the espionage standard.

By all indications, as far as the number of personnel is

concerned, it is a small service, but all of the members with whom I had dealings were highly professional. They were polished and astute fellows who handled anything from deception to praise, or from twisted truths to subtle threats with aplomb.

South Africa's relationship with MI6 in the days of the Bureau of State Security was a stormy one. The misuse of diplomatic cover in the 1970s resulted in formal liaison in London being prohibited. MI6's representatives in South Africa were also quarrelsome and as aloof as only a Brit can be.

The British realised early on that the liberation movements were going to play an increasingly significant role in South Africa's political future; they were thus careful not to be seen as flirting openly with 'the Boers', while merrily gathering sources in the struggle organisations. Give the devil his due. In the world of spies those who are quickest off the mark to foresee the unfolding of history are able to ensure they have the right sources at the right time in the right place.

On our continent, the British made masterful use of the sometimes over-hasty drive for independence by providing espionage training for newly developing intelligence services in African states. This was, of course, not for philanthropic reasons.

Through recruiting the best men during this training period, their agents and sources landed in positions close to the new heads of state. This was worth a hundred times more than all the large airports that were built by other former colonial powers in godforsaken places in Africa where, even today, very few aircraft land.

The British worked assiduously against South Africa's intelligence interests. For political exiles there were regular dinners in extravagant restaurants from London to Paris, the best single-malt Scotch whisky, Harris Tweed jackets, Stilton cheese, study bursaries for children and family, discreet discussions with influential people, holidays in select places frequented by the rich and famous ... In this way, many South Africans – wittingly and unwittingly – compromised themselves. The most tragic aspect of this is that in South Africa today some of them are sitting in the highest government circles – but they are vulnerable, especially to the British, who are now probably demanding their pound of flesh.

In my first testimony before the Truth and Reconciliation Commission (TRC) in 1997, I made this same point: that many senior ANC figures had, knowingly and unknowingly, provided information to intelligence services in other countries.[7] Nor was it only to the British: the Americans and Germans in particular were just as keen to know what was going on in South Africa. Indeed, Britain even wanted to step in and take control of the negotiation process in the early 1990s.

In the 1980s NIS's relations with the SIS slowly improved. We wanted to test the knowledge and insight the British had on our situation, and they were anxious to find out what was being planned for South Africa's future. Numerous meetings took place and finally we softened them up. Eventually they visited South Africa at intelligence chief level: the first visit was that of Sir Colin McColl (head of the service: 1989-1994) and thereafter the former lepers of NIS were also permitted to visit the SIS headquarters.

THE AMERICANS

South Africa's intelligence relationship with the Americans goes back a long way. Among NIS's best and sometimes senior operational members were placed in Washington to liaise with the CIA and in New York with the United Nations (UN) as their target. In fact, in the 1970s my predecessor, Alec van Wyk, had been the representative in Washington and, in co-operation with the FBI, was responsible for the unmasking of the South Africanborn spy Jennifer Miles, who was spying for Cuba.[8]

As far as raising and handling sources in America was concerned, it did not deliver a rich harvest for NIS. All our officially recognised people were watched with eagle eyes by the FBI. Before long, Pretoria instructed both offices in the USA to identify spy talent that could focus specifically on Africa. In this way, potential sources were identified who could later be recruited outside the USA.

As regards their own capability, the Americans simply did not have the same intelligence expertise about, and insight into, Africa as the Europeans, who had developed this skill thanks to their history as colonial powers. Their cultural superiority, coupled with a self-indulgent lifestyle, did not augur well for having good spies in Africa.

Their remarkable naivety and associated ignorance is perhaps best illustrated by a conversation I had in 1983 during the highly secret visit to South Africa of the enigmatic William ('Bill') Casey, head of the CIA. NIS hosted a showy dinner in the Concilium building's dining hall, which had been decked out especially for the occasion. I had the honour of sitting next to Mrs Casey. She was deeply concerned, she said, about the violence in the country and was worried about what would become of whites.

'From which country in Europe did you emigrate to South Africa?' she asked.

Initially I did not fully understand the question, but then I realised that she sincerely thought that someone with a white skin could not be born an African. I answered her as follows, 'Ma'am, I am the second son of the ninth generation of a German soldier of fortune, Johannes Bernhardt, who left Cologne in Germany in

1706 and two years later moved to the Cape and settled perma-nently in South Africa.'

With mock innocence I added, 'Do you know for how many generations the Caseys have been in America?' I am not sure whether she grasped what I was implying.

In the 1980s our interaction with the CIA continued on the highest level. After Stansfield Turner, Bill Casey appeared on the scene. He was an old fox from the days of the Office of Strategic Services (the predecessor of the CIA) and a confidant of President Ronald Reagan. He had an obsession with secret initiatives and believed with a sometimes childlike bravado that the clandestine dethroning of dictators and secret paramilitary operations against communist regimes were the main tasks of an intelligence service.[9]

In this delusion he had a faithful adherent in PW van der Westhuizen and his mates in Military Intelligence, hence the clashes between Casey and the American Department of Foreign Affairs over assistance to Jonas Savimbi's Unita movement in the Angolan civil wars, in which MI was closely involved.

However, secret military operations launched by intelligence services are seldom successful. They are time and again exposed by the media, and are usually followed by tedious commissions of inquiry in which the service concerned is publicly humili-ated. Intelligence services are very sensitive organisations whose members only perform optimally if they personally believe in what they do and are not merely carrying out orders. It is strange how a superpower that has burnt its fingers countless times with this type of action in, for example, Cuba, Chile, the old Congo and Iraq, cannot grasp this fact.[10]

The CIA will, of course, argue that they achieved a great deal of success in Afghanistan and that elsewhere in the world, especially with drone attacks, they have neutralised many terror units.[11] Naturally, tactically speaking this can lead to momentary successes, but the strategic question is: How many embittered 'terrorists' whose only aim in life is revenge against America or the West are created by every drone attack?

THE GERMANS

For years, the German intelligence service, the Bundesnachrichtendienst (BND), provided the old Bureau for State Security with considerable assistance with training as well as the protection of heads of state. NIS's relationship with the Germans took the form of many bilateral discussions and a number of visits were made from both sides. The younger members of NIS in particular benefited greatly from these. Overseas visits taught them that spies should view the world without blinkers and should always be aware of the bigger picture.

On visits to Germany as guests of the BND one had, for the most part, to put up with their Prussian precision, which could be very exhausting. One was not left in peace for a single moment. On one occasion when I implored them to leave me and Engela in peace so that we could enjoy a beer in a street café, they were astonished.

'To do that you will have to get a double to act as yourself, because our system does not make provision for such aberrations,' came the clipped answer.

We provided the Germans with information about Africa – which remained a hard nut for them to crack – in exchange for valuable information about the Eastern Bloc, particularly East Germany. Numbers of aspirant spies from the ANC were trained by the Stasi, the East German secret service that was held in great regard throughout the world.[12] Naturally, we wanted to know who was being trained there, in which areas, and so on. Bonn itself also had close links with the ANC and was terribly careful not to give us official information that would land them in hot water, politically speaking.

In the area of counter-espionage (see Chapter 7), NIS and the BND worked well together, as was evident in the inclusion of eleven West German agents in the exchange package with Kozlof. In a private room at Frankfurt's airport, Herr Ackermann of the BND and I celebrated the successful completion of the operation by singing '*Die Wacht am Rhein*' at the top of our voices.

With the fall of the Berlin Wall in November 1989 the BND started to believe that the German state no longer faced any danger. That Al Qaeda members operated from Germany as part of the attack on the World Trade Centre in New York on 11 September 2001 hopefully put paid to that false perception.

MOSSAD AND OTHERS

Intelligence services' capability and international standing are not necessarily proportional to their country's position in the international power constellations. Some of the largest powers have the weakest intelligence services while smaller countries often have the world's best services. Israel's Mossad is an example of the latter while, in my opinion, the CIA would not win many gold medals in an intelligence olympiad.

However, the Israelis also suffer from a large dose of obnoxious arrogance combined with what we call in Afrikaans '*die kortgatsindroom*'. Their overbearing attitude quite possibly hides a lack of self-esteem.

The other side of the coin is surely that the Jews' survival is constantly under such threat that they do not always put their minds to the art of 'how to win friends and influence people'. When all is said and done, intelligence services are there to ensure the continued existence of their countries.

Nevertheless, one couldn't help wondering whether they would be as arrogant and outspoken if they had to make the grade on their own and could not constantly fall back on the safety net of Big Brother America in their hour of need. Their behaviour was often like that of a spoiled child.

On my first visit to Israel early in the 1980s I was accompanied, as was often the case, by Gert Rothmann. General Yitzhak Hofi was the head of Mossad at the time, but most of the talking on their side was done by an overbearing senior Mossad member. He was as sharp as a needle, indeed too clever by half, and was full of advice for South Africa. But on the Middle Eastern problem on his doorstep, he was as silent as the grave.

After a frustrating day we were on our way back to the hotel and I ranted about the unpleasant discussion, which I had experienced as being rather insulting. The Israelis had a cheek to think that they could hoodwink this youngster so easily!

Rothmann listened patiently and then answered with sound advice a sack full of shekels could not buy: 'Doctor, remember, in the intelligence world it is always to your advantage if other people underestimate your intelligence.' An adage by the wise old Sun Tzu about how one should approach one's enemy is also relevant here: 'Keep a pose of inferiority and encourage his arrogance.'[13]

NIS's relationship with Mossad progressed in fits and starts because it was subsumed by co-operation in the military domain with the South African Defence Force. Nevertheless, we received excellent information from the Israelis about the political, economic and strategic situation in the Middle East and North Africa and, in turn, we provided information about southern Africa.

NIS maintained very good relations with the Italian foreign service, SISME, and their domestic service, SISDE. In the field of technology in particular, with the interception of information through satellite communication, we received vital assistance from the Italians. In my view they have one of the most underrated intelligence capabilities in the world. Espionage services can certainly not be rated according to the incompetence and corrupt practices of their political masters!

We also had contact with numerous other services from other countries – from the east to the west, the north to the south – in some cases only on occasion.

THE RUSSIANS

The Russians are in many respects like the Boer people: very candid, sometimes even crude, but they are honest, easy-going and certainly not showy or bombastic. They do not try to impress you with ostentation.

Russia's early eighteenth- and nineteenth-century history has always fascinated me. At that time Russia, together with England, Austria/Hungary and France, was a great power in Europe. Thanks to my interest in their history, I knew enough not to think, as did most of my military colleagues, that every Russian was a communist. They were every bit as nationalistic in their outlook on life as I was. For these reasons, from the first opportunity I had to get to know the Russians, there was a sense of familiarity – not that it was always easy!

The South African Communist Party (SACP) is one of the world's oldest communist parties outside of Russia. The KGB, certainly the most feared and notorious intelligence service of modern times, was for many years a faithful supporter of the SACP. During the Cold War the Soviet Union tried in every imaginable way to expand its interests throughout Africa at the expense of the former colonial rulers.

Armaments were pumped into southern Africa on a huge scale, especially into Angola and Mozambique, with far-reaching implications for our region which was plagued by bloody civil wars that claimed thousands of lives about which South Africa could also not wash its hands in innocence. NIS and MI waged a fierce war of words about this issue in the inner chambers of the intelligence community because South Africa had, of its own doing, become embroiled in a military struggle in Angola with the lackeys of a superpower whose military capability was simply overwhelming.

Yes, we were able to win skirmishes and certain battles and had other short-term successes, but it stands to reason that in the long run South Africa had no hope of emerging victorious from a military conflict with the Soviet Union. It was a fairly simple equation.

As early as 16 June 1981, with Gert Rothmann taking the lead, NIS used the negotiations on the Kozlof exchange to establish dialogue between us and the Russians. We wanted to go to the Big Bear in his lair and tell the Russians that we liked them, were busy sorting out our problems and didn't want outside interference. The Russians were initially as tough as nails and our talks with the KGB which took place in various European cities, often in Vienna, were an attempt to convince them of the value of a secret diplomatic channel.

The discussions took place with a KGB member I shall call Leo, who wasn't the least bit interested in trifles such as politics and diplomacy. However, at NIS we were convinced that we were on the right path and believed that if the superpowers left Africa to the Africans, we would be in a position to sort out our continent's problems far quicker.

We made slow progress. The first meeting took place in August 1984 when a delegation from NIS and the Department of Foreign Affairs[14] met the Russians, led by their ambassador, at the Russian embassy in Vienna.[15] The KGB used this intelligence link to request that NIS persuade the Mozambican resistance movement Renamo to release a number of Russians they had held captive since the previous year. MI had refused to co-operate on this matter.

In the end, it took the intervention of the prime minister, who issued an order to the South African Defence Force (SADF) to persuade Renamo to set the hostages free. This only happened in part because Renamo held back two Russian geologists, Yuri Gavrilov and Viktor Istomin. We did everything we could to convince the SADF to pull the necessary strings to get these two released as well, but to no avail. After the signing of the Nkomati Accord in March 1984 Renamo refused point blank to co-operate.

This protracted episode only came to an end in January 1988 in Vienna when the new liaison, Boris, shared the news in a rather emotional way that the Russians had irrefutable information that Gavrilov and Istomin had been dead since May 1985 after an attack on Renamo's headquarters at Gorongoza in Mozambique. Our Russian colleagues were very upset because they presumed that we had really known all along that the two were already dead. It was only after months of talks that relations improved and they finally accepted that we really had no knowledge of the deaths.

This may seem like a trifling incident in the larger context of events but in the brotherhood between spies, mutual assistance creates the crucial trust which later makes the significant, seemingly impossible meeting of minds possible. It seemed that this insight was beyond the understanding of some of our military colleagues.

At last, on 29 March 1987, Rothmann made the breakthrough towards which we had worked for so long after he demonstrated fully to the Russians the mutual advantages that could arise on a range of fronts thanks to discussion and co-operation. The Russians agreed to the establishment of a high-level secret communication channel.

However, they were seriously worried about whether the Americans had been informed of the KGB's contact with NIS and continually asked for assurances that this was not the case. This we were able to give them categorically. The Russians heard repeatedly that we were not the lackeys of the USA and that, in its own right, South Africa was a very important regional power, indeed a continental power in Africa. At that stage we realised that Moscow's expansionist dreams for Africa were crumbling and that we should take the gap.

It was only at the end of October 1987 that Moscow finally gave the green light for the head of NIS to meet them for talks in Vienna. This took place on 17 May 1988.

At the meeting I informed the colleague (call him 'R') that I had a highly sensitive message to relay from my head of state but that we first had to clarify a few other matters.

The first was that we were not convinced that the channel of communication between NIS and the KGB was serving its real purpose. We were not sure whether Moscow recognised it as an official liaison channel with Pretoria. As a result, we did not know if our messages simply stalled in the KGB bureaucracy or if they ever reached the highest authority in Moscow. We were aware of numerous attempts by the Russians to liaise with South African diplomats, businessmen, academics and church leaders, whereas they could get all the information they required first-hand through NIS.

Secondly, we were worried that the Russians were not playing their rightful role in the peace processes in southern Africa. Through our sources in the frontline states we knew that the Russian leader, Mikhail Gorbachev, was exercising pressure on the Cubans and the Angolans to reach a settlement in Angola, because Russia was reluctant to continue carrying the financial burden of the conflicts in southern Africa. In addition, I told R, it did not look good that they were being browbeaten by the Americans in the peace process regarding South West Africa's independence.

Thirdly, R was told repeatedly and emphatically that we were not pawns of Washington or the West. In fact, the CIA and the British Secret Service (SIS) were actively undermining our interests. South Africa would not allow itself to be dictated to by Washington, London or Moscow, I said.

Two weeks later a summit would be held in Moscow between President Ronald Reagan and Gorbachev, and we were convinced it would be short-sighted if the KGB did not enlighten the Russian leader fully about developments in southern Africa. They certainly knew where they could lay their hands on the best interpreted and most strategic information in this regard.

Fourthly, the Soviet Union knew that neither the ANC nor any other revolutionary group had the military capability to overthrow the South African government by force. This also applied to the frontline states. We knew that the KGB's own analyses showed that the ANC could not win by force of arms. Moscow should rather convince the ANC to abandon its armed struggle and to take part in the peaceful political process in South Africa.

Fifthly, we knew that the most recent military offensive in south-eastern Angola had cost the Soviet Union millions upon millions. However, we argued that Moscow could end its undermining activities without any significant loss of prestige. South Africa was ready to help with the constructive development of southern Africa and hoped that the Russians would become partners in this reconstruction and revival process.

Sixthly, there were numerous other spheres of co-operation that could be successfully explored by Pretoria and Moscow. In addition to the fields of mining, agriculture and diamond dealing, a great deal could be achieved with joint research initiatives and co-operation in the medical field and with energy provision (for example oil from coal).

I handed over the sensitive message from the South African president to R with the request that it be delivered urgently to Moscow. It read: 'The South African government is prepared to discuss covertly the possibility of signing the Non-Proliferation Treaty with the government of the Soviet Union provided that South Africa's security interests, political autonomy and other interests are recognised and guaranteed.'[16]

The message was a way of making the Russians aware that we were not the Americans' lapdogs and that we were also well able to conduct talks with Moscow on the important strategic issues of contemporary world politics. At that stage I was already heartily sick of our constant attempts to ingratiate ourselves with the Americans on the Non-Proliferation Treaty. In the light of the American legislation on comprehensive sanctions against South Africa,[17] we naturally received very little in return for our bowing and scraping to the Americans. It was more honourable and more balanced to strive for a distinctive and less subservient independence in international affairs.

R undertook to relay this message and his careful memoranda on our discussion to the highest authority in Moscow. That same night I sent a comprehensive encrypted report to PW Botha on the finer details of our conversation.

Exactly two weeks later R provided some feedback. South Africa was advised to raise the matter of the Non-Proliferation Treaty for consideration at the International Atomic Energy Agency (IAEA) in Vienna. The Russian mission in that city had already received a directive on their actions in this regard. He was positive about the other matters put forward via the secret channel and indicated that further developments could soon be expected. He did not refer to the status of the channel at all. I learnt later that, according to Russian logic, this meant that it had been accepted.

For the first time in decades, on the international front carefully worded but positive sounds about South Africa were beginning to eminate from Moscow's circle of influence. During the celebration to mark the 25th anniversary of the UN's Special Committee against Apartheid in New York in 1988, the representative of Ukraine, Hennadiy Udovenko, said circumstances in South Africa were no longer the same as 25 years before. He went on to aver that 'meaningful change' had taken place and that the time had come to move forward with a political settlement.

From Washington it was reported that pressure had been exerted on Udovenko to make this statement – shortly before he had delivered his speech, a Russian diplomat had been observed pressing a document into Udovenko's hand.[18]

However, considerable time would pass – more than two years – before more significant breakthroughs were achieved, thanks to the liaison channel with the KGB. It was nevertheless worth every jot of trouble, time and expense. It was an achievement of world-class proportions to build, in absolute secrecy, a mutually beneficial relationship with a country that had once been a sworn enemy.

CHAPTER 7

UNMASKED!

It is March 1989. Mike Kennedy, deputy head of NIS's counter-espionage unit, and I find ourselves in the hallowed halls of the British Secret Intelligence Service (SIS) in London. It is eleven o' clock in the morning, but we have certainly not come to drink tea.

In fact, our announcement to Christopher Curwen, head of the SIS, caused him to swallow a gasp. But, as behoves a good spy, he shows little of this and quickly regains his composure: 'Can I pour you gentlemen a whisky … a single malt, perhaps?'

The reason behind his attempt to defuse the crackling tension was simple: Curwen had just been informed that we had caught his spies spying on South Africa's nuclear weapons capacity. This is the kind of news the head of one of the most respected intelligence services in the world does not want to hear on an empty stomach.

There were a few brief attempts at denial, including from the SIS's official representative in South Africa, Mike Thicket, who also attended the meeting. I was very respectful, but asked that we not waste one another's time with cat-and-mouse games. I offered to show them photographs and play them tape recordings of talks and video recordings of secret meetings to support our claims.

What rubbed even more salt into their wounds was a letter from the South African head of state[1] for the attention of the British premier, Margaret Thatcher, in which he objected in the strongest possible way to this undermining by our former 'conquerors'. Ironically enough, in those years Thatcher was one of a very small number of Western leaders who supported South Africa; she did so openly, but not without criticism.

That evening Mike and I drank a small glass of whisky and toasted – without compliments to Her Royal Highness – this signal achievement of NIS, which afforded me the greatest personal satisfaction.

Months later Curwen wanted to know from me: 'How did you do it? You caught some of our best operators. We have retraced our steps but haven't been able to find our mistake.'

I responded with a counter-question: 'Thanks for the compliment, but what were your best spies doing in South Africa? I would have thought they would be in Moscow. Or in one of the Eastern Bloc countries. What threat do we pose to you?'

I didn't really receive an answer. Nor did they on how we had gone about catching the British spies.

Curwen, who was later awarded a knighthood, gave me an immensely satisfying piece of news when he told me how the Iron Lady had hauled them over the coals about their South African blunder.

More than a year later, Mike and I went to Washington on a similar mission to confront the American Central Intelligence Agency (CIA) about their spies, some of whom had been arrested together with the British spies. A letter of protest for the attention of President George W Bush was also handed over. [2]

South Africa was also a target of the espionage services of Germany, France, the old Eastern Bloc countries and Russia, in the form of the KGB and GRU, respectively the civil and military intelligence services. Many of these efforts had been successfully terminated or 'turned around'. The Russian 'agents' were mainly South African diplomats or officials from various state departments such as foreign affairs, trade and industry, tourism, mineral and energy affairs, and agriculture, and were stationed in South African embassies and missions overseas and locally. They were approached and, in many cases, recruited and handled by officially declared intelligence officials as well as those who were operating incognito.

All of these countries were in search of inside information about political, military and economic matters – in that order. Those who had been banned from the country – that is, political exiles who were members of the liberation movements – became sought-after targets, especially as South Africa moved towards a new political order and it was to be expected that some of these exiles would become important roleplayers in the new dispensation. Naturally we had no control over this but we were, for the most part, well informed about what was happening in this arena.

When the SIS and the CIA were confronted, they were given just enough information to show that we had an irrefutable case against them. Usually, in such cases we did not provide the names of the South Africans who had been approached or recruited by them, but only the name of the handler or sometimes – if it suited us – the other way around. The purpose of this was to keep them guessing about what we knew and didn't know. If they could not establish the full extent of our information, they were forced to abandon all their operations. In this way operations we had no knowledge of also had to be scrapped.

Later some of the supporting agents who had helped the British were handed over to their embassies and quietly sent back to London. The undeclared intelligence officers[3] who were involved in the operations were recalled to London before South Africa could declare them undesirable persons.

The same applied to the Americans, except that with them more people and a greater number of cases were involved. Generally speaking the Americans were less focussed in collecting information than the British. This was presumably because they had more manpower and virtually unlimited funds. The Americans also recalled their spies who had been involved in these incidents.

The CIA and SIS naturally thought that their organisations had been penetrated by NIS and we watched closely how they searched for our 'moles' in their ranks. The primary purpose of counter-espionage is precisely to penetrate the opposing intelligence service and, to a certain degree, to 'take control' of some of its operations.

Over the years the KGB approached various South African officials and businessmen overseas – and also in the neighbouring states of Angola, Mozambique and Botswana. We were reasonably successful in nosing them out and would then launch a number of interesting 'double-agent operations' against them. This involved persuading some of their agents (mostly in exchange for not being unmasked) to spy for South Africa as well, so that we could gain access to the information they had about the KGB. This also placed us in a position to feed them false information. Some of these operations were carried out successfully for eight or more years.

One such an unmasking that I can now disclose for the first time is that of the Polish spy Colonel Jan Wierzba. He was apparently (and indeed!) a qualified engineer, but what he did not tell his neighbours was that he was also a member of the Polish intelligence service who was sent here to spy on South Africa's nuclear weapons capacity.

For about fifteen years he worked at power stations and engineering enterprises in South Africa. He was a thoroughly likeable fellow, exceptionally reliable, voted for the National Party and made the correct anti-communist noises. As an employee and engineer he built up a good reputation and eventually succeeded in being appointed to a post at Armscor.

He began to collect information actively with the help of a South African supporting agent and on various occasions made contact with his Polish handlers who visited the country as Polish airline staff. Later he met his handlers in Europe, as well as members of the KGB in Austria.

Wierzba's case shows how extremely patient a spy has to be before he can start his real work. We were equally patient. When you are dealing with a good spy it takes on average eight years from the time he begins to operate until he or she is arrested. When we were reasonably certain that Wierzba was spying on South Africa's nuclear secrets, we followed his movements intensively for about four years.

As is the case with any other covert spy, he had to meet his handler(s) physically at least once a year, or provide them with irrefutable proof that he was still alive (a so-called sign of life) and that the information they were receiving was indeed coming from him. This was to ensure that he had not been captured in the meantime or that 'his' messages were not perhaps coming from NIS instead. This was quite possible!

We soon had enough proof to take action against him, but we had a long-term objective: we wanted to determine precisely how he was operating, but at the same time we had to limit the possible damage he might cause. We therefore began to 'manage' or manipulate the information he was passing on to his handlers – obviously without him knowing. For this reason we strung him along, observing his every move.

Eventually we had about a roomful of documents and proof of his activities: from which petrol he filled up with to where he had his hair cut. He ate breakfast almost every day in the same restaurant and, more often than not, we sat at a nearby table – without him ever suspecting we were there. Every scrap of information might be important to complete the puzzle. The other aim was to establish precisely how his mind operated, because we could use this to train our spies.

We knew from the outset that we were never going to charge and prosecute Wierzba. While doing so would score us a few points in the eyes of the public, he was worth far more to us than that. His mode of operation, together with the knowledge as to how he approached things, later enabled us to arrest numerous other spies.

After he was taken into custody in the mid-1980s he was thoroughly debriefed.[4] There was no real point in conducting an interrogation because we already knew everything about him. Naturally he wanted to know only one thing, 'How on earth did you catch me out?'

We gave him no answer. He was eventually sent back to Poland and handed over to their intelligence service.[5]

CHAPTER 8

A WORLD WITHOUT RULES

The Germans have a saying: *Der Beruf des Spions ist so schmutzig, nur ein Gentleman ist dazu fähig.* (Espionage is such a dirty business only a gentleman can practise it.) It comes down to this: it does not matter how you get to 'the truth' – everything is allowed. Your duty is to obtain the information that will ensure the wellbeing of the state and to pass it on to the right people.

It stands to reason that if something is so important that it must be acquired at all costs, there are few (if any) rules for how it should be done. This environment creates so many moral and ethical dilemmas that you sometimes wish you had never been privy to this or that information.

On more than one occasion I received messages from my counterpart in Paris, Berlin or London that went more or less like this: 'Your Minister P is here. Last night he slept in hotel B with a woman we know as QR. I can give you the room number if you are interested. She works for the KGB. I think you should be aware of this. If your minister needs distraction of this nature, we can give him the numbers of more beautiful and safer women.'

I learnt very quickly that an intelligence service cannot be the moral custodian of ministers and others. To a large degree their way of life is their own business. For us, the point was not that the minister was cheating on his wife. The point was that his behaviour was creating a security risk for the state.

As a result, NIS was obliged to keep an eye on the minister. In light of our overseas colleague's communication it would be gross negligence not to do so. If it then became clear from our own observations and the interception of conversations that the allegation was indeed true, we knew the risk to the state grew by the night.

What do I then do with this information? Do I give it to PW Botha and say, 'Look what your minister is getting up to.' Or do I hope that it was a single moment of weakness?

I usually confronted the man himself. This was one of the most difficult conversations under the sun.

Some immediately asked, 'Does PW know about this?'

Others fumed with anger and at first denied everything. When this no longer sufficed, I was blamed: 'Who the hell gives you the right to spy on me?'

Luckily this was not a difficult question to answer. I usually said, 'Look, we have a problem. Do you deny it, or not? Are you going ahead with these shenanigans, or are you going to stop? If you think your pride is being unduly wounded, go and tell the prime minister. I am giving you the chance to stop your nonsense. If it continues we will go and see PW together.'

That was usually the end of the story.

In this way I tried to end the risk his extra-curricular activities held for the state, and to give the man a chance to come to his senses.

Through this, I also added some guidelines for myself: To keep such information absolutely confidential and not to divulge it to anyone else. Not to use it in any way for personal gain, or for that of a political party or opponents.

Another controversial way of acquiring information is the interception of telephone conversations and, these days, of electronic messages such as e-mail. The interception of postal items was another method but this has largely fallen into disuse.

Intelligence workers find it difficult to escape the perception that they often listen in to telephonic or other personal conversations at will without the suspect's knowledge. These actions will never be well received by the public, but at the same time it is an internationally accepted way of gaining information about (suspected) enemies of the state. These days the information collected in this way is crucial for foiling the plans of smugglers, drug dealers and terrorists in particular.

NIS did not escape controversy in this respect. In the late 1980s we tapped the phone of Chris Ball, managing director of Barclays National Bank, after we learnt that he was an ANC sympathiser. It came to light that the bank had granted a loan to the value of R150 000 to a client to pay for newspaper advertisements commemorating the 75th anniversary of the founding of the ANC and calling for the unbanning of the organisation.

I was overseas at the time and my deputy passed this information on to PW Botha, who could not resist the temptation to divulge it in Parliament and ride roughshod over the bank chief. Ball denied that either he or the bank had any prior knowledge of the advertisements. It raised a huge furore: about Ball's alleged sympathy for a banned political organisation and about the interception of his calls.[1]

Pik Botha waylaid me in a lift and admonished me with a stern warning that NIS's blunder could lead to the fall of the government. The uproar took on such proportions that I offered to resign, but PW rejected this out of hand and later defended us tooth and nail in Parliament.

The incident brings to the fore another dilemma that an intelligence service has to face: should one provide the head of state with information that is not critically important to state security but that he could possibly – and, if you knew him well enough, would probably – use for political gain?

It can become even more complicated: what do you do if the head of state himself or the minister to whom you report becomes a security risk for the state due to his lifestyle or personal traits? Must you reprimand him? May you withhold information from him, even if he asks for it?

Something simple that people often lose sight of is that a telephone has two points. Thus, if Helen Suzman complains that her phone has been tapped this is (i) correct but (ii) also incorrect. The fact is that her phone has not been tapped, but that she is talking to people whose phones are.

If someone, even a member of Parliament, talks repeatedly to someone else who is actively undermining the state, it is only a very dumb spy who does not realise that something is going on. In such an instance, you have one of two choices: you submit a special application to the post office to tap their telephone (in those days they were landline phones), which was the quickest and cheapest way of finding out what was going on, or you send a team to follow and observe the person physically, which is both difficult and expensive.

None of these methods will ever be popular with the public, but then again intelligence services are not in the business of winning popularity competitions. By its very nature, the work they do violates the current culture of protecting human rights.

We certainly weren't specifically interested in people's bedroom matters or telephone conversations, but we were on the alert if their activities could be exploited by enemies of the state. Yes, it was a violation of their right to privacy. No, it is not an absolute right behind which they could hide in all circumstances. The state's right to safety affects the entire population and thus weighs more heavily than an individual's right to privacy.

This is a recognised point of law and is not difficult to grasp.

Ethical and moral questions are far more complex, and a head of an intelligence service must of necessity make such decisions alone when they arise. Similarly, a covert spy must also make many moral decisions on his own, often with little more than his conscience and convictions as a guide.

Attempting to delineate the activities of an intelligence service with legislation is a worthy exercise but in practice laws play a limited role. Legislation is indeed important, because it can protect you if your cover is blown – if one of your projects is made public. However, spies are creative people who have to act unconventionally or they will never be successful.

When you have to obtain crucial information, virtually anything is admissible. There are essentially no limits to what you may do if the safety of the state is on the line.[2] In this I concur with Cardinal Richelieu, Armand Jean du Plessis (1585–1642), to whom the following is attributed, 'I am prepared to make a deal with the devil if it is in the interest of the state.'

When the state needs vital information and you manage to acquire it, you are never asked, 'How did you go about getting it? And was it legal?'

One tactic our people used with great success was so-called 'false flag operations'. It entailed recruiting someone as a source on the pretext that he or she had to supply information for, say, the CIA, while in fact the information was destined for NIS. As could be expected, during the apartheid years many people preferred working for the CIA – and being paid in dollars – than working for NIS.

All of this meant that an intelligence chief was a very powerful person with an enormous amount of freedom. He decided who or what would be spied upon, where and how he was going to apply financial and human resources and what would be done with the collected information, as well as what he was going to pass on to his political head and what not …

This called for absolute integrity and moral judgement of the highest order.

I was not spared the bitter cup of impossible decisions.

Needless to say, NIS had numerous sources within the ANC and other organisations in the years when the liberation movements operated from neighbouring countries, planning and carrying out acts of terrorism against South Africa. From time to time, based on the information they had collected, the South African security forces attacked ANC bases in Mozambique, Zimbabwe, Zambia, Botswana, Angola, Lesotho and Swaziland.

In a few cases I was told at very short notice about an impending attack. Sometimes several of our sources were in the bases or places earmarked for attacks.

For the most part I was not informed at all – the security forces argued that if they told us and we warned our sources they would take to their heels and everyone would know immediately that trouble was on the way, in which case they would flee. Although I could see their point, it left me powerless and angry.

When I was informed beforehand, the dilemma was even more acute. If we warned the source and he left hurriedly, his comrades would know he had been informed. This was tantamount to a death sentence. If the ANC did not finish him off, he would in any case be lost to us as a source.

What does one do?

Apart from it being a dreadful call to make, it was not a clear-cut decision. There was always the chance that an attack could fail, or succeed only partially. This happened often. But it could also be that the attack, from the security forces' point of view, was highly successful and that your source was killed.

It was not only a matter of losing a fellow man – a colleague of flesh and blood – but most of the sources had been recruited and trained over many years with the greatest circumspection and at great cost. In my experience, reliable human sources are worth far more than the submarines and bombers that impress us so much.

It is an impossibly difficult choice that keeps you tossing and turning at night. And your eventual decision brings you very little peace of mind because you never know with certainty whether you made the right call.

It was at times like these that I instinctively knew: I had to get away. I needed complete and utter silence.

I then made the necessary arrangements with Engela and at work, packed a few things into the car and took off to the Karoo, to a place south of Beaufort West where a friend has a mountain hut on his farm. It is totally isolated, barren and inhospitable, at least an hour's drive on a difficult road that winds up the mountainside.

On the first day I would walk into the veld and shoot a springbok, and cook food for myself. For three days I would just sit there lost in thought. I would go to sleep early and speak a great deal with the Great Man above. And I listened.

The wide expanses, the grass plains and the quiet took me back to the world of my youth. There were many similarities but also a cardinal difference: in the meantime there was a loss of innocence. I could no longer look at the world through the eyes of a child.

I would think of a poem by EA Schlengemann, a few lines of which give the Namib Desert a voice:[3]

Maar saans as die mis oor my west'like strand
Soos 'n lykkleed my kaalte bedek,
En die nagwinde kerm oor my eind'lose sand
En skadu's my lengte oorstrek –
Dan word ek meteens met weemoed omgewe,
Al bly ek hoogmoedig en wreed,
En ek smag na die wellus van groenheid en lewe,
En sug in my eensame leed.

I am sure that from time to time all spy bosses and spies have to do some introspection. For this, silence and isolation are essential. We struggle over whether the power the information gives us is always used correctly. Sometimes we just want to be alone so that in every minute of every day we are not bombarded by difficult decisions about our fatherland.

At such times, under the Karoo stars, I shared my nagging problems and doubts with God. Like his grace, this was enough for me.

One of the misconceptions about intelligence services is that all who work in the field are deep-cover spies. This is certainly not true.

Naturally the employees in the transport department did not work with highly secret information. Nor was it necessary that our medical doctor had to know what everyone did; indeed, this was to be avoided. Like all good intelligence services across the world, we also worked on a need-to-know basis. This meant receiving only the information you needed to do your work, and no more. If you started asking for details about what your colleagues were doing, eyebrows would be raised and the question would be asked why you wanted to know.

(This applied to me, too. For example, if I received highly secret information about a planned coup in Kenya, I did not ask where the information came from or how it was acquired. I only wanted to know whether the information was reliable. There are good reasons for this approach: suppose you fall into the hands of a hostile country or espionage service. The only thing they will want to know is who your sources are. It is to your advantage if you genuinely don't know.)

Furthermore, NIS was also an ordinary state department where, every day, several people sat behind desks and wrote reports. But this is not the kind of material suspense movies are made of.

'Operational personnel' is another term for spies, and they are usually divided into two categories: covert spies and deep-cover spies. Both have to collect information not generally available in the usual manner – that is, openly (overtly). This is where the term 'covert', which means 'secret' or 'disguised', comes from. In the context of espionage this implies an element of illegality.

Deep-cover spies all have a so-called living cover, which means that they have other jobs that they do openly. Or they may work for one or more companies that were founded as a front for their spy work – if you call such a company you may get through to someone who sells life insurance or something similar, but this is not really what he or she does.

His wife and children do not even know he is a spy. A good spy goes to his grave without ever being unmasked. While it is hard to determine, one can reasonably assume this happens every day somewhere in the world.

Spies lead an exciting and dangerous life. They handle extremely sensitive sources and must assume that they are constantly being watched. If you operate in another part of the world and are caught, you are in deep trouble. The adrenalin that is inevitably part of this kind of life can become addictive; such spies find it almost impossible to do normal office work.

A spy faces many challenges. The most demanding aspect is often not recruiting someone such as a minister of an African state as a source, but how to obtain the information physically from him. After all, he can't leave it in an envelope with his secretary! The very old technique of 'dead letter drops' is still used today. The source leaves the information in one form or another at a pre-arranged place and the handler collects it there. They are never seen together.

This is the basic idea, but the way in which it is done and adapted depends on the ingenuity of those involved. A man jogs every day through the park, or every second day; he does some stretching exercises, jogs further … week after week. One day he goes through the whole procedure again, bends to tie his shoe-laces and, unseen, picks up a memory stick that has been left in the grass, does his exercises and jogs off as usual.

The possibilities are endless. This kind of thing becomes a lifestyle; it calls for a specific type of personality and it must be accommodated within the framework of a state department.

For obvious reasons, NIS's deep-cover spies did not work in the same building as we did; I hardly ever visited them, because people could recognise me and draw conclusions. I met some of them on occasion in safe surroundings far off the beaten track, but until this day I don't know what their real names are. I don't need to know.

It is thus by no means an idle claim to say that a spy leads a lonely life. Spontaneity is virtually out of the question. Most of the time they are like actors on a stage. As time passes many begin to wonder who they really are, what they are actually experiencing, what they truly think.

And don't expect recognition or praise for what you do, even if you have rescued your country from disaster. Some or other politician – probably more than one – will claim it on your behalf.

Another general perception amongst the public is that espionage services throughout the world, under the protection of the law, regularly kill 'enemies of the state'. This is not entirely untrue, and it is understandable that such an assumption is commonly held.

In countless James Bond-type movies and spy thrillers the hero not only collects information about the enemy in every possible and impossible manner; he also personally does away with them after pulling off all kinds of superhuman tricks while yielding to a beautiful woman or two.

But far more credible than this fiction is the fact that various intelligence services, such as the CIA, have a paramilitary capacity that plans and carries out eliminations. It is also a fact that – especially in the old Eastern Bloc countries and the Soviet Union – espionage services were used to keep the political head of the country in power at all costs. His troublesome competitors had to be removed. Underlying this was a totalitarian outlook on the state and its functionaries.

In a democracy the security of the state is also of paramount importance, but the prime minister (or president, or monarch) is not the state. His or her personal (political) interests are secondary to the interests of the state, and he or she must rule according to the will and the interests of the entire population.

In principle I am not against the argument that a person who poses a deadly threat to the state and endangers society should be eliminated. Osama bin Laden is an appropriate example. In addition, I believe that a person must be prepared to take responsibility for his or her own deeds. This should also apply to someone like Edward Snowden, the former IT system administrator of the National Security Agency, who placed the lives of thousands of people in danger with his reckless revelations.

The moment an intelligence service discovers that someone is spying on it for a hostile country, the suspect will be scrutinised for a long period to find out, among other things, who is helping him. Revelations such as those made by Snowden about the identity of agents and sources immediately expose an entire network of people whose lives are placed on the line virtually overnight. This is treason – treason against them and against his fatherland. For this reason I have no sympathy with Snowden and fully understand if the Americans are out for his blood.

But – and I feel very strongly about this – it is not an intelligence service's task to carry out such operations. When I assumed my duties at NIS, at the very outset I made this clear to everyone. We debated the matter and there was general consensus that 'eliminations' were not the task of an espionage service. I can categorically state that such operations were neither planned nor implemented in my time as head of NIS.

Firstly, they have no place in a department whose only task is to collect and interpret information. We were therefore neither equipped nor authorised to act in this way.

Secondly, assassinations and other forms of elimination never solve the underlying problem. There is no guarantee that the victim's successor will not be more radical or efficient.

Thirdly, assassinations make everyone more suspicious and make it even more difficult to find solutions. It is a fact that the role of Special Forces in resolving conflict is completely overestimated.

Fourthly, eventually such operations come to light and then your organisation is vilified. It makes the recruitment of sources even more difficult than it already is. The same applies to the essential communication channels with the services in other countries. Nobody trusts a gang of murderers.

By this I don't want to give the impression that the world of espionage is a world of elves and fairies. It is a tough environment with very few rules in which angels do not survive.

And yet – and this is something of which I am today still very proud – after 1994 when the Truth and Reconciliation Commission began to investigate human rights abuses and members of the security forces confessed to everything they had been up to, not a single member of NIS had to testify about what he or she had done or about how guilty they felt about their actions. This tells me that nobody was forced – ordered by a superior or by 'the system' – to do anything that went against their principles. It also meant that in the past, while carrying out their duties and often having to make difficult decisions, they were already clear about the morality of their deeds.

A somewhat controversial aspect of espionage that did not cause me to lose any sleep was employing women in our operations. To my own shame I must admit that it was only after quite a number of years that I realised what a unique and significant role women could play in the service.

Practical examples illustrate this in the best possible way. Once we were in an intense discussion with the intelligence chief of another country with whom we wanted to establish ties. There were all kinds of hitches and it became a battle of wits as each side tried to outdo the other.

I launched into an argument and received a gentle kick under the table from one of NIS's female employees. Immediately I realised that I was on the wrong track.

We paused for a quick smoke break. Then she told me, 'You

have misunderstood him. It is not X to whom he is referring. He has Y in mind.'

It is without doubt a genetic truism: women have far more emotional intelligence than men and they use it in ingenious ways. They pick up waves and tremors of which I am totally unaware.

And while I pause to reflect on men's frailties, here is another example: we wanted to do a presentation on the ANC to the head of state of an African country. By this time, respectfully, I was an international expert in the field, but I knew he was probably saying to himself, 'Here's this bloody Boer spy again. What rubbish is he going to come up with this time?'

Luckily I realised beforehand that this would probably happen, and I also knew that blonde women in particular interested this man immeasurably. So I stepped aside for one of my colleagues who was herself very knowledgeable.

The president hung on her every word, asked her a range of questions on certain points, made a few jokes ... the discussion took almost twice as long as usual. When I suggested that we should excuse our presenter, his reaction was: No, no, please she must stay; he had more questions to ask.

There was no argument about the content of her presentation. He agreed with everything she said.

Often things did not end there. In this instance we still needed sensitive information from him. By now it was evening and we were having a few drinks in the bar. My colleague was expertly trained and knew how to ask the right questions, all the while smiling coyly and using the right body language and another glass of wine or two to keep him talking. We got the information we needed.

Nine out of ten times the gentleman would want to prolong the evening, suggesting that they continue the discussion in his hotel room, but I was there to keep a fatherly eye on my colleague. If need be I could become very rude and step in with all six foot plus of me, and that would be the end of it. Everyone went to sleep in their own bed.

CHAPTER 9

SECRET DIPLOMATS

It is not always the flamboyant winger or the battering ram of the scrum who scores the try.

Intelligence services have been responsible for some of the world's most spectacular diplomatic successes. The reason for this is simple: espionage services create a direct and *confidential* liaison channel between one head of state and his counterpart in another country. Furthermore, professional spies do not seek the glory and recognition that are usually associated with so-called diplomatic breakthroughs.

Over many years NIS's employees negotiated successfully with heads of state and other prominent figures across the world and were responsible for numerous sensational successes. But even today, very little is known of these. This is particularly true of the period of South Africa's diplomatic isolation in the 1980s when NIS initiated and maintained interstate relations that would still today amaze our friends and foes alike.

When we informed our colleagues in Foreign Affairs about these discussions, they bristled with irritation and accused us of interfering in their sphere of influence. One can understand their anger, but did they seriously think that because of bureaucratic etiquette we should stand back while we were able to make breakthroughs for South Africa? Should we simply allow the unique opportunities that the intelligence environment offered to go unutilised?

On one occasion my valued and very capable colleague from

Foreign Affairs, Neil van Heerden, told me heatedly that they were fed up with having to go in through the back door. It was now high time, he said, that South Africa should be able to use the front door. Allow me to quote a bit of Boer wisdom and suggest that the back door is nearer to the kitchen and hospitable, cosy bonhomie; the front door often leads to the sitting room with its pretence and formal atmosphere.

In the 1980s in particular, NIS built up excellent relationships with many heads of state in Africa. This illustrates that especially in times of diplomatic isolation there is a need for reliable channels of communication.

The value of a direct channel between heads of state, often facilitated by intelligence services, can scarcely be overestimated. This, by the way, is one of the reasons why intelligence services have to fall directly under the control of their heads of state. The direct and personal conveyance of messages and impressions has many advantages, including cutting out any manipulation by middlemen, who, alas, may well include colleagues and ministers of other state departments.

However, secrecy holds the greatest value. The worldwide insistence on absolute openness in interstate relations, as promoted especially by the news media, is a colossal blunder. For the most part it is simply incorrect to assume that public opinion is informed or knowledgeable enough to make meaningful contributions to the often rapid and complicated unfolding of events in the field of diplomacy.

PW Botha and Nelson Mandela were in continuous, indirect contact with each other for more than two years before it was announced to the world. One shudders to think what the implications might have been if, from the start, this process had been subjected to the fanfare, speculations and tall stories journalists often dish up. Without doubt it would have cost South Africa its peaceful revolution.

Secret liaison may also conceal embarrassment and confusion. If mistakes are made, there is no need for public apologies to follow. Via a confidential communication channel the parties can speak honestly and openly and emotions can be freely expressed so that the other party can assess the gravity of the situation. Good spies quickly learn to take careful note of people's emotions. It may be a ruse for some, but it remains a fact that during emotional outbursts the truth is sometimes crudely but honestly expressed.

In this vein I have a priceless memory of an incident that took place in the early 1980s during the visit of Klaus Kinkel, the head of the BND (the West German intelligence service), to meet PW Botha in the old Verwoerd building in Cape Town. Kinkel, accompanied by a German *Mädchen* as interpreter, strode into the office on the eighteenth floor, full of Prussian bravado.

Botha was incensed by the verbal attacks on South Africa by the German ambassador at the United Nations and before long Kinkel fell victim to a tongue-lashing. The poor interpreter lost her nerve completely and fell silent, unable to handle the verbal onslaught any longer.

Botha did not always handle such disputes gracefully, that's a fact. Nothing was softened or spun into protective diplomatic wool. The advantage was that thereafter both parties knew exactly what the other's standpoint was, and what points of agreement there were.

Later, when we shared a glass of wine to pour ointment on the wounds of German self-respect, Kinkel admitted that they had been insensitive to the political sentiments of some groups in South Africa. Needless to say, the incident was confidential and did not lead to any public embarrassment.

However, Bonn had a better understanding of South Africa's sensitivity about German diplomatic opportunism thereafter.

VIA AFRICA TO THE REST OF THE WORLD

Early in the 1980s it became crystal clear to us that it was critical for NIS to forge a bridgehead into Africa. This was certainly also where NIS's primary intelligence future – and its greatest test – lay.

The importance of relationships with the French, Americans, British, Germans and others was obvious given that they are former colonial powers with extensive business and other interests in South Africa. But the heart of the threat against South Africa lay in Africa. The newly independent states wanted to wipe out the last white enclave on the southern tip of the continent, and every state felt it could play a role in this process. As a result it was more important and a bigger challenge to establish liaison and communication links here than with all of the European countries put together.

Virtually the entire African continent was hand in glove with our biggest enemy, the ANC. Our continent was not our friend; indeed, throughout the world South Africa was being criticised, slated by the leaders of Africa before audiences who wanted to sing with them in the choir and who contributed lavishly to their campaign coffers. Nevertheless, we went to talk to them.

So, what did we do in the 1980s in Africa?

Along with my senior and operational colleagues we made contact with several countries but especially with what we regarded as the Big Five: Nigeria, Egypt, Kenya, Uganda and Zambia. There were also contact and links with other states but we weighed up the situation carefully and decided to concentrate on the most important roleplayers – also as far as their hospitality towards the ANC was concerned.

In truth, we were on a diplomatic mission. The main and critical difference was that it happened in secret and was kept confidential. The goal was to explain to them that South Africa was moving away from apartheid and that we wanted to work out a new political dispensation in co-operation with all significant political groups.

Our message went more or less like this: 'We are not approaching political reform from a position of weakness. Forget that. The ANC can talk in vain about overthrowing the South African government by force. We are going to reform because it's the right thing to do. We want to put an end to the bloodshed in Angola and Mozambique and also to the terror attacks in South Africa, because no one is benefiting from them. We want to help build up the African continent and can make an enormous contribution, but this cannot take place in a climate of armed conflict. Therefore, we ask you to close the ANC camps in your countries. We know they are causing you many problems.'

The discussions with heads of state and senior intelligence people were tough but frank and wide-ranging, extending to everything under the sun. I told them I was there with the authorisation and full knowledge of President Botha and that from time to time I would bring letters from him. 'I cannot make decisions on his behalf but I speak on his behalf. He has sent me. Whatever you tell me I will convey directly to him.'

Formal interaction with Africa by the Bureau for State Security, NIS's predecessor, was limited. Liaison with Swaziland, Lesotho and Botswana was regular, but it faltered at times. However, there were good relations with Malawi, and a permanent office had been established in Zaire which we appropriately called 'Warmpatat' (Hot Potato).

Over the years NIS had maintained a good relationship with

the Zimbabwe Central Intelligence Organisation (ZCIO), which was called the Central Intelligence Organisation (CIO) before Zimbabwe's independence in 1980. The CIO's head at the time was the British-born Ken Flower, an experienced spy who had to be approached with kid gloves.[1]

An example of the tangible advantages of having good ties between intelligence services is seen in the case of the South African spy Odile Harrington. She was 26 years old when she was recruited by the security police in 1986 as a source and was sent to Zimbabwe to spy on the ANC. According to a report in the *New York Times* she was 'an idealistic, poignantly unqualified amateur enticed into the underworld of espionage and exploited by her handlers to infiltrate the African National Congress'. Shortly after her arrival in Harare, she put snippets of information and a photograph of an alleged ANC member into an envelope, addressed it to someone in South Africa, and asked a policeman who guarded an ANC safe house in Harare to post the letter![2]

She was tried, found guilty of spying and sentenced to 25 years' imprisonment, after which she was held in the notorious Chikurubi prison. Here, according to her evidence, she was cruelly assaulted and denied food.

I had a good relationship with the head of the ZCIO at the time and over the years regularly raised the issue of Harrington's release. He was a friendly old fellow, but remained pessimistic about this because according to him, President Robert Mugabe was 'difficult'.

One morning in November 1990, while I was in a management meeting, I received an urgent telephone call from him: 'If you want Miss Harrington you must come and fetch her *today*. I managed to get Mugabe to change his mind, but tomorrow it may be another story.'

We immediately arranged for a plane and, less than two hours later, took off from Lanseria with, among others, NIS's doctor and one of the female members of staff (with a small bag of make-up) on board. My Zimbabwean counterpart met us at the airport and gave us the address of a house where we would find Harrington.

Everything went well and by five that afternoon we were back at the office. I phoned Rusty Evans, Deputy Director of Foreign Affairs, and informed him that Harrington was safely back in South Africa and in our care.

He exploded. 'Who the hell gave you the right? We are busy with that. Keep your nose out of our business!'

This made me equally angry and I didn't keep my cool either. 'Listen, Rusty, you and your minister can both go to blazes! This is how Zimbabwe wanted to handle it. The woman is here now. You can get her – and all the limelight – tomorrow.'

At the press conference the next day at the Union Buildings, Evans sat beside Miss Harrington. As usual, Pik Botha was also close by.

From the late 1980s onwards we were regular visitors to some of the most important capital cities and countries in Africa – from President Museveni's tent under the leafy trees in Kampala to Kenneth Kaunda's camp on the banks of the Luangwa; from sipping champagne with my friend Assih under the night sky in Togo to boat trips with the Egyptian minister Omar Suleiman[3] on the Nile, where one was overwhelmed by the marvels of God's creation. I was equally overwhelmed by the wonders of that early civilisation which also made me ponder deeply what had led to its downfall.

In 1983, with the opening of the NIS office in Lomé, the capital city of Togo in West Africa, we were often like the proverbial first-year student on campus, but we learnt quickly. If Togo gives the impression of being an insignificant little country, take a look at an atlas and note that it lies very near Nigeria and was thus close to one of NIS's most important intelligence targets. From an operational basis such as this espionage activities are much easier and are potentially subjected to less professional scrutiny than would be the case in Nigeria, for example.

NIS was in Togo with the approval of President Gnassingbé Eyadéma. Our people also developed a good working relationship with the intelligence service head, Assih, whom I would rather have as a collegial friend than an enemy. He is currently a guest of the French government somewhere in France after he apparently tried to carry out a *coup d'état* with the help of the French, the former colonial power in Togo.

While on my first visit to Togo I waited anxiously in the hotel's foyer for the people who were due to collect me at 09:00 for the appointment with President Eyadéma at 10:00. But in Africa one must learn to wait. After seven hours of waiting we were eventually seated in the president's office and received the grace to pretend that such delays were fully acceptable. It was not only in Togo that one was subjected to this kind of testing behaviour.

In my opinion undue emphasis is placed on this aspect of African culture (that time is apparently not a factor). After all, I think it is correct to say that heads of state from Africa are always on time for appointments with the British queen or the American president.

My discussion with Eyadéma was the first of many. He was not unduly concerned about the political complications in South Africa. He was more interested, in typical dictatorial manner, in giving me an account of his achievements, and then embarked on a long lecture about all the injustices of colonial rule. On various occasions he ate caviar and drank French champagne of the best vintage, while everywhere in his poor, struggling country one could see the results of his policies.

We learnt a great deal in Togo, particularly about the communication systems that had to be installed under the most difficult circumstances on the roof of the NIS residence in a typical suburb of Lomé. Our people had to learn how to find their way in the completely different living conditions of Togo and did pioneering work in the process. We visited Togo regularly and spent hours discussing aspects of our future actions and operations in West Africa. At night the talks frequently centred on the role South Africans were able to play and, indeed, had to play in the development of our continent.

The French intelligence service kept a close watch on our activities and were probably not enamoured with our interference in their sphere of influence in West Africa. However, we did not see it as a clash of interests and were careful not to supersede them in any way; in fact, in certain areas we even worked together.

A modern training centre for the Togolese intelligence service was later built outside Lomé; NIS contributed the lion's share as far as the planning and funding were concerned. Thanks to this success, among others, our access to the rest of the continent could be extended considerably and soon we began to liaise with the most important states and leaders in Africa.

A few years after establishing the Togo operation we opened an office in Lagos, Nigeria. Through their national security advisor, General Aliyu Mohammed Gusau, we made contact on the highest level with President Ibrahim Babangida. This meant that we could give them first-hand information about what was happening in southern Africa. In exchange, we were supposed to receive useful information from the Nigerians, but this was not really forthcoming.

However, this was not the end of the world, because we regarded Nigeria as a focal point for exerting influence and wanted to inform the Nigerians on a higher level about political developments in South Africa. Nigeria was an avid supporter of the ANC. In January 1977, Thabo Mbeki became the ANC's first representative in Nigeria and was placed in Lagos, which was then the capital city.[4] We thus had the unique opportunity of explaining to the Nigerian leadership that the ANC was not the only roleplayer in southern Africa and that the South African government was serious about a new political dispensation.

In this way we hoped that Nigeria and other African countries would adopt a softer, less acrimonious attitude towards South Africa and would begin to curtail the ANC's armed activity. To a certain extent this hope was realised.

Faux pas

The offices we opened in other countries in Africa in the 1980s, the high tide of the apartheid years, are an example of NIS's success, but faux pas over which we sometimes had very little control also occurred.

In the second half of 1981, among other routine visits I went to the regional office in Durban where a member of staff, Martin Dolinchek, asked if I would meet an acquaintance of his who wanted to discuss an important project with me. This person turned out to be the mercenary Mike Hoare. His ambitious plan was to carry out a *coup d'état* in the Seychelles to remove the leftist president Albert René – who had himself come to power through a *coup d'état* – from office. This would give South Africa strategic landing rights in the Indian Ocean and a convenient lookout post on the movements of vessels in the area.

It was a foolish and harebrained plan and I left 'Mad Mike', as he was known, under no illusion as to what I thought – I emphasised that NIS would have nothing whatsoever to do with his proposed adventure. However, Hoare pressed on regardless and on 25 November he took off from the Matsapa airport in Swaziland on a Royal Swazi National Airways flight bound for the Seychelles. With him were 45 mercenaries, of whom about half were ex-servicemen from the army; among his 'soldiers' was Dolinchek – without my knowledge or approval.

They fashioned themselves as a beer-drinking club, Ye Ancient Order of Froth Blowers, and according to later evidence in court, on the way to Mahé they had already lived up to this name. In Mahé, a customs official at the airport discovered an AK-47 in one of the beer-drinkers' rucksacks. A fight broke out; one of mercenaries was shot dead and a few others were wounded and arrested. One of those arrested was Dolinchek. The rest managed to hijack an Air India Boeing that had just landed in Mahé and forced the pilot to fly to Durban.

Flight control in South Africa suspected trouble. Hoare and his men were taken into custody at the airport outside Durban, later put on trial and, one after another, sentenced to jail terms. In his autobiography, General Magnus Malan mentions that a member of NIS (presumably Dolinchek) had introduced Hoare to members of MI and that, after various discussions with Hoare, army officers had supplied him with weapons. However, according to Malan, no members of the defence force had taken part in the failed coup.[5]

Every self-respecting intelligence service in the world will do everything in its power to bring its spies back alive, no matter how badly they have behaved, if they are arrested or imprisoned. In the end, the state paid the ransom of a few million rand for Dolinchek's freedom.

Needless to say, the Seychelles fiasco was big news and many fingers were pointed at NIS – after all, I had met Hoare prior to the failed coup, and a member of NIS was directly involved in the incident. Naturally everything could be explained, but my policy was that it was part of spy ethics not to talk about one's work. The disadvantage of this, however, was that one cannot defend oneself publicly against false accusations. We issued a concise statement that NIS had not been officially involved, and then fell silent.

IN A TENT IN ENTEBBE ...

The Zambian capital, Lusaka, was for many years the ANC's headquarters in Africa. It was here that the political propaganda war and the military onslaught against South Africa were planned and co-ordinated. In and around Lusaka there were often thousands of ANC supporters who were on their way somewhere for further training or who were waiting to leave on so-called military missions to South Africa. High-profile leaders of the ANC regularly hung out at the Pamodzi Hotel.

It was often apparent that President Kaunda had little knowledge of the full extent of the ANC's activities in his country. Nevertheless, from the mid-1980s NIS began to liaise directly with him and members of his intelligence service, the Zambia Security Intelligence Service (ZSIS). Our goal was firstly to create a discussion channel through which Kaunda could be well informed on political developments in South Africa and secondly to make his country less hospitable towards the ANC.

Early in May 1989 I was privileged to enjoy a lengthy discussion with Kaunda over lunch on the banks of the Luangwa, surrounded by natural beauty that is among the best in the world. Kaunda's talks were always philosophical and full of admonition that we had to make peace in Africa and ensure that peace be maintained.

The following month, two senior members of NIS, accompanied

by two representatives of our Department of Foreign Affairs, visited Kaunda in Lusaka. The conversation moved to Swapo's treacherous attack across the northern border of South West Africa despite the UN's Resolution 435 to influence the upcoming election. The men also took with them an official request from the South African president that Kaunda use his status as elder statesman to bring Sam Nujoma, the leader of Swapo, to his senses.

Kaunda assured them that the Swapo forces in the western part of Zambia were fully under the control and supervision of his army and that he would not allow any violation of Resolution 435. However, between the lines he admitted that Nujoma was being strongly influenced by President Robert Mugabe and that prior to the invasions the two had met on a regular basis.

I personally met with Kaunda a number of times, either in his office in State House in Lusaka or in the Luangwa nature reserve. What I appreciated about him was that he did not turn his back on his identity. He ate his food in a genteel manner but with his hands, with a handkerchief beside him. In this way he showed his refusal to shy away from his culture and ethnic identity.

Kaunda has always worn his heart on his sleeve and cries easily; all those who know him will confirm this. In those days, when he related stories about the injustices black people were suffering at the hands of the whites, tears welled up in his eyes. When I tried to comfort him by saying perhaps it was not *that* bad, he cried even more. Then he added, 'But you Boers are really not too bad. I trust you more than I do the British who are so superficial and pretend they are friendly.'

To meet President Yoweri Museveni in his tent under the shade of overhanging trees on the grounds of State House in Entebbe, Uganda, is an experience as authentically African as can possibly be. He never received guests in his official dwelling; all were met in the tent pitched on one side of the lawn. He delighted in telling visitors that it was from this same tent that he orchestrated his military incursions against Idi Amin until he eventually dethroned him. In this way he ingeniously kept alive the image of himself as a guerrilla fighter against the rule of Amin.

Of all the leaders in Africa whom I have met – including Olusegun Obasanjo, Ibrahim Babangida, Hosni Mubarak, Daniel arap Moi, Kenneth Kaunda and Eduardo dos Santos – Museveni made the biggest impression on me. He has a strong character, in a different way than most of his counterparts. He is courteous and a good listener, but when he speaks you listen to what he says.

He argues convincingly. His most important point was: 'If only you Boers would come to understand that you can't hold on to political power on your own. I understand why you are doing it. You don't trust us black people. But I am also an African and we cannot be friends with you if you insist on ruling alone as a minority government. We know you have exceptional skills and abilities that we need in Africa, and we are not angry with you, but please try to see our side of the story too.'

A great advantage of a confidential discussion channel such as this one was that we could bring the message home to the most important African leaders that South Africa was breaking away from apartheid and was on the path towards working out a new political dispensation in consultation with all the citizens of the country. These were candid talks because neither side ever feared that the mere fact that the discussions took place, not even to mention their content, would appear on the front pages of the next day's newspapers.

That we succeeded in establishing what was actually an additional diplomatic liaison channel in Africa at a time when South

Africa was isolated internationally was, in my view, a major breakthrough.

Furthermore, we helped to create a less favourable climate for the ANC in a number of 'host countries'. By 1988/89 active support for the ANC's terror attacks against South Africa had decreased somewhat.[6]

The 'Africa project' was one of NIS's greatest successes.

CHAPTER 10

A NECESSARY 'COUP'

In my youth in South West Africa and as a student at the Free State University in Bloemfontein, politically speaking and in other respects I held a conservative outlook on life. In certain respects I am still conservative today – for which I offer no apologies.

However, in the early 1980s some of my thinking changed in important ways.

A few months before my appointment at what was still the Department of National Security at the end of 1979, I was asked to deliver an address at the Federasie van Afrikaanse Kultuurvereniginge (FAK, an Afrikaans cultural organisation) in Bloemfontein. In my address I said that 'in future the protective political milieu the Afrikaner has made his own through the power of his inherent outlook on life and the world' had to be maintained and that 'the policy of multiple political sovereignties for South Africa's black people [read: apartheid] is an honourable and worthy attempt' to make peaceful co-existence possible.[1]

At this meeting, completely out of the blue, I was elected to the executive of the FAK, which says something about the mindset of Afrikaners at the time. A few months later I was appointed as a member of a commission of enquiry into security legislation. Conservatives could justifiably expect that I would oppose any liberalisation of this legislation.

On my arrival at National Security I was still of the opinion that the South African security forces could crack down on the revolutionary ANC and all its allies and that with the necessary legislation and associated force the government could nip their plans and ideas in the bud. On this strategy and its viability, a number of discussions were held in the inner circle of the department. Furthermore, for four days a week we were exposed to the information collected by NIS.

Over the next two, three years, all these factors combined to gradually convince me that the validity and workability of the political policy and military actions South Africa was using were no longer appropriate. This conviction also took hold of me thanks to the influence of my colleague Mike Louw, a dyed-in-the-wool supporter of the old South African Party (SAP) from Prieska. I realised that our political and military approach offered nothing in the way of a permanent solution, that the country's most burning question needed a political and constitutional answer and not a military-strategic one. In time I realised that one damages one's conscience by denying the truth about 'the truth'.

I would like to think that I am an intellectually honest person. One consequence of this is that one must always be prepared to test one's opinion against new information and, if necessary, to adapt one's viewpoints and convictions. This, and not some Damascene conversion, gradually led me to new insights on the road ahead for the country.

In this I was part of an intense process of fermentation in Afrikaner and government circles about the political direction the country should take. A critical forum where this process took place was the State Security Council (SSC), which became the terrain for intense debate and wars of words behind the scenes – also between me and some military leaders.

In contrast to what many people believe today, PW Botha was not the founding father of the State Security Council or the concept of the 'total onslaught'.

The origin of this theory can be traced to the Cold War (1947–1991) era and the conviction in the West that the Soviet Union (USSR) was out to use every possible means in its power to achieve world domination. The triumph of Mao Zedong's forces in China in 1949 and communist-inspired revolutions in Greece, Malaya, Korea and Indo-China led to the American doctrine of containment whereby America, thanks largely to agreements made with regional powers, tried to halt the USSR's expansion of power.

In South Africa, military strategists saw a similarity between these developments and the establishment of Marxist governments in Mozambique and Angola, coupled with the escalating Border War (1966–1989). They saw merit in the ideas developed by the French military strategist General André Beaufre in the 1950s, based on his experiences in the Algerian war of independence.

Although the French won virtually all the skirmishes against the rebels, in the end they had to admit defeat. According to Beaufre the reason for this was that the French were unable to win the loyalty of the Algerians and could not convince them that they would have a better future under French rule than under the rebels. Beaufre argued that the appropriate reaction would have been to maintain a strong military presence but also to 'take away the enemy's trump card' by introducing ground-breaking reforms to create hope for a better future.

Beaufre argued that the 'total onslaught' on all aspects of life by revolutionary movements that were trying to take over control of the country could only be counteracted by a 'total strategy'. He was invited to visit South Africa in 1974 and delivered a lecture in Pretoria to senior officers of the military. He made a great impression on the head of the defence force, General Magnus Malan, who applied Beaufre's analysis to the South African situation. The 'total onslaught' doctrine and the response to this in the form of a 'total national strategy' took on official status in the White Paper on Defence which was presented to Parliament in 1977 by the Minister of Defence, PW Botha. Because of this he is often seen, incorrectly, as the founding father of this strategy.[2]

During the term of office of Botha's predecessor, Advocate John Vorster, the State Security Advisory Council (SSAC) was set up in 1972 as the outcome of a commission of enquiry into security matters headed by appeal judge HJJ Potgieter. The SSAC was fairly inactive until 1979 when it was changed into an effective, integrated management mechanism under Botha's premiership and its name was shortened to the State Security Council (SSC).[3]

The core function of this body was to provide the government with advice about security matters. In this regard it was not unique; many countries, and also the liberation movements, had similar mechanisms. In the case of the ANC it was known as its Politico Military Council.[4]

The SSC, along with three similar bodies (for economic, welfare and constitutional matters) was, in fact, a Cabinet committee. The latter three committees were in charge of the National Welfare Management System and the SSC was responsible for the National Security Management System.

By law the SSC comprised the president (as chairperson), the most senior minister in the Cabinet, and the ministers and departmental heads of the military, the police, the Department of Justice, the Department of Foreign Affairs and NIS. In this manner, each of the relevant state departments was required to make a contribution as far as state security was concerned, or at least to reflect upon such matters.

Although partly and justifiably the SSC can be accused of

creating an extremely powerful inner circle, its decisions served as recommendations that were laid before the Cabinet which, technically speaking, could reject them. This probably only happened very infrequently.

Another misapprehension about the State Security Council was that it was a bunch of likeminded politicians and officials who were wangling to oppress the black population even more.

As someone who was directly involved in this council, it is my honest opinion that it was a bona fide attempt to keep the country on an even keel in a time of crisis. The minutes of the SSC back up the assertion that we often spent long hours struggling to manage economic, welfare-related and social circumstances in the country to avoid the revolution that was being planned in some circles.

After 1994 I pleaded before the Truth and Reconciliation Commission (TRC) that these minutes should be made public because I believed that the council, despite certain blunders, had nothing to hide and because making the minutes public would put an end to the suspicions and rumours about the SSC.[5] Unfortunately, Minister Kobie Coetsee opposed this move and got his way.

Secondly, the SSC's work cannot be described as scheming and plotting, because there was no unanimity about how the onslaught against the country should be countered, although eventually a broad consensus did evolve.

Thirdly, the SSC was not focused on the oppression of the population. Yes, states of emergency were declared in some regions and civil rights were restricted, but these measures were aimed at maintaining a reasonable degree of law and order so that a climate could be created in which preparations could be made for a negotiated settlement.

In my opinion the sustained and irrefutable information delivered by NIS played a big role in persuading the members of the SSC that a political settlement was South Africa's only hope for peace and prosperity. Some ministers such as Chris Heunis, Pik Botha and Alwyn Schlebusch did not need to be persuaded. Along with a few others, they continually warned against the dangers of economic collapse, international isolation and the option of going it alone. In the end – in agreement with NIS's interpretation of the situation – only a political solution would resolve the conflict, they argued.

Heunis was an intense and hard-working man with an exceptional intellect and a memory like an elephant. However, he sometimes became entangled in long discourses and often interrupted himself with new ideas that confused his listeners. He spoke with such urgent haste that General Jannie Geldenhuys, who sat beside me in the SSC, once asked discreetly, 'Is the speed at which one speaks an indication of one's intelligence?'[6]

In meetings of the SSC Pik Botha, the Minister of Foreign Affairs, always made his presence felt. He was a unique political personality and was often responsible, both in the council and outside, for brilliant contributions. He and his department made a vital contribution to ensure that international thinking and morality was heard and considered in the SSC and other security structures.

For the SSC to work efficiently the country was divided into different geographical regions that coincided more or less with the provincial borders that were drawn up in 1994. In each area a joint management centre was set up that allowed the authorities to co-ordinate the management of security matters in that area.[7]

The SSC met every second Monday at the Union Buildings in Pretoria or at Tuynhuys in Cape Town, with the result that decisions could be implemented quickly. The council was expanded to include a working committee and a secretariat.

The working committee was an important body that did all of the preparatory work for the SCC. Its members were the heads and senior officials of the four state departments that comprised the SSC. A great advantage of the working committee, of which I was a member, was that the members could air their opinions freely and plans for the implementation of state policy could be implemented away from the prying eye of their political heads, who often had their own agendas.

Here, through the years, there was intense debate that might easily have led to fighting had it not been for the good-natured and wise guidance of the chairperson, the South African Defence Force's Lieutenant General André van Deventer.

In the revolutionary upheaval in which South Africa was embroiled in the 1980s it was not only important for the government to maintain law and order but also to win the struggle for the hearts and minds of the population. It was no secret that large parts of the black, coloured and Indian population were resentful about discriminative laws and poor living conditions which were laid directly at the door of apartheid policy.

This often led to explosive situations that could be defused by the mechanisms of the SSC and the involvement of the defence force and certain state departments. What it came down to in practice was that the SADF in particular could, in record time, build a school, clinic or a road, or repair a blocked sewerage system, while through the ordinary bureaucratic channels it would take months or even years to finish such projects.[8]

Naturally this intervention was not popular with state departments keen to do their work, because technically their line functions were taken over by the National Security Management

System. It was, in a certain sense, a (necessary) coup of the administration of the country – the autonomous functions of some departments were taken over by the Security Management System, implying the following: 'Your processes and work performance are not good enough for the circumstances in which the country finds itself. We are taking over now and will help you provisionally to get things done.'

It was easy to understand why the council became a controversial body. However, for me the critical question was: Were the Security Management System and the SSC there to establish a military dictatorship and ruin all chance of constitutional negotiations? Or were they trying to create a climate in which people could sit around a table and discuss the country's future, rather than glaring at one another over the barrel of their guns? [9]

Members of the Cabinet who were not part of the SSC rightly felt that they had been excluded from what was proving to be a forum where crucial policy decisions were made; they grew increasingly critical of the top officials of the security community and accused them of going all out to empower themselves and rule the country. Nor was the SSC popular with most of the elected politicians, who alleged that unelected officials and securocrats had taken over the government.

Although PW Botha understood this, he found it hugely frustrating that the police, who, after all, were primarily responsible for the maintenance of law and order, seemed unable to do so consistently and successfully. At the same time he realised that the goodwill of the broader population was indispensable for the promotion of peace and prosperity. Added to this, he was a doer who had great respect for the SADF's ability to accomplish things quickly and efficiently.

In the SSC he saw an opportunity to use the SADF for

projects that were equally important as being militarily prepared. Unfortunately this also gave undisciplined elements in the security forces, such as the Civil Cooperation Bureau (CCB), the opportunity to carry out all manner of illegal actions.

The SSC also undertook certain controversial projects such as giving paramilitary assistance to Mangosuthu Buthelezi and the Inkatha Freedom Party, something I opposed strongly.[10]

Another initiative that was considered but not decided on was the establishment of a so-called third force, a security component that would fall 'between the police and the military' and help to maintain stability in the country. This would solve the problem of the police's apparent inability to maintain law and order and avoid having to make use of the military for this purpose. It was pointed out that countries such as Spain, Italy and France used similar institutions to deal with this problem. A commission was instructed to look into the desirability of having such a force.

From the outset I was against a third force for two reasons. If a state department is not functioning successfully, everything possible must be done to ensure that it does so. Creating another state institution would be an artificial solution. The other reason – in my view, a decisive one – was that yet another roleplayer in the security sphere would definitely lead to even more conflict over each roleplayer's turf. There were already more than enough cat fights about this.

The commission that investigated this matter – of which I was not a member – recommended that a force of this kind should not be set up. The SSC approved this recommendation and, no matter how disappointing this might be for some people, no decision was ever taken to establish a so-called third force.[11]

The name did, however, become a convenient hatstand on

which to hang all kinds of illegal actions by elements in the police and the defence force (such as the shootings on trains, the planting of car bombs, and the murders of certain political activists). If someone chooses to label the activities of the CCB or the operators from Vlakplaas as the work of an 'official' third force, that is their choice, but it is factually incorrect.

I have often had to answer the question: Was NIS not aware of the murders by CCB or Vlakplaas members? And if NIS indeed didn't know about them, why not? After all, isn't an intelligence service supposed to know everything?

However, the fact is that no intelligence service knows everything, and no right-minded person expects it to. It is not an all-seeing eye that sits somewhere in the universe and observes absolutely everything. And intelligence services do not spy on other state departments. This is an unwritten rule, because every department and its head are responsible for making sure that none of its members undermines the state.

Intelligence services are not institutions that investigate 'ordinary crimes' and prosecute offenders. Therefore, when – in the course of our normal activities – NIS became aware of the activities at Vlakplaas, I informed General Johan van der Merwe, the Commissioner of Police, about this. As far as I was concerned, by doing so I had discharged my responsibility.[12]

When we learnt, once again in the normal course of collecting information, that the defence force had acted in contravention of the Nkomati Accord and provided weapons and assistance to the Mozambican rebel movement Renamo and its leadership, I discussed the matter with the president and said to him, 'Sir, we cannot do this.'

He told me to broach it with General Constand Viljoen, the head of the defence force. When I did so, Viljoen got all hot and bothered and accused NIS of spying on the military. He had the habit of treating those who argued with him as if they were troops on the parade ground. On that particular day I had had enough, and I bristled.

'Listen, General. What you don't understand is that the state has an official policy on such matters. You are in contravention of that. If you don't stop this [the help to Renamo], I'll make the information public. Who gives you the right to undermine state policy?'

It became an unpleasant conversation because, typical of a military officer, Viljoen was accustomed to giving commands rather than discussing matters. However, eventually the assistance to Renamo was indeed stopped.

Naturally we also kept an eye on the far right and the many organisations that sprung up on that particular plot of land – and often wilted just as quickly. Here one constantly had to differentiate between those who were exercising their right to express and organise themselves politically and those who crossed the line with activities that undermined the state.

Furthermore, you had to be wary of what PW Botha might do with the information you gave him. He could easily grab your report and use it to castigate the Conservative Party in Parliament the next day. This would put the fat in the fire and get NIS into deep trouble for spying on political parties.

By the mid-1980s, we at NIS and most of the members of the SSC realised that a negotiated settlement was the best possible way to defuse South Africa's political crisis. The other, closely linked, realisation was that such a settlement could only be successful in a climate that was stable enough for people to discuss peace in an orderly manner. In the South Africa of this stormy time we at NIS believed that using an instrument such as a state of emergency was necessary to maintain stability.

How can you discuss peace if you are busy waging a war?

The irony inherent in this question illustrates why so many peace initiatives (such as in the Middle East between Israel and the Palestinians) are doomed to fail: people who are shooting one another cannot at the same time sit around a table and talk about how to resolve their problems.

In the SSC there was no consensus on the desirability of the state of emergency regulations of 1986-1989. The police were in favour of this, because it gave them broad powers to go after riotous elements. The military was unsure about what they wanted. Foreign Affairs was against the prolonged state of emergency because it would lead to yet more economic sanctions. At NIS we had a keen awareness and understanding of this, because sanctions did indeed have grave economic and social implications, but we had to weigh this up against the alternative of unrest and chaos with scant prospects of a political settlement.

By that stage, among the SSC members NIS already had a reputation as a body that did not have a radical ideology, allowed itself to be led by the facts, made balanced judgements and held views that were in the interests of the country.

The SSC, military and police, despite mistakes and other shortcomings, played a crucial role in maintaining relative peace and order at a stage when the country was a smouldering powder keg. Had it not been for these institutions, bloody civil war and scorched earth would more than likely have been South Africa's fate.

In later years the SSC and, by implication, NIS were blamed by some for not being able to foresee that the Tricameral Parliament that came into effect in September 1984 would heighten political unrest because it excluded black people.

People who don't understand how the state worked at that time may find it difficult to believe that the Tricameral Parliament (that gave coloured and Indian people a measure of participation in the country's legislative process) was not discussed by the SSC. To the best of my knowledge this did not happen at all, certainly not in any depth.

The reason for this is simple: It was a party political matter that was discussed and finalised in Parliament and the political arena, while the SSC was focused specifically on issues of security. It stands to reason that a new constitutional dispensation such as this had security implications; therefore, at NIS we discussed it internally.

One of the greatest challenges of statesmanship and politics is not only to do the right *thing* but also to do it at the right *time*. The question is: Realistically speaking, what was achievable at the beginning of the 1980s, particularly in white politics?

I am convinced that if the new political dispensation in 1984 had also given black people political power at the highest level, the chances of a right-wing coup would have been dangerously high. This would probably have led to civil war. Bear in mind that the Soviet bloc was still a powerful player at this stage and that the liberation movements received substantial military assistance from that quarter.

Our viewpoint at NIS came down to this: the Tricameral Parliament was certainly not the final solution to the country's political conundrum, but it was a step in the right direction. We certainly did not see the new dispensation as an attempt to form a power bloc of white, coloured and Indian people against black people.

As far as I am concerned, those who now use the benefit of hindsight to argue that the initiatives of 1989/90 should have been introduced earlier are misinformed and naïve.

For a typical servant of the state such as me, it was a great source of satisfaction that at least coloured and Indian people were also drawn into the running of the country. It is very easy to criticise the civil service, but to ensure that it functions properly and efficiently is quite another matter.

Chapter 11

TALK – BEFORE IT'S TOO LATE

By the mid-1980s, our *wye en droewe land* ('wide and sad land') that NP van Wyk Louw had immortalised in his poetry was a turbulent, bleeding country. Violent protests, bomb explosions in public places, consumer boycotts and violence committed by both sides were the order of the day.[1]

ANC saboteurs caused damage of millions of rands' to state targets such as Sasol, the country's prestige oil-from-coal refinery, and the Koeberg nuclear power station outside Cape Town. At the air force headquarters in Church Street in Pretoria a car bomb exploded, killing nineteen people, seven of whom were air force personnel. In total, 217 people were injured.[2]

Parts of the country were what today would be called a 'stateless state'. In these areas there was virtually no service delivery by the state because law and order had broken down in accordance with the ANC's plan to make the country ungovernable. Despite the assurance of the police that everything was under control, at NIS we knew this was not the case. The relationship between white and black had deteriorated and mutual suspicion was increasing.

In the black townships the political violence reached a gruesome crescendo in the form of necklace murders, with so-called people's courts or kangaroo courts executing those suspected of collaborating with the government. Suspects were tied up, a car tyre was placed around their necks, petrol was thrown over them and they were set alight. According to police statistics 406 people died in this manner between September 1984 and April 1992. In this period there were 80 507 incidents of unrest in which 9 280 people died.[3]

In this climate of lawlessness the law enforcers' hands did not remain clean either. It later came to light that many political activists were killed. In August 1985 foreign banks called in their loans to the government after Chase Manhattan refused to renew its loan facilities to South Africa. The international value of the rand fell and a financial crisis ensued, while at the same time the Border War in Angola and support to Renamo in Mozambique were costing the country billions.

In isolating South Africa internationally, the ANC was highly successful. We became the polecat of the world. In the UN and on countless other international platforms South Africa was kicked out, isolated and insulted, labelled an illegal minority government that in many ways was likened to the horrors of Nazi Germany. Economic sanctions and boycotts, oil embargoes, sports isolation, cultural marginalisation, diplomatic isolation and even excommunication from religious bodies followed.

The relevance of constitutional institutions such as the (white) Parliament came under pressure because the large majority of black people viewed it as a useless instrument for political change. They organised themselves into numerous extra-parliamentary parties and groups. The resignation in 1986 of Dr Frederik Van Zyl Slabbert, leader of the Progressive Federal Party, from the legislative assembly undermined the legitimacy of Parliament even further.

The reaction of the average white person to these chaotic circumstances was one of fear for the future and distrust in black people, with a resultant deterioration of race relations, a hardening of sympathetic attitudes and a widespread feeling that black people should be 'put in their place'. Right-wing members of Parliament who were against the idea of power sharing between white, coloured and Indian people in the Tricameral Parliament broke away from the National Party (NP) and formed the Conservative Party (CP) which, in May 1987, replaced the Progressive Federal Party as the official opposition. Afrikaans language and cultural organisations, as well as many of the churches, experienced division along political lines and traumatic disagreement.[4]

The Afrikaners' tried and trusted option of retreating into a protective laager in the face of an outside threat grew stronger in some circles. For many in the armed forces and police, it went without saying that the whites had to 'fight to the bitter end' to retain power.

However, there were also those both inside and outside Parliament who held other opinions about which course to take. At NIS the majority of us believed that a political solution to the country's most pressing problem – and therefore the unavoidability of negotiations – was the only way out. Already in the early 1980s a senior member had the courage to suggest that we should hold discussions with Nelson Mandela, who was still incarcerated on Robben Island serving his sentence. People such as Mike Louw and the intellectual stars in our research component began to argue ever stronger in favour of the negotiation option. As far as they were concerned, the sham fighting of the wars in Angola and Mozambique had to be replaced by internal political negotiations.

A growing group of like-minded allies gradually took shape. Minister Chris Heunis and the Department of Constitutional Development worked enthusiastically on a political solution. As a seasoned politician who had wide experience on national, provincial and local government levels and who, in addition, had a friendship of many years with PW Botha, Heunis was in his own right an important roleplayer. However, he did not have the department or the officials to support him fully.

Minister Pik Botha and the Department of Foreign Affairs, on the front line of the external onslaught against South Africa, were also strong proponents of a negotiated political settlement. In this regard a true stalwart was the director general, Dr Brand Fourie. There were also other state departments that supported a settlement process – some secretly, because they were afraid to arouse the suspicion of the president and his confidants in the security forces.

Others, such as Dr Kobus Loubser of the Department of Transport, and his successor Bart Grové were both man enough to take strong stands on the crippling economic consequences of the wars in southern Africa. They were also strongly against implementing restrictive economic actions in neighbouring states such as cutting off rail and road links, regularly commenting on the futility of these measures in the long term.

There were also strong voices raised outside government circles on the need for a political solution. For years people such as Helen Suzman and Dr Van Zyl Slabbert had spread this message in Parliament and among the wider public. Businesspeople, religious leaders, academics and even prominent sportspeople added their voices to the growing choir in favour of a political settlement process. As far as internal resistance politics was concerned, the United Democratic Front (UDF) and later the Mass Democratic Movement (MDM) joined forces with what seemed like countless other organisations to stir up public resistance and violence, while the government refused to negotiate on anything that smacked of 'political surrender'.

For the uninformed, all of these attempts had some merit. If the government was too stupid to see the writing on the wall, they themselves would take the initiative and force the authorities to act. They were, of course, completely unaware of what the government was doing in secret by the late 1980s.

What was the government's overriding strategic reaction to the domestic and foreign onslaught on all fronts?

It rested on two pillars: the phasing in of political reforms and the maintenance of law and order and general stability. As part of the process of political reform, permission was granted (as early as 1979) for the formation of black trade unions; some race-based laws and 'petty apartheid' measures were repealed; and a new constitutional dispensation (the Tricameral Parliament) was introduced in 1984, which gave coloured and Indian people limited political participation.

The motives behind these reforms varied from cold political realism to moral objections against the assault on people's dignity.

The government's reaction to the domestic onslaught, in its effort to maintain law and order and ensure the safety of the man in the street, was to use harsh security measures against those who incited terrorism. In July 1985 a partial state of emergency was announced; a year later this was extended countrywide and it was then renewed year by year.[5] The media was heavily muzzled and no reporting was allowed on political unrest. Via the SSC a semi-dictatorship of security was created to keep the administration of the country on an even keel.

In real terms, both pillars were geared to weakening the position of 'the enemy' by means of strengthening one's own. The basic point of departure was a tried and trusted one that had been proved correct over decades: comprehensive political reforms, which inevitably bring uncertainty, can only be successfully implemented if introduced in a stable and reasonably orderly society.

The tragic irony is that most National Party politicians, including members of the Cabinet, were not sure how *verlig* (enlightened, inclined towards reform) the prime minister (later president) actually was. One couldn't really blame them because at times PW Botha moved forward progressively and then suddenly became stubborn and refused to budge if he felt he was being pushed in a certain direction. His disastrous Rubicon speech in August 1985 was a case in point.[6]

What made the relationship with Botha even more difficult for many NP parliamentarians was that he later became increasingly ill-tempered and would not tolerate any contradiction.[7]

Everyone knew that the armed forces and military matters were close to Botha's heart, although he had left the portfolio of defence in October 1980. It was also widely known that in the opinion of most of the generals and brigadiers the country's problems should be sorted out by military action. People who did not subscribe to this particular view knew – or believed – that they were on thin ice.

In my view, under the surface the climate was far more favourable for negotiation than it appeared to most observers, but many were reluctant to make their voices heard and say where they stood. Years later, when the unrest was over and the struggle won, some of them related tales of their heroic deeds with progressive-minded friends under the oaks at Stellenbosch, but when they had to stand up and be counted in the SSC and elsewhere, they were as quiet as mice.

I had built up a very good personal, confidential relationship with PW Botha; as a result of my work I sometimes spoke to him more than once every week and had held hundreds of discussions with him. Therefore I can say with reasonable certainty that by 1986 he had accepted, perhaps with reluctance, that a negotiated settlement was the best option to solve our political predicament.

I believe that NIS had succeeded in making Botha rethink and reassess his political position and had activated his sense of justice. We had dozens of conversations with him and I often discussed the potential of 'soft power'[8] (including diplomacy, bargaining and negotiation) to defuse conflict situations.

Another relevant factor was that he had access to the reliable information NIS provided to him on a daily basis. This showed incontrovertibly that one could not halt the broader course of history, and in the South Africa of 1985 this meant that the political emancipation of the black population and the recognition of their rights were inevitable.

In the end, irrefutable information, just as it had done for me five years earlier, changed Botha's perceptions. This also had a great deal to do with trust, because he knew I was not trying to hoodwink him or sell him down the river.

It did not mean that he suddenly experienced a political conversion. This was simply not in his pragmatic nature. At the same time his practical tendency made him open to realising what was achievable and what would fall short; what would work and what would fail; what was fair and what was unjust.

These were insights he came to over time and that were not always clear cut. As is the case with most of us, he struggled with these issues right up to the time of his retirement from politics.

In politics and affairs of state it is of crucial importance to be able to read the signs of the time and to recognise the opportunities the course of history offers.

In the late 1980s the disintegration of the Soviet Union as a world power – and the collapse of communism – offered South Africa a unique chance to make the necessary and appropriate changes on the political landscape.

NIS's liaison partners in Europe – particularly the Germans, French, Italians and Spanish – kept us informed about developments in Eastern Europe, as we did for them on affairs in Africa. Early in the 1980s it became clear that the Soviet Union's role in Angola and elsewhere in Africa was on the wane. Analysts began to predict the fall of the old USSR, almost unthinkable at the time.

The implication for South Africa was that the USSR's military and financial support to the MPLA in Angola, and particularly to the ANC, was set to decline, which meant that the ANC would become more vulnerable. According to our information it was highly unlikely that the British, Europeans or Americans, for example, would take over the Russians' role in this regard. In a nutshell, the weaker the ANC was, the more advantageous it was for us to negotiate with them.

Also of great importance were the positive sounds behind the scenes from African countries (such as Egypt, Uganda, Kenya and Zambia) towards South Africa, particularly on the basis of our assurances to them that negotiations with the ANC were just around the corner. Some of these countries were fed up with the problems the ANC camps were causing them and about the organisation's attitude, according to them, of superiority and a desire to dictate to others.

Another critical aspect was that although international developments offered us a unique time slot, the available time was limited. One aspect of this was Mandela's advanced age; by 1986 he was already 68 years old.

We realised all too well that if he died a prisoner, it would do incalculable damage and have dire consequences for the entire country. It did not require the wisdom of Solomon to realise that negotiations taking place in the likely climate of violence in the aftermath of his death would virtually seal our fate. With Mandela at the helm of the ANC there was a good chance that moderation and fairness would prevail in the search for a peaceful resolution to the looming South African revolution. If we missed this opportunity, increasing terrorism and bloodshed would be the fate of all South Africans. Furthermore, Mandela's international stature had begun to take on such lofty proportions that campaigns for his release from prison had become something of a holy crusade; millions of people in all parts of the world identified with the campaign to release him.

Another critical way in which the aspect of limited time became relevant is the fact that successful negotiations with lasting advantages for all parties must take place in conditions where a healthy balance of power prevails. In my opinion it was NIS's greatest strategic insight that we had to negotiate while the balance of power was of such a nature that it took place between equals. After all, you can't negotiate with your back to the wall.

If there is no question of anything approaching equality between the respective stakeholders in the discussion, negotiation is often a one-sided affair in which only the conditions of the handover are discussed. It was our considered judgement, based on expertly interpreted national and international information, that we should not hesitate any longer, because the scales were beginning to tip against us. We couldn't allow the Union Buildings in Pretoria to be taken over by an unruly mob as had happened to the Bastille in Paris two centuries ago!

Henry Kissinger, one of the most renowned diplomats of the modern era, bequeathed us the insight that diplomacy is not about making peace but about power relationships: 'Peace, therefore, cannot be aimed at directly. It's the expression of certain conditions and power relationships. It's to these relationships, not peace, that diplomacy must address itself.'

CHAPTER 12

A CAUTIOUS STEP

'President, we just have to realise fully what we are in for when we begin to negotiate with Nelson Mandela. The eventual outcome is inevitable and will be a majority government, with him as the president.'

These were more or less my words to President PW Botha in May 1988 when he asked me to head up a small government team to conduct exploratory talks with this symbol of the black liberation movement.[1]

'I understand that very well,' was Botha's clipped response. He was apparently somewhat irritated by my uncalled-for prediction. 'There is no need to preach to me.'

What I, and no one at NIS, knew at that stage was that Kobie Coetsee, the Minister of Justice under whom prisons also fell, had already held a few talks with Mandela. The preamble to these was that in 1985, on a flight between Johannesburg and Cape Town, Coetsee had met Winnie Mandela who was on her way to visit her husband in the Volkshospital in Cape Town. Coetsee used the chance to extend a gesture of goodwill and also went to visit Mandela at the hospital.[2]

This was followed by sporadic meetings between the two men over the next three years – for the most part at the Coetsee home – while Mandela was serving a life sentence in Pollsmoor. I saw Coetsee regularly, especially at the State Security Council, but he did not utter a word about his early talks with Mandela.

Why he handed this task over – or had it taken away from

him – we will certainly never know. He was often busy with a variety of plans and schemes, which apparently only he knew about. Coetsee was nevertheless an intelligent man and I am certain he wanted the talks to continue, but perhaps he didn't have the time or the stamina for them. Years later, at a function, he said in a speech that one of the reasons I had been chosen for the task was that I could be so *hardegat*. I valued the compliment.

Botha's instruction was that I should report back to him directly on the talks with Mandela. He demanded that these meetings be conducted in the strictest secrecy. Not even the Cabinet was to know about them.

The other members of the team were Fanie van der Merwe, Director General of Justice, under whom the Department of Prisons resorted; Mike Louw, Deputy Director General of NIS; and General Willie Willemse, Commissioner of Prisons (later Correctional Services), the only member of our group who was known to Mandela. He and Mandela had known each other since 1971 on Robben Island and were well acquainted. Later it was striking to see how much mutual respect these two men had in their interaction.

Van der Merwe possessed remarkable expertise in conduct-ing negotiations; Louw was a likeable man with wise insight and balanced judgement; and General Willemse was an outstanding administrator whose competence was to prove invaluable in the time ahead.

On a sunny Wednesday afternoon, on 25 May 1988, the four of us found ourselves in the cramped, grey office of the commander of the Pollsmoor prison outside Cape Town. The office furniture was typical of that of many a senior state official: a settee, Morris chairs, a bookcase and an oversized desk.

It was hardly ideal for a meeting of five people and, with a view to being the meeting place for talks that would probably determine the future of the country, perhaps even less appropriate. We were tense, aware of the enormity of the moment, but also inwardly elated about the prospect of being part of it all.

The last rays of the winter sun washed over the beautiful Constantia valley, Zeekoevlei and beyond, before sinking over the False Bay coast. Then the statuesque, imposing figure of the world's best-known prisoner, appeared in the doorway flanked by two warders.

Prisoner 46664.[3]

Nelson Mandela wore the standard blue overall and boots of the prison service, yet emanated a dignified and firm but friendly presence. With a gallantry that one hardly expected from someone who had been sitting in jail for 24 years, he extended his hand to each of us in turn.

Although we did not know one another, he was at ease, joining the exchange of pleasantries about the weather and the difference in our ages.

Meanwhile, the coffee and tea appeared, and Mike Louw took the opportunity to tell the joke about the 'tea boy' who was confronted by a lion at the Union Buildings. Thereafter the officials refused to go to work – not because they were afraid of the lion, but because they were no longer given any tea!

Together with the coffee and tea, tasty sandwiches were served on one of those oval stainless steel trays so characteristic of the civil service. Unusually, the sandwiches were cut into savoury triangles and shredded lettuce leaves had been scattered over them. Mandela applied himself with enthusiasm to the snacks, enjoying them immensely; it was almost heart-rending to see and I immediately made a mental note of this.

I tried to put myself in his 'political' shoes. In his head I was probably the big boss of a bunch of apartheid spies who had been responsible for the murders of prominent ANC cadres. But now he had to sit and talk to this 'Boer spy'. Actually he didn't want to do this at all, because he distrusted me, and he would soon make no secret of this.

Furthermore, as a venerable man of almost 70 who set great store by his culture, it was difficult, almost insulting, to have to negotiate with a young whippersnapper of 38. He probably said to himself, 'I asked to talk to the president and this is who I get instead!'

For this reason, Willemse's presence was of great importance. He didn't talk much, nor was it expected of him to do so, but he made Mandela feel at ease; hopefully Mandela was also aware that here was a man who would hold a protective hand over him.

Everyone did their bit to try to create a relaxed, congenial atmosphere – something that does not come easily to me, particularly with strangers. Despite the relative geniality, we all knew that we had not come together to drink tea and chat about the weather. The elephant in the room – the burning issues about the country's future – could no longer be ignored.

I began by saying that the government saw this discussion, and hopefully more that would follow, as a matter of great significance. We were gathered there on the express instructions of the president. We were all aware that the country was on the brink of a violent revolution and we had to try to avert this by reaching an understanding.

As far as the government was concerned, I explained, the search for a peaceful political solution rested on two points of departure: on the one hand, the acceptance of black people's reasonable and realistic demand for a one-man-one-vote system in a unitary state;

on the other, the acceptance of white people's legitimate concerns about a majority government that had unbridled power in a constitutional dispensation in which their interests and those of other minority groups could be disregarded and overridden.

I said we regarded the meeting at Pollsmoor as an opportunity to clarify matters on the highest level, and to find out whether the two parties, the government and the ANC, were prepared to reach an agreement on these cardinal issues.

I explained that as far as we were concerned, there were three stumbling blocks in the way of a political agreement: the ANC's use of violence in their effort to come to power; the influence of the South African Communist Party (SACP) within the ANC; and the fears about the abuse of power and the constitutional guarantees that would be necessary to allay these fears.

We did not elaborate on these. The plan was to get Mandela talking so we could get a sense of his thinking and what his plan of action was.

Prisoner 46664 was well prepared.

He gave us a clear picture of his own views and those of the ANC. According to him the ANC was also against violence, but had been left with no alternative because over decades the request to talk to the authorities about black people's political rights had been turned down time and again. On communism and its influence on the ANC, Mandela said that he was not a communist himself and that the Freedom Charter was by no means a blueprint for communism. He claimed once the negotiations on a new constitutional dispensation had begun, the relationship between the ANC and the SACP would become irrelevant.

Finally, he said the discussions would have to be held without any preconditions because the goal of honest negotiations was precisely to find solutions to differences of opinion. We did not resort to splitting hairs; the main task was to collect information. The time for serious debate would soon follow.

The two and a half hours that were available flew past and there was no time to talk about the question of a constitutional model.

As we later came to expect of him, Mandela used the last few minutes to raise new issues. The one was his criticism and concern about the release six months previously of the hardened communist Govan Mbeki, whom he felt would not contribute positively to a climate of negotiation. The other matter was an earnest plea for the release of his old comrade, Walter Sisulu. This was a contentious issue and, over the nearly eighteen months that followed, the delay in releasing Sisulu led to many verbal clashes between me and Mandela.

We then parted company – I felt that everyone seemed reasonably satisfied with this first meeting. There were no serious confrontations and no derailment. We agreed to meet again as soon as possible.

At the same time, we became aware once again of the vast differences between us. We realised that what lay ahead was not going to be a Sunday school picnic.

The next day I reported in great detail to the president on the course of the discussion. In his typical manner, PW Botha warned: 'Well, then. Now don't allow yourself to be mesmerised too much by the old man.'

On 1 June 1988, within a week of the first discussion, the next meeting took place between the government team and Mandela – this time in the home of Willie and Elsie Willemse, appropriately named 'Kommaweer', on the Pollsmoor grounds. Elsie had prepared a delicious meal and, like many unsung wives of officials, played her part in creating a relaxed and pleasant atmosphere.

At the outset I told Mandela that we were most appreciative of the serious and sympathetic way in which he had handled our previous discussion. With the help of excellent food and drink the defences were lowered on both sides; I took the opportunity to talk to Mandela about the kind of work we did in NIS and our modus operandi. I assumed, and it later transpired that I was correct, that he was convinced we were out to get the ANC by whatever means possible – including assassinations – and to stop the organisation in its tracks.

I explained that NIS's task was not – unlike the intelligence services in Eastern Bloc countries of the time with which he was familiar – to keep the king on the throne. In other words, we served the state and not the ruling party. Tomorrow, or the day after, there could be another party in power, and then we would proceed with the collection of information that was necessary to ensure the security of the state.

'Our work is not to watch people who want to vote out or out-manoeuvre the leader of the ruling party, or who are busy with all sorts of party political misdemeanours. You can take my word, we don't do this. Besides, there is much more important work to do.'

On one occasion, at a later discussion, he asked me: 'And if by chance you come upon information that is damaging to the king, what do you do with it?'

Mandela was intelligent and pragmatic enough to foresee that this might well happen. I did not suggest that it was an easy deci-sion, because there is a grey area between state security and party politics, but I did give an indication of what my role would be: 'Then it is my responsibility to decide whether the information only has personal advantage for the king in his capacity as politi-cian, or if the state also has an interest in it.'

This is one of the reasons why an intelligence service has to

Left: As a young boy and pupil of Otjiwarongo High School in the former South West Africa in 1963.

Above: My father, Nicolaas Evehardus Barnard (front, third from left), was chairperson of the student representative council of the Bloemfontein Teachers' Training College. Many decades later my son Nico would follow in his grandfather's footsteps when he was elected chairperson of the student representative council of the University of the Orange Free State (UOFS).

Above: It was love at first sight when I met Engela Brand as a student. We were married in 1972.

Below: I have always had great respect for advocate and former president CR 'Blackie' Swart (far right). Here we are at the annual CR Swart memorial lecture at the UOFS in 1976, along with the rector professor Wynand Mouton and minister Fanie Botha.

My appointment as head of the Department of National Security, the later National Intelligence Service (NIS), from the halls of academe at the age of 30 had the media buzzing.

Top: A new dispensation for the intelligence community was crafted around this table in Simon's Town. Clockwise, from left to right: Lt Gen PW van der Westhuizen, Brig Martin Knoetse, Maj Gen Johann Coetzee, Brig Jan du Preez, Lt Gen André van Deventer, ID du Plessis, R Adm WN du Plessis, Brig Frans Steenkamp, André Knoetze and myself. **Bottom:** Shortly after my appointment to the Department of National Safety I was invited to present a talk at Windhoek High School. My father, who was chief inspector of schools at the time, also attended.

Above: In Chicago in November 1983, at the invitation of the CIA, with Jannie Holmner (left), who was my secretary for many years. **Below:** Shortly after my appointment as head of NIS I was taken on an overseas tour to meet some of my peers. Here I am in the Hall of Mirrors at Versailles outside Paris, France.

Top: I met Pope John Paul II in the Vatican in 1984 as a member of the entourage of president PW Botha and his wife Elize. **Bottom:** With my colleague Cor Bekker (far left) on a visit to Taiwan in 1981.

Top: This photo was taken in Havana, Cuba during the negotiations with the Cuban government on the war in Angola. Sitting next to me is Neil van Heerden of the Department of Foreign Affairs, and alongside him is Gen Jannie Geldenhuys, head of the Army at the time. **Bottom:** A *bosberaad* at a military site in Vhembe in the early 1980s, with among others Gen Magnus Malan (third from left), then minister of Defence, and Gen Constand Viljoen (second from left), then head of the Army.

Top: Engela and I with two KGB generals whom we hosted at our beach house in Kleinbaai. Next to Engela is Ivanov (pseudonym) and to my right is Artemov (pseudonym). **Bottom:** My core staff who stood by me through the years: Back, from left to right: Johnny Lourens, André van Wyk, Elsa Schutte, Christo Smit, Jannie Holmner. On the armrests of the couch are Tina van Wyk (left) and Rene Kuhn (right). In the front Christa Malan sits left of me, and Alta Strydom on the right.

Top: Spies also need a break from time to time: with my colleague Gert Rothman on a mission to Mauritius. **Bottom:** In 1984, the political journalist Alf Ries (to the left of Botha) and I celebrated our birthdays on the SAA Matroosberg with president PW Botha and his wife. On the far right is André Brink, political reporter of *Die Volksblad*.

Top: NIS's good relationship with the Zimbabwe Central Intelligence Organisation made possible the extradition of the South African spy Odile Harrington in 1990. Harrington is to my right and Dr Abel Hugo, medical doctor for NIS, is standing next to her. To my left are other NIS staff. **Below:** Head of the British Secret Intelligence Service Sir Colin McColl (with the hat) on his first official visit to South Africa in the late 1980s.

Top: At the preparatory talks that led to the Nkomati Accord with Mozambique in 1984. Left of me are Gen Magnus Malan and Pik Botha, then minister of Foreign Affairs. **Bottom:** Mike Louw, deputy director-general of the NIS and my right-hand man for many years, at the NIS farewell function for me in January 1992. With him is my wife Engela.

On 5 July 1989, PW Botha and Nelson Mandela met in Tuynhuys. I was pleasantly surprised and very relieved by how friendly Botha was that day.

In the bottom photo are, from left to right, Botha, Kobie Coetsee, then minister of Justice, myself, Gen. Willie Willemse, Commissioner of Prisons, and Mandela.

Top: Engela and I with her parents, Floors and Lizzie Brand – mainstays throughout the years. **Bottom:** With my mother Daleen, a woman like no other.

On a number of occasions our children were invited along with us to visit Mandela. In the top photo are our oldest son, Nico, his wife, Paula, and their children, Lukas and Addi, with Mandela in Johannesburg. Below are our youngest, Niela (left), and middle son, Hannes (right), with Mandela in Cape Town.

Top: Where my soul is at peace – next to the fishing waters on the Namibian coast. **Bottom:** My first buffalo, which I shot in the mid-1980s in the Zambezi Valley in Zambia.

report directly to the head of state and not to a minister, who may have his own agenda regarding the head of state and could use the information he acquires to further it.

I tried to explain that the security information collected by a good and ethical intelligence service provides survival options for the state. The discussions we were busy with were an obvious example of this.

Mandela listened to me rather nonchalantly. I did not expect him to accept everything I had said lock, stock and barrel. In the West there were also intelligence services that moved far beyond the boundaries of collecting and interpreting information. From his perspective, why would South Africa not fall in this category?

Nevertheless, it did not become an issue and was only broached again once or twice – hopefully, I believed, because Mandela had realised that he could take my word for it.

That was not all we spoke about that evening. We started to feel each other out and began teasing out the finer points of the major topics we spoke about. Before we knew it, four hours had passed and it was time to say goodbye.

From the outset, I conducted most of my talks with Mandela in Afrikaans. I explained that English was not my home language, and while I realised that it was not his home language either, I could not always express myself accurately in English. The last thing I wanted was that there be any misunderstanding between us for linguistic reasons.

Mandela's understanding of Afrikaans was good and he was happy enough that I spoke to him in Afrikaans. I sometimes had to explain the meaning of a word and there were times when he found it necessary to give further explanation of a concept or a phrase. In this way we helped one another.

He usually greeted me in Afrikaans in his rather husky and measured tone of voice: "*Môôôre, doktor! Hoe gaaaan dêt?*" I took this as a sign of goodwill.

CHAPTER 13

THE SWORD *AND* THE WORD

Even before the very first talks at Pollsmoor, the four of us from the government knew that the question of violence would probably be the most difficult and controversial topic of the negotiations. It is the greatest symbolic weapon in the hands of any liberation movement and should not be discounted. At the same time, for those groups at the receiving end of the violence it often becomes a stumbling block to negotiations.

When addressing Parliament in January 1985, President PW Botha offered to release Nelson Mandela if he agreed to reject the use of violence as a political weapon.

A month later, at a massive public gathering held in the Jabulani stadium in honour of Archbishop Desmond Tutu who had just been awarded the Nobel Peace Prize, Zindzi Mandela read out her father's reaction to Botha's offer. A few sentences made two matters clear: that Mandela had thought long and deeply about his and his people's rights and the attainment of their freedom, and that he was not prepared to abandon the use of violence. As he put it:

'I cherish my own freedom dearly but I care even more for your freedom. [. . .] I cannot sell my birthright, nor am I prepared to sell the birthright of the people to be free. [. . .] What freedom am I being offered while the organisation of the people remains banned? Only free men can negotiate. [. . .] Your freedom and mine cannot be separated.'

And the promise: 'I will return.'[1]

From the beginning of the talks, Mandela had made it clear that neither of the parties should set conditions for the other party. He and the ANC were prepared to talk to the government but only if they were not bound to any preconditions.

Mandela admitted that the ANC did not have the military might to overthrow the South African government and agreed that the ANC was 'not doing so well' militarily. On the other hand, he was convinced that the government would, in the long run, not be able to counter the ANC by force.

His viewpoint was that once the negotiation process was under-way, the need for violence as a means of solving problems would disappear. In other words, the momentum of the peace process would make the use of force redundant. He had apparently under-estimated the loose cannons of the ANC, who regarded violence as central to any revolution.

Mandela sometimes wavered between positions regarding the use of violence. He claimed that he was initially against the use of violence but that in the 1950s and 1960s he had agreed to its use because all of the ANC's peaceful attempts had been treated with contempt by the NP government and he had become convinced that it was the only solution.[2] Using lengthy monologues, he tried to show that the use of violence was historically justified and made frequent reference to the Boers in the Transvaal and the Free State who had taken up arms against British imperialism between 1899 and 1902. According to Mandela, the Boers had proved that mil-itary defeat could be converted into political victory.

Eventually it is not by choice, but because one is forced by humiliating circumstances that one starts fighting for what one believes in, Mandela declared. He gave credit to the gov-ernment's reforms and said the president had shown great courage but that black people demanded political power in

Parliament. 'That is where political power is. Without that we are helpless.'[3]

He asked, 'How can you, who have yourselves fought more than one war of independence, not understand our urge for freedom? Remember, we have great respect for the Boer generals and have all read Christiaan de Wet's book, *Die stryd tussen Boer en Brit*. It is almost like a handbook for us.'*

In this way Mandela wanted to demonstrate to us: We know your history. We know what you did. Now please understand that we have the same aspirations as you.

He implored us to try to understand that violence was the only weapon that the oppressed majority could use against an authority that refused to listen to reasonable political demands.

It was an ironic situation in which Mandela found himself: while he knew very well that the armed struggle on its own had no chance of success, he fought tooth and nail for the right to use violence – even though the armed struggle was little more than a symbolic gesture.

In his autobiography he puts it in so many words: 'Although MK was not active, the aura of the armed struggle had great meaning for many people. Even when cited merely as a rhetorical device, the armed struggle was a sign that we were actively fighting the enemy. As a result, it had a popularity out of proportion to what it had achieved on the ground.'[4]

The remarks of a high-ranking MK member and, later, a prominent politician to MK cadres who were serving prison sentences

---

* This book was written over a number of years. I first began working on it in 2002. At that stage I was in possession of transcriptions of some of my discussions with Mandela. These were compiled at the time by officials of the National Intelligence Service and the Department of Correctional Services. The quotations by Mandela used in this book, unless otherwise indicated, were taken from these transcriptions. The transcriptions that were in my possession unfortunately no longer exist.

on Robben Island, when he visited them in 1992, should be seen in the same light. He had to handle a tricky situation: the MK cadres who were due to be released in the foreseeable future were not inclined to be sweet-talked by the words about negotiation, peace and reconciliation that had become part of the national vocabulary since 1990. They wanted blood and glory, but now had to be persuaded to think differently because they would not march in glorious victory through the streets of Pretoria.

Comrade Politicus now had a simple message: 'Comrades, you are the heroes of the revolution. You have taught the Boers a lesson; you have forced them to give up. You have not suffered in vain in the icy forests of Eastern Europe and in the camps of Angola. It was not a futile exercise. Posterity will remember you for the sacrifices you have made. Viva!'[5]

The relative incapacity of the ANC's military prowess created another dilemma for Mandela. In the short term any chance of an armed takeover was a figment of the imagination; and in the long term it could only lead to widespread bloodshed. Thus, realistically speaking, he had no choice other than to negotiate if he wanted to enjoy the fruits of the liberation struggle in his lifetime.

The matter of Mandela's release was never a point of debate on the agenda. We all accepted it as a given and very early on we referred to it openly. For us it was by that stage merely a matter of the particular circumstances and the climate in which he would walk out of prison. A political vacuum was not an option.

Mandela undertook to work towards a moratorium on the use of violence immediately after his release in such a way that no political group, including the government, would be humiliated. He acknowledged that there were two camps in the ANC on the question of the use of violence. One group felt that the 'diplomatic approach' was the obvious solution and that holding talks with the government was indeed the best approach. The other group was strongly against this idea and believed that 'the only thing that the government … [and] the white man, will understand, is violence.'[6]

Mandela was adamant that he would not entertain the idea of abandoning violence before his release; nor would he agree to a temporary suspension. According to him this would make him look like a puppet of the government while the government itself was 'relying on naked force to solve [its] problems'.[7] He alleged that the government's overt attempts to destroy the ANC had in fact strengthened the organisation and had united the international community against the apartheid state. The government would be allowing a golden opportunity to slip through its fingers if it did not reach an agreement with the ANC while a moderate leader such as Oliver Tambo, who was against violence, was still at the helm of the ANC.

It was as clear as day that Mandela could not make any concessions on violence and at the same time retain the support of the radical wing of the ANC. Years later many of these comrades spoke with nostalgia about how they dreamt of one day, à la Fidel Castro in Havana, marching through the streets of Pretoria and taking over the Union Buildings, the symbol of white power. The indoctrination in Mosow, East Berlin, Lusaka and even London gave rise to many terrorist dreams that changed to nightmares in which there was only talk of revenge.

It is true that violence and terror are sometimes the only weapons available to those who are oppressed and disenfranchised, but we told Mandela in no uncertain terms that the government would not sit with its arms folded while the ANC planted bombs and landmines and killed innocent civilians.

A myth that the ANC tried to keep intact is that thanks to the actions of its military wing Umkhonto weSizwe it defeated the South African government militarily.[8] This is pure nonsense. Planting bombs in a Wimpy or landmines on a deserted farm road, or opening fire as Apla members did with AK-47s on a church congregation and then running away cannot be seen as military conquests.

The truth is that the ANC's armed onslaught was in many respects an abject failure. Where did the ANC set up a military base on South African territory, or even just a camp, as prescribed by the theory of revolutionary warfare? In fact, they were not even safe in neighbouring states.

The practice of necklacing was one of the most loathsome and despicable methods of terrorism which has ever been used in the history of human conflict. To make matters even worse, it was lauded by Winnie Mandela, no less, who trumpeted it from public platforms as the designated method of freeing the black majority. No peaceful progress was even vaguely possible, we said to Nelson Mandela, if leaders of the ANC preached such forms of violence.

The government was deeply shocked by the fact that many ANC attacks, for example the planting of bombs in public places, were focused on soft and defenceless targets. True freedom fighters do not wreak havoc against defenceless women and children. We had enough information to prove that calls to extend the struggle to include white suburbs were increasingly being made by the ANC leadership and that the violence looked set to gain a decidedly racist overtone.

Mandela's comment was that he knew nothing about such plans. 'Naturally you wouldn't know about this, sir, because you were isolated from these things,' was my reaction.

At this stage the radicals in both the security forces and the ANC were probably asking themselves what the alternative was to events on the political front. The right-wingers would have said to themselves, 'This peace initiative of PW's with political reforms and concessions ... If it lands on the rocks, what then? Then we will be in for a hell of a fight. The ANC's terrorists will storm our white suburbs and shoot people. We must be prepared for that.'

And on the other side, the radicals in the ANC in all probability would say to themselves, 'PW Botha is deceiving the world and Madiba too. He will never give up political power. We must turn the screws, extend the struggle to the suburbs and retain the initiative.'

The differences between the ANC's political leadership and the MK cadres on the ground showed that there was little or no control over the ANC's terror attacks. Mandela admitted this grudgingly. NIS had plenty of proof that MK was undisciplined and that the military leadership paid little attention to political authority.

But it would be short-sighted for us to delight in this. The challenge for us and Mandela was to get MK to consent to any possible agreement.

Mandela was also reasonably uninformed about the dynamics and sentiments in white politics. We explained to him that crucial elements in the security forces and a substantial portion of the government's traditional supporters had little enthusiasm for any settlement process. It was unthinkable to announce this as the new political gospel while the ANC was planting bombs and landmines.

The ANC's highest executive body, the National Executive Committee (NEC), came increasingly under the influence of MK's leaders and it appeared that the radicals had a stronger influence on the course the ANC was taking. If Mandela expected the government to keep its security forces under control, the same applied to the ANC's control over MK. After all, the government could not take future undertakings – by Mandela or anyone else – about the control of MK seriously while there was chaos in the ANC camps. At that stage NIS had reliable information on torture, rape, kangaroo courts and executions taking place in Angola.[9] Naturally Mandela was poorly informed about this and was clearly troubled when told about it.

This inglorious past later returned frequently as a nightmare to haunt the ANC and not even the subsequent manipulation of commissions of inquiry could paper over the disputes and bitterness.[10]

By November 1988 the discussion on violence gained a new dimension. The president asked that we inform Mandela he was prepared to meet him, but on the express condition that Mandela would give him his personal assurance that he does not support the use of violence as a method of reaching a political solution.

Mandela listened to this message with dismay and obvious consternation. Had we not made any progress with our talks, he wanted to know. He said negotiation had to be free of fear – that with a revolver pointed at one's head talks could not be frank and entirely honest.

While these are wise words, to achieve peace in the affairs of state, the sword and the word are inseparable.

Mandela was told that Botha also had a support base that accompanied him along the road he had to travel. The president had to retain his credibility among his voters, and the positions he had taken on key issues and had maintained over the years could not simply be changed overnight.

Botha did not expect Mandela to make a public statement or speak out about the question of violence. The requirement was that he would agree to assume a personal stance that he was not a proponent of the use of violence to reach a political settlement.

The emphasis on the strategic importance of a *personal* stance should not go unexplained. This was our manoeuvre to create space for Mandela so that he did not have to accept personal responsibility for the violence-mongers in the ANC – who we realised would not listen to him on this issue and might damage his credibility irreparably.

I wanted to know from Mandela what he was going to do if, after his release, he was unable to persuade the ANC that the violence had to end. Would he then rejoin the path of armed struggle with his resistance movement, which would in turn force us to arrest him again? Or would he choose his own course and venture along the path towards a peaceful settlement on his own?

He evaded this question astutely: 'Yes, that is a difficult question. I cannot discuss a question like that with you. That is a matter between me and my organisation.'[11]

On PW's requirement concerning violence Mandela remained stubborn and stood his ground. Among other remarks he said that as one of the founders of Umkhonto weSizwe it was unthinkable for him now to call a halt to violence openly; to do so at this stage would dash all hopes of peacefully defusing the revolution. Furthermore, it would completely destroy his image and his credibility. As he put it: 'The image which I have amongst my people must remain intact and under no condition must I make a statement that destroys that image.'[12]

He countered by asking us what we would do if, on behalf of the ANC, he began laying down conditions such as pulling all troops out of the townships, lifting the state of emergency and releasing all political prisoners unconditionally before any negotiations could begin.

I did not agree with Mandela that the legitimate task of a government to maintain law and order could be equated with the actions of a political organisation to gain power by means of force. The two cannot be compared. Yet it did highlight the dilemma of the use of force and the search for a peaceful constitutional solution.

He had to take his organisation with him, which would be impossible if he went to them with the message: 'I was ordered to renounce violence and … give assurances as an individual that I will not turn to violence as a solution.' That would have turned him into a lone individual who was rejected due to his concessions to the government, and the talks with him would not have led to anything. Mandela supported our standpoint in this regard with his statement that unless he had the support of 'his people', he would be 'totally useless' to the president.

I realised that nothing good would ever come of undermining Mandela's leadership stature. We did precisely the opposite by trying to promote his prestige in the ANC so that he could hold the organisation together and lead it. Although he was the impressive Nelson Rolihlahla Mandela, he was nevertheless sometimes uncertain about the role he would play when he walked out of prison one day.

Gradually, both the team and Mandela came up with new formulations on the question of violence. Mandela began to talk increasingly of his role in normalising the situation. Thanks to the insights of Mike Louw and Fanie van der Merwe, the team took the view that the government and the ANC were both in favour of a non-violent solution to the country's political problem.

On the question of violence, Mandela threw the ball back into our court.

In reaction to Botha's conditional offer he suggested that Botha rather make a public statement which drew attention to the position Mandela had taken during the Rivonia Trial, namely that he had never belonged to any organisation other than the ANC, and that Botha had made sure his stance on the matter was still the same. The implication of this, according to Mandela, was clear: it would confirm that he was not a communist.

Mandela went on to suggest that Botha declare the following in public: 'I am convinced that this man is not a communist and [that] … if released he will work for peace … [and renounce] violence.'[13]

If the president made a statement to this effect, Mandela solemnly undertook not to react by denying anything. Thus, his silence would be construed as an acceptance of Botha's statement.

This was in all likelihood an honest attempt by Mandela to make it possible for Botha to get out of the corner into which he had painted himself, but it would not serve the purpose. On what basis could Botha suddenly declare that he was convinced that Mandela was not a communist and now no longer supported violence?

I spoke bluntly to Mandela and did not pull my punches; these were not the sort of games one tried to play with PW Botha. He could happily forget about that. It was nevertheless my duty to convey the message to Botha – which I did, with great caution. He barely reacted at all.

Nevertheless, the suggestion did clearly underline the fact that although Mandela was very keen for the settlement process to be a success, he did not want to lose any credibility along the way; he wanted to remain in control of the constructive process.

He even went so far as to say that as much as they wanted to come home, the ANC members in exile did not want to shed blood; above all, he said, 'there is really no question that the revolution [is just] around the corner'. [14]

CHAPTER 14

MANDELA GETS A WIDER VIEW

From the time of the first meeting at Pollsmoor in May 1988 we realised that Nelson Mandela could not participate in the talks about the future of South Africa as a prisoner in prison clothes.

It is to Minister Kobie Coetsee's credit that he played a crucial role in accommodating Mandela in a normal homely environment where he could live like a normal person, although with limited freedom of movement.

Underpinning this was the belief that prisoners cannot be equal negotiators. Mandela, our team believed, could not be clad in boots and a prison service overall and be brought from a prison cell to contribute to such an important discussion. It is to the credit of the team of officials that from the outset they realised that the talks were not being held between 'conqueror' and 'conquered' but between parties who accepted that no solution was possible unless it was reached between equals; the one could not progress without the other in the search for answers.

It was already clear that in all likelihood Mandela would be South Africa's next head of state, and as patriots it was our task to prepare him for the full spectrum of the life that awaited him as head of state and world icon. When the time arrived we wanted him to represent our country with grace and distinction – unlike Paul Kruger, president of the Transvaal Republic, who, in the late 1800s, had visited the British queen and reputedly launched his chewed lumps of tobacco left and right over the royal table!

Many different possibilities were considered. Eventually it was decided that it was in everyone's best interests if Mandela was settled on his own in a comfortable house. But where?

The Brandvlei prison in Worcester was considered, as was the prison outside Malmesbury and many others in the rural areas. The surroundings had to give Mandela safety and privacy. His move should not be publicised, or we would have to deal with crowds of toyi-toying people. In addition, the place chosen had to be situated nearby so that I and the other members of the team, all of whom had other responsibilities, could get there reasonably easily and quickly. At the time I was also involved in the negotiations on South West Africa's independence and frequently found myself in airports across the world.

General Willemse suggested a house on the grounds of the Victor Verster prison between Paarl and Franschhoek. It was situated on one side of the grounds and the head of the prison service assured us that he could persuade the present occupant to move out because the house was needed for an important national purpose. But all this could not be done overnight.

Meanwhile, in August 1988 Mandela was diagnosed with tuberculosis and was first admitted to the Tygerberg Hospital and then to a clinic in Constantia, outside Cape Town, where he received treatment until early December. As a courtesy I visited him there twice, but naturally we did not have any serious discussions about state matters.

A considerable stumbling block arose with his new home: the furniture there belonged to the official who had lived there previously, so the house had to be completely refurnished. Our hearts sank at the thought – doing this via the Department of Public Works and the state tender process would take months. Who came to our rescue?

NIS! A good intelligence service is not subject to the suffocating bureaucratic regulations that apply in the civil service.

I telephoned a particularly efficient member of the service in Pretoria, who landed in the Cape a few hours later. Within two days the house was fully equipped, from knives and forks to bed, table and curtains – likely the quickest that any house had yet been furnished by a woman!

A day or two after his discharge from hospital Mandela moved into the house.[1] It was a reasonably modern farmhouse with three bedrooms. There was a swimming pool on the spacious plot that was planted with shrubs and a few pine trees. The only aspect of his new accommodation that Mandela disliked was the barbed wire above the surrounding fence. However, it was not there to keep him inside, but rather to keep unwanted guests out![2]

To give Mandela gradual exposure to the outside world, senior correctional service officials took him on excursions across the peninsula. He was driven around Cape Town, along the coast, through some white suburbs. He later wrote: 'It was absolutely riveting to watch the simple activities of people out in the world: old men sitting in the sun, women doing their shopping, people walking their dogs. It is precisely those mundane activities of daily life that one misses most in prison.'[3]

He was allowed to walk along the beach, and he drank tea at roadside cafés together with his guards. This could have caused all kinds of ructions if people had recognised the world's best-known prisoner, but nobody did.[4]

It would have been in no one's interest to keep Mandela sheltered from, and uninformed about, developments in the ANC and in the country at large or to cut him off from the ANC. Only on the grounds of first-hand information would he be able to make good decisions and only through contact with his comrades would he be able to consolidate his position in the ANC.

The government team realised that although he kept his advisory channels secret, he did not have, as we did, the advantage of ongoing consultation with other reliable advisers.

From the outset we understood that he needed the backing of the ANC in all of the important decisions he had to make and in each undertaking that was asked of him. We knew the ANC was deeply divided over the desirability of a peaceful settlement. With this in mind we knew intuitively that it was important and in the interests of the peace process for him to be able to communicate regularly with his support base so that he could inform them and gain their support for the settlement process. No matter how much he claimed that his communication with his supporters was a consultative process, he handled the initial stages of our discussions on his own.

Mandela was an opportunistic interlocutor. If it suited him, he avoided answering a question by using the need for consultation with the Rivonia group, other ANC leaders and ANC supporters as an excuse. If he saw an opening and could take the gap, he was self-willed, stubborn and even dictatorial in his unilateral decision-making. These, alas, are the characteristics of a great leader.

Mandela had a close, confidential relationship stretching over decades with members of the Rivonia group, including Walter Sisulu, Andrew Mlangeni, Raymond Mhlaba, Elias Motsoaledi, Wilton Mkwayi, and Ahmed Kathrada.

This relationship had been built up largely in the turmoil of the struggle and had survived for more than a quarter of a century, forged by mutual hardship. After Mandela's move into the house at Victor Verster, arrangements were made for the group of old comrades to visit him regularly. We were not so stupid as to think – as some people later expected of us – that we should isolate him and negotiate a one-sided agreement. In any case, he was far too astute to fall for that.

The conversations with his comrades, which took place from September 1988, were penetrating. Mandela told his comrades about his secret talks with the government and informed them that the government's team, which accepted his bona fides in the search for a peaceful solution, was very knowledgeable although it was poorly informed about the ANC.

Time and again he undertook not to give way on majority government, the armed struggle, or ties with the South African Communist Party (SACP). He repeatedly assured his comrades that they should trust him and said that he was slowly but surely making progress.

Here and there the comrades were concerned about Mandela's optimism and they often warned him not to trust the government too easily. (Indeed, they said Mandela should not allow himself to be mesmerised – PW's warning to me! Fear that negotiators will develop too much understanding and sympathy for an opponent is a universal risk during talks. However, this should not be confused with critical insight into the opponent's opinions.)

In turn, Mandela warned his group of comrades that they should send out a positive message about settlement talks with the government and help to persuade the masses that they should not foment senseless violence, which would give the government a golden opportunity to accuse the ANC of a breach of faith.

When this group of leading ANC personalities was eventually released in October 1989, most of them did anything but keep their promise to exercise a stabilising influence. On 29 October at Soccer City in Soweto, the Mass Democratic Movement (MDM) arranged a splendid welcome. SACP flags were waved everywhere and songs of praise in honour of Umkhonto weSizwe reverberated around the stadium.

Speaker after speaker exhorted the masses to continue the struggle. Kathrada spoke of the attempts by the government to introduce reform and denounced it as just another form of apartheid, praising whites who had shown the pluck to visit the ANC in Lusaka. Sisulu was more controlled and asked the masses to pursue the liberation struggle in an orderly and peaceful manner. The Swedish premier Ingvar Carlsson, in a message that was read on his behalf, promised to impose further sanctions on South Africa, which drew thunderous applause.[5]

We regarded this event as a test run for Mandela's release. At the same time it was an opportunity for the revolutionaries to let off steam. We could not justifiably expect those who had been released to repudiate everything for which they had been languishing in jail for a quarter of a century just because we (through Mandela) had asked for restrained action. Not even Mandela could move this mountain.

Although many of the speeches made the hairs on the back of the necks of our colleagues in the security forces rise, it was heartening to observe that the old guard was still accepted as the leaders of the masses. Also reassuring was the fact that the ANC had accepted organisational responsibility for the gathering and that reasonable order had prevailed.

The secret revolution of behind-the-scenes talks and negotiations was aimed exactly at preventing the frenzy of the inflamed masses such as during the public executions of the French Revolution and the storming of the Bastille in 1789, and the murder of the tsar in the Russian Revolution of 1917.

Gradually Mandela was permitted, partly as a result of his request, to receive an increasing number of like-minded people, including South Africans and a few from beyond our borders. In this way, he was prepared for the wide range of opinions and viewpoints in the world outside the prison walls to which he was about to be exposed. A telephone was later installed so that it would be easier for him to make contact with people. Of course, this also held certain advantages for us at NIS.

In addition to his wife, Winnie, and other members of his family, the visitors included prominent ANC figures who informed Mandela first-hand about the most recent tendencies in the organisation. In turn he asked for his guests' patience and informed them optimistically, but often selectively, about his talks with the government's team.

During one of Winnie's visits in July 1988 he told her that during the past month there had been promising developments that gave him great hope. The discussions, he said, were at a critical, delicate stage, one that would hopefully lead to increased trust on both sides, but called for patience. Unfortunately he was not at liberty to give her any other details.

Mandela warned the ANC leaders who visited him that these discussions were gaining momentum and that they should immediately start preparing for negotiations, because the government's people were ready, well trained and thoroughly prepared.

Had he known that this was not the case! Not even the Cabinet was aware of the secret talks and, furthermore, as most of its members could not – or would not – read the signs of the times, there was no talk at all of such preparations.

It is inappropriate to mention all of Mandela's guests and the reasons for their visits here but a few are indeed relevant.

With Dullah Omar and Ismail Ayob he spoke of the internal

dissent in the ANC and gave fatherly advice about how to solve this issue. These two comrades warned him that COSATU would become an important political factor and that many of the leaders of this organisation were not in favour of negotiation. In conversations with Albertina Sisulu, Murphy Morobe, Cyril Ramaphosa and Cassim Salojee, he sketched the course of the talks with the government team in some detail and warned them to show an understanding of white people's fears. He asked that Afrikaners be included in discussions about the future of the country because they held the political power and 'we can learn to understand how they think'. During this visit he alluded to the possibility of a listening device, saying: 'I don't think we are alone.'[6]

Albertina Sisulu thanked him sincerely and said that after his explanation they could give the people guidance on what was going on. Morobe said he understood that the government was afraid of mass action and gave Mandela the assurance that it would not occur. The leadership of the ANC would not allow the radical machinery of the MDM to take control of the process.

Mandela warned them that the reports he was receiving indicated that the youth were radical. Furthermore, he was disturbed by the inflammatory actions of Harry Gwala, a firebrand and hardened communist who had been released in November 1988 after he had lost the use of both his arms due to motor neuron disease. Despite this, he was closely linked to the bloody conflict between the ANC and Inkatha in the Natal Midlands that had led to the suspension of his membership of the central committee of the SACP.[7] Mandela condemned the actions of Gwala, who was also a member of the ANC's executive committee, in remarks to some of his visitors.

He placed great emphasis on the point that the government was ahead of the ANC as far as preparations for negotiations were concerned: 'I want us to be in front [ahead] of them. That is what I want.'[8]

With the veteran politician Helen Suzman, who had visited Mandela previously on Robben Island, the discussions dealt with the tense relationship between the ANC on the one side and the Inkatha Freedom Party (IFP) and Mangosuthu Buthelezi on the other.

They also discussed the role of the Conservative Party (CP) and what could be expected from white right-wingers. Mandela said that he understood white people's fears but was of the view that after five years of democratic government these fears would be allayed. He told Suzman that although sanctions had forced the government to adjust its policies, he was not in favour of sanctions because they damaged the economy.

Mandela explained that the initiative for the talks with the Government had come from him. Suzman advocated that he meet with the British ambassador to South Africa, Sir Robin Renwick. This request would be repeated by ex-judge Jan Steyn of the Urban Foundation.

Mandela's conversations with various people at the house on the Victor Verster grounds were a resounding success. They allowed him not only to play a confidential role in advancing the secret revolution, but also to gain a better perspective on international affairs and the undercurrents in his political power base.

It also meant that his mythical, almost superhuman image gradually made way for the realistic image of a talented and charismatic leader with singular characteristics.

How did we know what Mandela and his comrades said to one another in the house at Victor Verster? Well, no intelligence service worth its salt would fail to keep a record of conversations of such critical historical significance – especially if Mandela himself was part of these talks.

And no true freedom fighter – Mandela was, after all, one of the founders of Umkhonto weSizwe – would be so naïve as to think his conversations with a spy boss would not be monitored. Mandela was nobody's fool.

The use of bugging devices was an open secret. We never discussed it. Some of the prison guards at Victor Verster knew about it and presumably told Mandela, but at no stage did he broach the topic or voice his disapproval.

The reason for this was probably very simple. Mandela was very aware that he was not the supreme elected leader of the ANC, that he did not have a mandate to engage in the talks and that he thus had to make absolutely sure that throughout the proceedings he had the ANC leadership's support to continue with the initiative. I believe the recording of the conversations was a kind of insurance policy for him. If it was ever necessary for him to prove what he had undertaken and not undertaken to do, the evidence was on tape.

In an ironic and indirect fashion, the monitoring strengthened our mutual trust. Once, when he wanted to speak about Winnie, he took my arm and said, 'Come, let's rather go out and talk under the tree.'

But at the tree there was also a recorder! When we moved into the tree's shade I looked up into the branches and said, 'Let's talk elsewhere in the garden.' His face showed the slightest of crooked smiles and we walked away.[9]

From NIS's side, we handled the monitoring as ethically as possible. We never made any of the pronouncements by Mandela's guests public, nor did we use any of Mandela's utterances against him later during the official negotiations or at any other time.

By the winter of 1989, when Mandela's release moved even higher on the agenda, we often encouraged him to invite IFP leader Mangosuthu Buthelezi for a visit.

In 1975 Buthelezi had been a prominent member of the ANC Youth League when he formed the National Cultural Liberation Movement (NCLM) in Natal, cast in the same mould as a cultural organisation formed by the Zulu king, Solomon, in the 1920s in reaction to British and Afrikaner domination. The NCLM soon became known as Inkatha ('crown'). The ANC and the Pan Africanist Congress (PAC) were both banned organisations by this time, which left a vacuum for black political aspirations.

When we raised the topic of Buthelezi visiting Victor Verster, Mandela became vague and evasive. He seemed very reluctant to receive Buthelezi as a guest.

He would have to consult his comrades on the matter, he said; he was clearly playing for time. Behind the scenes he tried with all his might to consult on this thorny issue with his comrades in Lusaka, the Rivonia group and the struggle structures within the country, including the United Democratic Front (UDF) and the Mass Democratic Movement (MDM). However, they were evasive; on occasion, he complained to Winnie that he was very dissatisfied that the ANC had not given him an answer to his offer to speak to Buthelezi and to try to make him part of the settlement process.

Buthelezi and Inkatha, ostensibly a cultural organisation but in reality far more than this, had rejected the ANC's armed struggle and undertook to end apartheid by non-violent means. There was intense competition between Inkatha and the ANC over which organisation was the true representative of the political aspirations of the Zulu people. In time, this boiled over into a bloody and protracted conflict that since the 1980s had led to the death of thousands of people, especially in KwaZulu-Natal.

It did not take prophetic insight to realise that the ANC warlords in KwaZulu-Natal were not in search of peace; they simply wanted to fight it out to prove once and for all who wielded the political sceptre over the Zulu people.

Buthelezi, who was by no means a lackey of the government and enjoyed considerable international esteem, cleverly took the initiative. In July 1988 he wrote to Mandela to wish him well on his birthday on the eighteenth. He did so 'on behalf of the 1.6 million black South Africans who have joined Inkatha, and on behalf of the Zulu King and the vast, vast numbers of people in Kwazulu ...' [10]

He included words of encouragement to Mandela, saying that he was sure to be released eventually, and continued almost poetically: 'You are our brother in the struggle. You are a father of the struggle and your liberty is our dearest wish'. He reiterated that he would not take part in any political settlement until Mandela was a free man.

Mandela would certainly have picked up the innuendo in Buthelezi's letter: that Inkatha was by no means an insignificant little party; that the Zulu king was closely associated with the organisation; and that Inkatha and Buthelezi were an integral part of the struggle, of which Mandela was *one* of the fathers.

Buthelezi continued in the same vein to say that apartheid would be obliterated but that this should signal the birth of a democracy. He issued an almost prophetic warning: 'We must avert a final apartheid posthumous victory as black opposes black and so destroys black, that none can be left the victors.' He referred to their 'black brotherhood' and reminded Mandela of his past role in opposing enmity between black people.

Mandela was somewhat disconcerted by the message and

the direct reference to violence between black people. He was visibly taken aback, clearly not well informed about what the ANC warlords planned and preached in KwaZulu-Natal and the blood-soaked extent of the conflict among the Zulu people. He was obviously not keen to listen to the information we had on this and listened in silence. We left the matter there.

A year later, Buthelezi wrote to Mandela on his birthday once again. After expressing the hope that it would be Mandela's last birthday in jail, he reported that real peace between black people had still not been realised: 'We know that anger in the very air will continue to breed black-on-black violence on the ground until somehow there is a kind of catharsis and everything is laid to rest. Our commitment to work for peace between black and black and to join black to black in the common pursuit of a just society will continue.'

Mandela did not hesitate to discuss this question with his visitors, but he refused to discuss it with us. I am not sure what his motivation was in this regard, but I imagine that he was distressed, even embarrassed, about this violent discord in black ranks while he held up the struggle (even idealised it) as a harmonious effort for a noble cause. He may also have wanted to prevent us from trying to drive a wedge between him and Buthelezi.

During a visit from Helen Suzman in July 1989, he told her that the Rivonia group in Pollsmoor had approved a visit between him and Buthelezi but that the ANC in Lusaka had refused to give permission. This meant, to his disappointment, that he and Buthelezi were unable to lay the differences between the ANC and Inkatha to rest.

In a letter to Buthelezi, Mandela expressed the hope that the cordial relations that had existed in the 1970s between Buthelezi, Oliver Tambo and their respective organisations would be speedily restored. The 'most challenging task facing the leadership today is that of national unity,' he wrote.

Mandela described political disunity as a fatal error that had to be avoided at all costs. Wisely, he did not choose sides in the conflict, and said, 'I consider it a serious indictment against all of us that we are still unable to combine forces to stop the slaughter of so many innocent lives.'

He made no secret of his consternation, 'In my entire political career few things have distressed me so as to see our people killing one another as is now happening.' He foresaw a horrendous outcome: 'As you know, the entire fabric of community life in some of the affected areas has been seriously disrupted, leaving behind a legacy of hatred and bitterness which may haunt us for years to come.'[11]

These were prophetic and wise words, which, alas, fell on deaf ears.

CHAPTER 15

NEGOTIATING OUR OWN PEACE

Dissatisfied, on a night in May 1988, I sat in a plane from London on my way back home after yet another tedious round of talks about South West Africa's independence. On instruction from the president, I had been included, somewhat against my will, in the South African negotiation team. The secret talks with Mandela had only just begun and I had enough on my plate.[1]

I mulled over the day's events and saw, in my mind's eye, all the emissaries and observers in the proverbial contest arena: South Africa, Angola, Cuba … and in the wings: America and the Soviet Union …

Suddenly the reason I felt so disgruntled became crystal clear: this was *not* how South Africa was going to do it. Like small boys in a sandpit who were being watched over by big brothers to make sure the little ones played according to *their* rules. Not a damn!

Another thought came to me: negotiations are like love – the only participants should be those who are intimately involved. The same applied to our discussions with Mandela and, through him, with the ANC.

Attempts by other countries throughout the world to hijack the South African peace process were legion. For example, in March 1986 the so-called Eminent Persons Group (EPG) visited South Africa on behalf of the British Commonwealth in an attempt to establish how peace could be promoted in southern Africa.[2] One of the leaders of the EPG, General Olusegun Obasanjo of Nigeria, visited Mandela in Pollsmoor and arrangements were made for an official discussion in May after the group had held talks with the ANC in Lusaka and government representatives in Pretoria. For their own reasons, Pik Botha and the Department of Foreign Affairs supported these plans enthusiastically.

In the early hours of 19 May, a few hours before the group was due to meet with the government, the SADF attacked ANC bases in Harare, Lusaka and Gaborone, after which the EPG promptly cancelled its appointment and left the country. For years afterwards Pik Botha spoke reproachfully of how the military had ruined 'my peace initiatives'.

Later, the whole world seemed to want to give us advice; some parties certainly had good intentions. The attempt by the British ambassador to South Africa, Sir Robin Renwick – and, through him, the British premier, Margaret Thatcher – to become involved in the peace process is one of the best – or should one say worst? – examples.

About a year after the beginning of the secret talks with Mandela, headlines appeared out of the blue in British newspapers about a message from Mandela to Thatcher in which he had reportedly expressed his appreciation of the British involvement in the peace initiative. According to *The Guardian*, a 'third party' had delivered the message verbally.[3] An anonymous spokesperson for the British Foreign Office claimed that the full text of the message could not be made public. The report also mentioned that Mandela had thanked Thatcher for refusing to visit South Africa while he was still incarcerated.

Somewhere, there was a snake in the grass. PW was justifiably furious. I spoke to Mandela urgently to find out what was going on. It was an intense talk during which I explained that if our talks were held up as a consequence of pressure by the British on the South African government, the negotiation process would be utterly derailed. No self-respecting country, let alone one under PW Botha, would tolerate that.

Mandela categorically denied the existence of any such 'message' and, at my request, he sent a handwritten letter that same day to this effect to Renwick, in which he distanced himself from it. Mandela also agreed that this letter could be made public. In the letter, which was published widely in the media, he said, among other things: 'I must point out in this regard that I neither wrote such a letter nor dictated it to any attorney as alleged in the [news] reports.'[4] Mandela's co-operation in removing this obstacle to the negotiations was worth its weight in gold.

The British were not the only ones trying to stake a claim.

The American presidential candidate for the Democratic Party in the 1988 election, Michael Dukakis, suddenly developed a great concern for Mandela's health after he was admitted to Tygerberg Hospital. In a letter to Botha he wrote that the Mandela family was 'gravely troubled' by the fact that Mandela was seemingly neglected by the prison authorities while his health had clearly deteriorated. Mandela was not receiving due medical attention in prison, Dukakis wrote.

He asked that the family be allowed to have Mandela examined by a team of medical specialists of their choice to remove any doubt about his illness.[5]

Botha hit back in characteristic style. It is worrisome that an American presidential candidate could be so poorly informed, he wrote, and suggested that Dukakis check his facts before making derogatory remarks. He told Dukakis that his letter insulted the medical profession in South Africa: 'I am sure it did not escape your notice that South Africa pioneered human heart transplant surgery and that in many other areas of medical research it is also in the forefront.'[6]

Dukakis was dead silent.

At Kobie Coetsee's suggestion, Mandela had earlier been examined by the world-renowned Professor Heinrich Herzog of Switzerland, who reached the same conclusions as the specialist at Tygerberg. Coetsee often came up with clever tactical moves like this one to protect the credibility of the negotiation process.

The foreigners who posed as peacemakers had counterparts, as it were, inside the country: a wide range of people, from romantics and politicians to cynics and academics, held talks with the ANC, some perhaps with good intentions, others with no more than an eye on their own interests.

Between 1983 and 1990 about 1 200 South Africans met representatives of the ANC in exile in 167 gatherings or meetings attended by churches, legal bodies, businessmen, sportspeople, journalists and students. They came from a wide range of organisations, from Anglo American to the Broederbond and Orania.[7]

In 1988 and 1989, in the two years in which the secret talks between the government and Mandela took place, these meetings reached fever pitch. The path to Lusaka, London, Dakar and Switzerland was trampled flat.[8]

Most of these 'peacemakers' were full of injudicious idealism and completely misjudged the intensity of the ANC's power game in competing for political power. For the uninformed, these efforts were noble attempts. If the government was too stupid to see the writing on the wall, they would take the initiative to force the authorities to act.

Of these safaris, NIS's Mike Louw said that it was 'certainly inappropriate that these groups, because they were naïve, uninformed, or because they shamelessy promoted small sectional interests, were prepared to kneel at the feet of the ANC. The ANC should not be allowed to slip in through the back door. If it wanted to enter, it should do so honourably, through the front door.'[9]

The frustration felt by these unofficial negotiators was understandable: they honestly believed the country was hovering on the edge of a precipice and the government would do nothing to salvage the situation. The secret discussions with Mandela and, later, with the exiled ANC were, however, at such a sensitive stage that any public disclosure to put these amateur negotiators' minds at rest would have wrecked the peace process.

Mandela and I thrashed out this matter in detail when we met in March 1989.

I told him that, as in the case of foreign interference, the government could not be put in a position in which it appeared that it was yielding to the pressure of these domestic peacemakers. As a politician who always had to be mindful of his support base, he understood this only too well. He agreed that these mediators did not have the authority to make the settlement process succeed. I also asked him to use his influence with the ANC in exile, particularly the contingent in Lusaka, to ensure that they also viewed the approaches by all and sundry in this light.

We could not trust these self-appointed mediators; each wanted his own pound of flesh, which bedevilled our process. Mandela agreed: 'I don't want people to say that they have influenced me. I myself have influence and would like to negotiate in that spirit. This [negotiation process] is a domestic issue.'[10]

The basic problem with these 'negotiators' was that they represented no one but themselves. This was clear for all to see, and the government had already made it evident that a new political dispensation had to be worked out, which sports bodies, churches or even the mighty mining houses could not do.

Perhaps it was the deep emotional connection we both had with

South Africa that brought home both Mandela's and my realisation that negotiation, like a healthy marriage, had no room for outsiders.

How could a country's future be entrusted to people who had no political responsibility and had not been elected to positions of authority? Only the state and its representatives could negotiate a new constitutional dispensation, reach agreements and then implement them.

Confusion was another problem. Some of these self-appointed peacemakers thought that they had intimate knowledge of the government's thinking and conveyed it to the ANC, passing it off as authoritative. However, these were often mere speculations or even deliberate distortions. We then had to go to great lengths to put it right.

Naturally, the ANC welcomed contact with people who could be seen as leaders or who excelled in their field. They knew that matters were moving in the direction of a settlement; in anticipation, it was essential to identify and influence prominent people and groups. The discussions and safaris, then, were not as innocent as they seemed.

This was the ANC's chance to improve its international image: 'Look, we are not a bunch of terrorists. We smoke pipes, drink whisky and read *The New York Times*.'

One could also view this from another angle: imagine if – without consulting Mandela (a route we could have taken if we had wanted to) – we had conducted independent negotiations with the UDF, the PAC, the SACP, the Mbeki faction in exile, Inkatha and whoever else, to find out what they thought. Mandela would have been furious and said, 'What are you trying to do? You're pulling your old stunt of divide and rule!'

One of the great successes of the secret talks with Mandela was to get his buy-in that the peace process would be led and implemented by South Africans. Through this, we ensured his commitment to South Africa's sovereignty in the negotiation process.

Negotiations are indeed like love; nobody can love another on your behalf, and nobody can negotiate on your behalf. Agreements mediated by a third party often lead nowhere because the opposing parties did not come to an understanding from conviction.

South Africans were able to negotiate peace successfully because they did it themselves on home soil. We pulled it off and in the process we made a unique contribution to conflict resolution.

CHAPTER 16

RED AND DANGEROUS

I often reported back to President Botha on the same day of my talks with Mandela. With an eye on the impending negotiations, critical information regularly came from the ANC's inner circle that he had to be informed of.

At that stage I had free access to the president at all times – at any time of the day and sometimes also at night. That he always made time for this is surely an indication of how important it was to him.

Botha was always very interested in what had been said during the discussions: 'Is he someone who listens to reason?' he would ask. Or: 'Is he a man with whom we can make peace?'

I could see that Botha was struggling within himself. Should he make peace with the ANC and betray his people (he would have thought) or save his people by making peace? He accepted my judgement but remained worried that Mandela might outmanoeuvre me.

He never doubted that I should keep talking to Mandela. He often spurred me on: 'Keep moving ahead. You are doing the right thing.' But our discussions never gave rise to incisive advice from his side.

From the early 1980s the influence of, and support for, communist ideology was on the wane throughout the world.

However, within the ANC this was not the case. The South African Communist Party (SACP) was a formidable political movement and still makes its presence felt twenty years after the advent of democracy in South Africa. As is the case today, SACP members, although small in number, were an extremely influential group within the ANC, and the Party played a critical role in the struggle in southern Africa.

With good reason we were very concerned about the great influence exercised by the communists in the ANC. One of the most troublesome aspects was that the SACP had no respect for the free market system and would make sure, if they had their own way, that industry and mining would be nationalised if the ANC came to power. In their leaders we saw no sign of moderation, reason or attempts to effect a peaceful settlement.

Needless to say, the government took the SACP very seriously when its leaders in the inner circle declared with pride: 'If one looks at communist parties throughout the whole world, there are none that appear to have the same depth and level of influence as our Party has on the National Liberation Movement (NLM).'[1] Although in this instance there was no specific mention of the ANC, it stands to reason that the SACP must have had considerable influence in the ANC – the largest alliance partner – to have been able to influence the NLM.

The 'Inner Party Bulletin' (1986) is an informative document that expresses the following, among other sentiments: 'We must not be satisfied with the position we have undoubtedly won as the radical conscience of the liberation front. We must in addition become a radical force in our own right.'[2]

Naturally, the SACP remained on our radar; we acquired sources in its highest council chambers, especially in London, so that we knew what it had up its sleeve. It unsettled us that, despite Mandela's assurances, this group of influential people was the tail that wagged the ANC dog.

The danger became even clearer when the revolutionary statements of various comrades who attended a meeting were studied.
'Comrade B', as the anonymous comrades tried to disguise their
identity, was of the opinion that 'we are not strong enough to
impose our will or enter into negotiations from a position of
strength. At the same time we cannot say we reject negotiation,
because we have to widen our support by undermining the regime
while concurrently increasing our strength.'

'Comrade E' was unabashed in expressing the wide influence
of the SACP in the struggle: 'Our position in the NLM is strong
but unfortunately the best elements of our Party are hidden in it
and only the old members are known.'

On possible negotiations with the government, 'Comrade I'
said: 'The enemy wants to talk to a weak ANC and employs every
trick to achieve this and unless we quickly repair our weaknesses
on the ground we shall never succeed.'

From the outset, Mandela was reluctant to discuss anything
about the SACP and communism. He was obviously irritated
that spokespeople of the government were publicly labelling him
a communist. He denied in the strongest possible terms that he
was a communist and rejected the allegation that the ANC had
swallowed communist ideology hook, line and sinker.

He mentioned that in the 1940s he himself was worried about
the growing influence of the SACP in the ANC – so much so that,
during the Transvaal Congress of the ANC in 1945, he tried to
get a proposal accepted that SACP members could not concurrently be ANC members. This proposal was rejected because too
many influential members of the ANC were also members of the
SACP. Along with Oliver Tambo and Walter Sisulu, Mandela had
initially made concerted attempts to prevent ANC engagement
with the SACP.

Mandela went on to say that as leader of the ANC Youth League he had tried to kick out the communists, but was unsuccessful. The reason was that the non-communists in the ANC believed the organisation was akin to a 'parliament of the people' and that everybody should be allowed to join. In addition, the government was the common enemy – and in this struggle, any ally was welcome.

The ANC could not afford to shun or alienate fellow fighters in the struggle. The alliance, he explained, was a marriage of convenience.

Mandela admitted that there were elements of communist ideology for which he had some affinity, especially the socialist models of communism as they had found expression in France and England. According to him, these offered a better opportunity for all people, especially the disadvantaged, to make a decent living. He also found it commendable that communists worldwide supported the struggle for justice in word and deed.

He reiterated that he was not a communist and that the Freedom Charter, which had been accepted in 1955 at Kliptown by the Congress of the People, was by no means a blueprint for communism. Indeed, in 1956 he had written an article intimating that the Freedom Charter could lead to a blossoming of free enterprise activity within the black population.[3]

Mandela continually tried to portray the SACP positively. In this regard he quoted the British premier, Margaret Thatcher, who had said of Mikhail Gorbachev, 'I like Gorbachev. I can do business with him.'

However, Mandela neglected to mention that the Russian leader had begun to pull down the pillars of communism!

He then tried to express his viewpoint on communism by taking another tack, that of friendship: 'If we turn against our friends the communists, your government will have every right to ask: If that is the way you treat your friends, how can we trust you to keep faith with us?' He went on to remark: 'When you [the government], who are presently the enemy, demand that we get rid of the communists, who are presently our friends, you make it virtually impossible for us to act on this matter because to do so would inevitably create sympathy for the communists.'[4]

Because I had made a thorough study of communism and its social application, I felt obliged to point out to Mandela that it had not delivered the utopian workers' paradise it had promised. In practice, it was a fiasco. If he needed proof, he should take a look at Cuba – regardless of Fidel Castro's seven-hour speeches enthusing about all the wonders it had wrought there. The fact was that his people lived in poverty, had to queue for food, drove old decrepit cars and if you dared to use your vote against the Party or its politicians, you were locked up. The Soviet Union had rescued itself by moving away from classic communism.

I put it crudely to Mandela: it is really nothing other than a system in which a small, select group of people live a wonderful life thanks to dictatorial power, abusing the state to do so and waxing lyrical on all kinds of theories of equality while depriving others of these same privileges.

Mandela did not debate this with me but stated that he found the dogmatic and prescriptive nature of communism unacceptable. He preferred to borrow the ideological elements he found attractive. He made no secret of the fact that the nationalists in the ANC knew exactly what they were fighting for and would not allow their aims and ideals to be taken in tow by foreign ideologies.

Recent research shows that in his later years Mandela distanced himself from communism, but it is true that in the 1950s and 1960s he had a great deal of sympathy for this ideology.[5] Proof of this estrangement is the fact that his first overseas visit was not to Moscow or Havana but to New York and Washington. Indeed, many years passed before he visited Moscow.

If the government demanded that he distance himself from communism, Mandela argued, he would be obliged to abandon many valuable friends he had made in the past, which he was not prepared to do. The ANC would not allow a political opponent to force him to reject a proven friend. In this regard he made an insightful, moral remark: 'Once you are my friend, I will listen to what you have to say about other friends, but I don't want an opponent to tell me who my friends should be.'[6] One has to salute Mandela for this wisdom.

He agreed that many of the intellectual stars of the ANC at the time were also members of the SACP, and referred especially to Joe Slovo. By implication, Mandela admitted that the ANC would need its SACP comrades at the negotiation table to prevent their being outwitted by the government.

On the right to own private property – which, for communists, is a capitalist aberration – he made an interesting remark: 'The majority of [our] people will never have anything to do with Marxism-Leninism. The workers aspire to change their position, to get better houses, better living conditions. They want to own [material] things.'[7]

This was an honest remark that comforted us. The degree to which this desire is responsible for materialistic offences and corruption by the black elite today would make Mandela turn in his grave. However, at that stage it was reasonably certain that the ANC, with Mandela at the helm, would not introduce a classically communist policy of class struggle and large-scale nationalisation. When Thabo Mbeki and the leaders of the external wing of the ANC became part of the negotiations, it soon became quite clear that they were committed capitalists.

Mandela underestimated the influence of the SACP and held it against us that, according to him, we believed our own propaganda about the ANC. However, we showed him the many pronouncements in ANC publications and by its leaders that embraced communism enthusiastically and glorified the key role that the SACP was playing in the struggle. We wanted to show him that he was out of touch with the ANC's prevailing ideological tendencies.

Mandela sugar-coated this prickly topic by saying that once formal negotiations between the government and the ANC had begun, the relationship between the ANC and the SACP would become irrelevant.

The hours-long discussions about communism clarified a few cardinal issues.

The first was that Mandela, despite an ideological flirtation with communism, was by no means a dyed-in-the-wool, Stalinist communist. Instead, he was what one might call a crypto-communist who had made elements of communism part of his political philosophy. He was a proud and driven black African nationalist who sought out and made friends and allies who would support him and his organisation in their endeavours to reach their ideals. He believed in nationalism and claimed that apartheid was robbing black people of this.

The debates, including those on the questions of violence and a future constitutional model, continued – hour after hour, day after day and blow by blow. At times they were brutal, hard-hitting and painful. But the longer they continued, the better we began to understand and respect one another's fears, expectations and dreams.

Mandela had an old-fashioned gallantry reminiscent of the

manners of a British aristocrat. The way he received visitors was a good illustration of this.

We had an appointment at least twice a month and when I arrived at the house at Victor Verster, I would always be dressed in my customary suit and tie. He would receive me at the door and, as always, I would take off my jacket. Before I could do anything with it, he would take it from me, despite my protestations, and hang it up.

Then I was asked first about my health, then whether Engela was well, then how the boys were and, finally, 'What would you like to drink?'

I felt it immediately: he was the genteel host and I was now in his territory.

But it was more than this. He had a presence one would expect of a future president, which he used very naturally.

Unlike many other influential people, Mandela was at ease with the power of his presence. He carried it in a way that put the people around him at ease. It was not a studied performance – it was his nature.

Of course, he could also be stern and severe if something he felt strongly about was under discussion, but he was never arrogant. Despite his stature, he was humble. His persona was devoid of any self-importance or snobbishness. But like all people he enjoyed the admiration of others, especially in his later years.

No other leader in modern times has, to my knowledge, possessed this combination of engaging qualities.

The initial course of our discussions was also a revelation. I would usually open the conversation with one of the major issues, or something in this vein. He would remain utterly silent, listening attentively, for perhaps twenty or thirty minutes.

'Are you finished?' he would usually ask.

Then it would be his turn, but within the first few minutes I would want to interrupt him to comment on something.

'No, no!' he would reproach me, sharply. 'You have had your turn. I am talking now. Now you can listen to me.'

After many hours and several months, the discussions took on a more 'Western' style, if one could call it that, and we were more inclined to interrupt each other when telling each other stories. But I sometimes yearned for the polite and dignified way in which Mandela preferred to conduct discussions.

CHAPTER 17

THE LEADER FALTERS

After his usual Christmas holiday at the Wilderness on the Cape south coast – and the celebration of his 73rd birthday on 12 January 1989 – the president and Mrs Botha returned to Cape Town to face the new year's activities and responsibilities.

On the morning of 17 January, Botha made time for one of his favourite ways of relaxing by horse riding along Noordhoek beach. It was a windless summer day but on his return to Westbrooke, the official residence, he asked the staff: 'Do you hear how the wind is blowing?'

This remark brought questioning looks, because no one had heard the wind blowing.

That night Botha awoke with a severe headache and felt nauseous; he went to the bathroom and collapsed, where his wife found him on the floor in the early hours of the morning. A physician who was summoned gave him an injection and stayed with him to monitor his condition. When Botha awoke later that morning he complained that his left arm and leg felt 'strange'.[1]

At about the same time I took a flight to Johannesburg. Shortly after we landed, I received a message to go immediately to the VIP lounge where an urgent call awaited me. It was Ters Ehlers telephoning from Botha's office and he was audibly upset: 'Doctor, you must please come to Cape Town immediately. There are major problems here.'

I asked what the matter was. All he would say was, 'Something is seriously wrong. The boss is not himself.'

I turned on my heel and caught the first flight back to Cape Town, where Ehlers informed me that Botha had suffered a stroke. He was in the intensive care unit of 2 Military Hospital in Wynberg.

The president's office expected me to keep an eye on matters. After all, history tells us that palace revolutions can arise at any place and time. Happily, order and stability was part of the inheritance of Botha's rule. The administration of the country, including the security forces, went ahead without a hitch.

I purposely avoided any idle chatter about crown princes and successors.

Later that afternoon a bulletin was issued on Botha's hospitalisation; it stated that his condition was stable following a 'mild stroke'. In due course it became apparent that it had been anything but 'mild'.[2]

This was the beginning of the end of PW Botha's 53-year-long political career.[3] It would hold wide-reaching consequences for the country and NIS.

CHAPTER 18

WHITE FEARS, BLACK ASPIRATIONS

The three central issues in the talks with Mandela – the ANC's use of violence and terrorism, the influence of the communists on the ANC and a future constitutional model for the country – continued to be debated from May 1988 to the end of 1989.

None of these were easy, but the question of how a new constitutional model could be put in place and which form it should take was especially complex. How could a country move peacefully from one political dispensation to another, particularly if it involved the transfer of political power from one racial group to another against the backdrop of a history of racial tension?

Deep-seated power interests – the power of the South African state against the now-evident power of the ANC backed by the black majority – had to be reconciled. The state still had superior military power and could, for the most part, maintain law and order and render services, but the legitimacy of its authority to do so was on the wane.

The liberation movements, on the other hand, were far weaker militarily, but were increasingly challenging the authority of the state and disrupting its service delivery while the legitimacy of their struggle in the eyes of most South Africans and the international community had increased significantly.

Throughout, the basic question remained: how could the will of the majority in their quest for democracy be addressed in a peaceful manner? From the outset the government's team took the stance that an interim transitional government had to be brokered with the input and participation of all the major roleplayers. At the same time, someone had to rule the country in an orderly manner through the painful birthing process of the new dispensation.

Early on we reached a clear agreement with Mandela on a fundamental issue: that the government and the ANC were the undisputed main roleplayers in the discussions about the country's future.

'I don't mind how many parties are included in the deliberations,' was Mandela's reaction. He wanted to negotiate with the NP because it was clear that the ANC was the thorn in the NP's flesh. He went on to say: 'In reality it is the NP and the ANC who must talk and negotiate.'[1]

Another critical aspect on which agreement was reached was that neither the government nor the ANC should act in a way that undermined the other's role and influence in the negotiation process. This would endlessly complicate the settlement process. We also agreed that the leading roleplayers in what was by its very nature a brittle and sensitive process would both guard against party political opportunists, fifth columnists in the security forces and foreign do-gooders hijacking and wrecking the process.

The main issue was that an understanding was reached that Mandela would not be released into a vacuum, but into a climate of consensus about certain basic matters.

Quite early in our discussions Mandela explained that we had to accept the principle of majority government, which implied full political rights for black people. 'We fully understand that and accept it,' was our response. We assured him that this was also the position held by the president.

In the same breath we asked him time and again: 'Are you aware that many white people fear majority government, and that they have good reason to feel this way?'

From the outset Mandela was very accommodating about this and said it was a reality that would have to be addressed. On the far right of the political spectrum, the Afrikaner-Weerstandsbeweging (AWB) had already been formed in a garage in Heidelberg (Transvaal) in 1973; by the mid-1980s it was notorious for various, mostly distasteful, reasons.

In 1982 right-wingers gained a more civilised public image when a group of NP parliamentarians, in protest against power sharing with coloured and Indian people, broke away from the party and formed the Conservative Party (CP). In case anyone, including Mandela, doubted the viability of white conservatism, the CP became the new official opposition in the parliamentary election of May 1987, replacing the Progressive Federal Party.

Two years later, while our secret talks were underway, there was another election in which it was generally predicted that CP support would increase even further. It was therefore not without irony that Mandela expressed the hope that the National Party, whose political policy he had previously despised, would fare well in the election.

'I hope you win, because I don't want to start all over again [with settlement talks] if the CP wins,' he said.[2] The NP won this election but with a decreased majority: 48 per cent (in comparison with 53 per cent two years earlier), while CP support grew from 27 to 31 per cent.

To counteract white people's resistance to a black government, Mandela came up with the interesting suggestion that the proposed interim government should comprise 50 per cent black and 50 per cent white representatives, and that together they could rule the country for a transitional period of five to ten years. Such a dispensation, he reasoned, would give the two groups greater exposure to each other, which would in turn lead to responsible majority government in which the best candidates would be elected to rule the country. This was a noble ideal on Mandela's part, but after 1992 it disappeared in the quicksand of affirmative action during the formal Codesa negotiations.

The government team also asked Mandela what guarantee the white people had that they would not be exposed to the same orgies of chaos and bloodshed that had occurred during the 1950s and 1960s in other African countries.

When Mandela tried to find reasons for what had happened elsewhere in Africa after independence he showed his Achilles heel. As convincing as his arguments were about South Africa's political issues, those he used to explain away the delusions and blunders of megalomaniacal African political leaders were unconvincing. It came down to putting all the blame for Africa's dismal post-colonial history on colonialism.

I retorted that most countries on the continent had become independent 30 or 40 years ago; surely it was about time they stopped putting the blame for all their woes on other people and accepted responsibility for the chaos. We talked for a long while about the critical role of administration and service delivery and Africa's pitiful record in this regard.

Nine months after an agreement was reached on a ceasefire in the Border War, and the SADF had pulled out of Angola and, largely, from South West Africa, in the early hours of 1 April 1989 about 1 600 armed Swapo members crossed the border from Angola into South West Africa. A few hours before the UN's Resolution 435 came into effect, marking the official beginning of peace for South West Africa. The Swapo members were heavily armed with automatic weapons, mortars, surface-to-air missiles and a large number of anti-tank guns. They clearly had one aim in mind: to wipe out any remaining military presence in the northern part of South West Africa and to disrupt the upcoming election.[3]

The government team could hardly have asked for a better case study to hold up as an example of how agreements made in Africa are blatantly disregarded, and I wasted no time in bringing this home to Mandela in no uncertain terms: 'The agreement we will come to with you is of immense importance to us. If this is how Swapo and the ANC go about agreements, the process of settlement politics has suffered a setback from which recovery will be difficult.'

And this wasn't all, I explained: when I see the president again he will surely say to me, 'And so, Dr Barnard, what do you have to say now? You saw what Swapo did, and yet you want me to trust the ANC. What makes you think they will act differently?'

Mandela's initial defence was that he could not speak on behalf of other freedom fighters. He agreed that Swapo had made a grave mistake, but argued that he and the ANC should not be judged according to the deeds of 'people outside South Africa'.

I told him his opportunism was transparent. When it suited him, he understood the untrustworthiness of many errant leaders of African states – and we were expected to do so too. When it did not suit him, we were expected to understand that he could not be tarred with the same brush.

Out of the blue he launched into an attack on NIS and told me that the reputation of any African politician who had any kind of dealings with NIS would be shattered. In the same breath he said he had developed trust in me, but I had to realise that the ANC and Swapo were different organisations that could not be treated the same way.[4]

I could not resist the temptation to issue a light threat that I would have to tell the state president that he condoned Swapo's indefensible breach of faith.

Mandela suddenly changed his tune and admitted that everyone agreed that Swapo had committed a grave error, but we should not allow it to stand in the way of our own negotiation process. We both agreed on this wholeheartedly.

Although the talks with Mandela were wide-ranging and certain secondary issues were also touched upon, we did not discuss in any depth (and, as far as some were concerned, not at all) matters such as a federal system of government, a bill of rights, the content of a new constitution and similar issues. On other controversial questions such as affirmative action and the redistribution of land we did indeed spend a great deal of time because of the government team's concern that such steps would have a detrimental effect on efficient administration of the country and food security.

The aim of the secret discussions was not to reach conclusive agreement on governmental issues, but rather to learn about each other's opinions on important matters first-hand, to identify common ground and to create a climate of mutual trust and understanding.

Besides, any 'binding agreements' made during the discussions on matters such as a future constitutional model would frankly be undemocratic, unfeasible and inappropriate. These issues would be the responsibility of the democratically elected leaders of the country's various political groups.

TALKS WITH THE EXTERNAL WING OF THE ANC

As the secret discussions with Mandela progressed, we at NIS realised that it was strategically important to include the influential

ANC-in-exile in the settlement process. Although Oliver Tambo wielded a moderating influence over exiled members, there were also many zealous young pretenders outside the country.

It was our considered opinion that confining our negotiations to captive leaders inside the country would risk having the exiled leaders hijack and derail the entire negotiation process. Unlike some in the security community, we – who were actually responsible for the management and conduct of the early phases of the settlement process – did not believe that there was any lasting value in a divide-and-rule strategy against the ANC.

Had we subscribed to that strategy it would not have made any sense to include the ANC-in-exile, based by this time at its headquarters in Lusaka. It was far more important to work through one central focus of power, namely Mandela, who enjoyed wide support among his people. It would have been exceptionally foolish to try and negotiate with five or ten components of the ANC plus other, smaller struggle parties.

It was also clear to us that there were some differences of opinion between local struggle supporters and the external wing of the ANC. We were convinced that cat-and-mouse tactics in which we played the one group off against the other would only increase the chances of conflict and wrest the chances of reaching a settlement irrevocably from our grasp.

Mandela's ability to inspire solidarity was critical to the process. He realised this all too well. He also knew, as did we, that in the eyes of the young Turks, he and the old-guard struggle leaders were from a bygone era. Peace through negotiations was not their ideal for concluding the struggle.

It was true that thousands of ANC followers were living in dreadful circumstances in camps such as Quatro and Pango and in other hiding places elsewhere in Africa, where cruelty and suffering were the order of the day. At the same time, the ANC elite outside the country were enjoying a life of luxury. The colonial powers of yesteryear were able to salve their consciences by providing prominent freedom fighters with free accommodation in swanky hotels, single malt whisky and caviar on a tray. Smoking thick Cuban cigars and drinking glasses of cognac, they complained endlessly about the injustice and oppression in South Africa.

This comfortable and luxurious lifestyle did not go down well with ANC supporters and front organisations inside South Africa. They regularly had to flee for their lives from the clutches of the security police who often caused them inexcusable personal suffering and pain. Mandela was fully aware of the tension between the fat cats and the foot soldiers.

PW agreed that we should not embark upon secret discussions with the ANC-in-exile behind Mandela's back and also that our own Department of Foreign Affairs, because of the advantages confidentiality offered, should not learn of this exercise or be used as a channel of communication.

The plan to include the ANC-in-exile in the talks was discussed in detail with Mandela on three occasions. He was informed that the ANC-in-exile had put out feelers, through Thabo Mbeki via various confidential channels, to hold talks with the government. Several secret messengers who indicated that they were acting on behalf of Mbeki or the ANC made contact with NIS with similar messages. The British and American intelligence services also sounded us out directly in this regard. Therefore, unless we began serious talks immediately and with Mandela's full knowledge – and preferably also his consent – these self-appointed mediators would *befonkfaai* the entire process. (It was Mike Louw's job to tell Mandela what this word, a euphemism for 'bugger up', meant!)

It was explained to Mandela that Louw, my deputy, would be tasked with opening such a discussion channel with Mbeki. He could inform Mbeki first-hand about our ongoing discussions with Mandela and ask Mbeki coridally to ignore all other would-be intermediaries as he would now be in a position to talk directly to the government. Furthermore, this proposed channel would (hopefully) be established with Mandela's knowledge and approval.

Nevertheless, Mandela was still sceptical and suspicious. He did not explicitly say so, but we knew that when his lower jaw began to hang at a slight angle he was unhappy. We deduced that he was worried that we were trying to drive a wedge between him and the ANC-in-exile. 'I must warn you that such a move may destroy all the work we have done thus far.' He went on to say, 'You will be playing into the hands of those who say that NIS is not to be trusted because they are trying to divide us.'[5]

Mandela emphasised yet again that his position of trust in the ANC should under no circumstances be jeopardised.

Presumably in an attempt to resolve his dilemma without openly saying we were testing his trust in us, he asked us not to hold settlement talks with individuals but rather with organisations. As he put it, 'Let's talk to the ANC as a whole. Let's talk to the NP as a whole, you see?'

He labelled Thabo Mbeki[6] a 'gifted youngster', but made it clear that any talks with the ANC-in-exile should be held with Oliver Tambo himself, the president of the ANC. If we consulted with Mbeki, this would cast suspicion among his own group, and this could lead to discord. His very firm standpoint was that we would have to work with him (Mandela) and with Tambo: 'For the moment you will have to be satisfied with me. You can rest assured that I have my own means of keeping in touch with my people.'[7]

'Precisely for this reason we want to make sure that other individuals and powers do not cause division in the ANC and drive a wedge between the ANC and the government,' I explained. 'We could have started discussions on our own a while ago, but wanted first to get your co-operation because we don't want to sow suspicion and discord.'

However, my explanation had little effect. We parted company that day without having achieved anything.

Prior to the second meeting on 21 July 1989, where this matter was discussed, I asked Mike Louw to plead our case. He was very adept at conducting tough talks such as this. Furthermore, unlike me, he had more self-control and found it easier to remain calm.

And then Mandela snookered us. He remarked innocently that he had learnt that NIS was one of the best intelligence agencies in the world. We did not ask about his source, but nodded in the affirmative.

Well then, if that was so, why didn't we bring Mbeki secretly to the house at Victor Verster so that he could join our discussions? This was a low blow; for many reasons, such an exercise was highly inadvisable.

Nevertheless, we noted his implicit acceptance that talks with the exiled ANC leaders had to take place and that he was looking for a way to make this happen on his terms. As Mao Zedong put it, sometimes one has to retreat two paces to advance by five paces at a later stage.

We informed Mandela that such a meeting would only be possible in South Africa after a similar one had been held in Europe.

Louw wrestled long and intensely with Mandela on the involvement of the ANC-in-exile. He explained that a meeting did not mean we were going to negotiate. He also referred to the fact that the day of Mandela's release was fast approaching and there was still a great deal of spadework to be done before the real negotiations began in earnest.

But Mandela counteracted our every move. He said that such a meeting was premature and that we should realise that the ANC was not yet ready to take part in negotiations.

That was indeed so, answered Louw. Which was precisely why the ANC leaders in exile should be well informed of the current situation; this would give them the opportunity to prepare themselves for negotiations.

No, said Mandela. The ANC had to decide for itself who would talk to the government team. 'They may well decide on someone other than Thabo Mbeki.'[8] He objected that the NIS team wanted to prescribe from the government's point of view how it should be done.

It was clear that Mandela would not relent.

I later approached him again on the same issue and informed him that we were planning to go ahead in any case. The matter was too important; we could not allow him to thwart the process.

Time was beginning to catch up with us. FW de Klerk had already taken over as president and it was becoming obvious that Mandela's release was only months away – and before this happened, the external wing of the ANC had to commit to the settlement process. A specific and moral understanding was crucial to this.

We immediately put the wheels in motion for Operation Flair. I asked the esteemed Stellenbosch philosopher Professor Willie Esterhuyse to relay the message to Mbeki in England and to help make the arrangements for a meeting in Switzerland.[9] Esterhuyse, who had already developed a good personal relationship with

Mbeki, would at the same time serve as symbolic guarantor so that the ANC exiles could see that we were deadly serious about talking to the organisation.

With a new head of state at the helm and rumours of peace doing the rounds, there were stirrings in political circles and among officials. We realised that we had to start lifting the veil carefully and show that the peace process was under control and being managed effectively – even though no further details could be disclosed.

As early as 5 July 1988, with the help and full knowledge of PW Botha, NIS had piloted a decision through the State Security Council (SSC) to take out a bureaucratic insurance policy on the secret talks, of which the SSC was unaware. It read as follows: 'The Security Services and Prison Service should study the Mandela question continuously and remain in touch with the situation on the ANC leadership.'[10]

A little more than a year later, on 15 August 1989, FW de Klerk was elected as the new head of state. The next day we laid a proposal before the SSC which was evidence of Mike Louw's gift to say highly significant things in a way that only those who were well informed would understand. It read: 'It is necessary that more information should be obtained and processed concerning the ANC, and the aims, alliances and potential approachability of its different leaders and groupings. To enable this to be done, special additional direct action will be necessary, particularly with the help of National Intelligence Service functionaries.'[11]

Resolution no. 23 of 1989 was intentionally formulated this vaguely and later served the exact purpose for which it was intended.

It was when President De Klerk was informed about a meeting on 12 September in Lucerne, Switzerland, between

Mike Louw and Maritz Spaarwater of NIS, Thabo Mbeki and Jacob Zuma.[12] De Klerk was up in arms and wanted to know who had given us permission to take such a step. This specific SSC resolution was then respectfully brought to his attention.

CHAPTER 19

A WOMAN LIKE WINNIE

Revolutions, whether violent or peaceful, exact high personal prices. Those paid by Nelson Mandela and Winnie Madikizela were no exception. Their estrangement was an example of the high toll that thousands of South Africans on both sides of the liberation struggle paid.

Winnie is and was a very talented person. She was also an attractive woman. Even the old guard of security policemen with whom she had altercations on many occasions over the years often spoke of her being a beautiful woman, particularly in her younger years.

At NIS we were looking forward to her being South Africa's first lady and representing the country with dignity both here and overseas. She had all the potential to outshine the quintessential American first lady Jackie Kennedy.

But this was not to be.

Even before the secret talks with Mandela began, we realised that Winnie's tendency to court controversy and her future role as the 'Mother of the Nation' had to be handled in some way or another. She had to play a key role in the transformation process. Secretly we hoped that Mandela would have a restraining influence on her self-willed and untoward behaviour. If this could be used positively and she became an outspoken proponent of negotiation, we would gain an important ally in the peace process. If such a prominent and radical icon of the struggle were, figuratively speaking, to lay down her weapons – of which she had many – the benefits would be enormous, as she was an international figure in her own right.

However, to speak to Mandela about such a personal, sensitive and emotional issue was easier said than done. On several occasions when this question was raised I asked the rest of the team to leave the two of us alone, or I broached the matter when we were alone.[1]

Needless to say, Mandela was always uneasy during these discussions, but he handled them like a consummate gentleman. He never disparaged Winnie or made humiliating remarks about her. On the contrary, he always protected her and said how sorry he was that she had had to manage without him, that he had relinquished his duty towards her through his political involvement. This remained a very painful issue for him.

Winnie's revolutionary passion was irrepressible, however, and her pronouncements and behaviour grew more outrageous by the day. Throughout the world people took note of her notorious statement in April 1986 of how South Africa would gain its freedom using matches and necklace murders.[2] The ANC leadership, who especially under the guidance of Thabo Mbeki was doing its utmost to improve the image of the organisation overseas, was shook to the core by Winnie's behaviour.

During a discussion about Winnie and her role in the horrendous violence in the country, Mandela became visibly embarrassed and, after a long silence, remarked laconically and a little shamefacedly, 'You know, a man's wife is always right.'[3]

Often he listened in silence while I informed him about such things. Presumably he trusted me to give him accurate information. He was acutely aware of the ANC's embarrassment about Winnie and dismayed by her stubborn refusal to have anything to do with people who could assist her.

During one of Winnie's visits he told her diplomatically about 'positive developments' (without referring specifically to the talks with the government team), that these were extremely sensitive and that anything that she said or did might lead to 'them' asking, 'Can we trust this man if his wife is doing these things?' Later he added, 'If there is any mistake, it must be made by them, not by us.'[4]

Furthermore, Winnie was busy building a luxury home in Soweto, for which she did not have the money, while it was Mandela's wish that when released he would return to the house in Orlando West where he and Winnie had lived for the first few months after their wedding on 14 June 1958.

We observed these events with concern and thought a great deal about how we should act.

General Willie Willemse, who was later promoted to Commissioner of Correctional Services, came up with an excellent suggestion: that Winnie be allowed to move in with her husband at the Victor Verster house. That would keep her out of the lime-light – and away from many temptations – and give us a measure of control over her.

Mandela listened to the suggestion with a twinkle in his eye; Winnie refused point blank.

Her excuse was that she and her husband could not indulge in such privileges while Mandela's Rivonia comrades were still sitting in jail. She suggested that they should, in the interim, be content with day visits. She got her way. It was easy to read between the lines that she was not prepared to forgo her unfettered lifestyle.

That was merely the beginning. In December 1988 a 14-year-old activist, Stompie Seipei, was kidnapped and killed by members of Winnie's team of bodyguards who were known as the Mandela United Football Club. Jerry Richardson was found guilty of murder and Winnie of kidnapping and complicity in assault.

In February 1989 Mandela and I had a wide-ranging discussion about this new bomb that had exploded around Winnie. It was a difficult and uncomfortable discussion.

Mandela acknowledged that Winnie's behaviour was a major problem and said he was doing what he could about it. He admitted that there were issues between them and that he had talked to her many times already, warning her about her unacceptable public pronouncements and actions. At the same time he expressed his gratitude that we had discussed this delicate matter with him confidentially and directly and had not misused it to score any points against him.

To defuse the growing crisis, the ANC leadership formed the Mandela Crisis Committee (MCC). The telephone lines between South Africa and Lusaka hummed with activity. The MCC called on Oliver Tambo to intervene and said disparagingly of Winnie's behaviour: 'She shows utter contempt for both the Crisis Committee and the community.' Tambo was told in no uncertain terms that it was crucial for him to take action against this 'ghastly situation' that was 'developing before our very eyes'.[5]

Initially Mandela was extremely tactful towards Winnie when she visited him. He helped to find excuses for her involvement in some of the unfortunate things that had happened. However, he rejected her retort that the MCC was hand in glove with the security police and that the entire hullabaloo was a plot against her personally; he barely hid his impatience with this lame excuse. She bristled at his advice that she should keep out of the public eye for six months.

In time it became patently obvious that a serious estrangement had developed between the two. In October 1989, when Winnie turned up at Victor Verster without an appointment, Mandela refused to see her. She was obliged to write a message to him instead. In the note she tried to curry favour and said that the Mandela Reception Committee was making progress with the arrangements for when he was released.

Everyone was carrying out his instructions carefully, wrote Winnie.[6]

Mandela reacted officiously, disconcerted by the behaviour of the two women in his life – Winnie and their daughter Zindzi – who avoided him because they did not want to be held accountable for their wrongdoings. To a confidant who visited him,[7] Mandela said he had been struggling for over two years to get Winnie to give him a statement of her banking transactions. He also lamented the way in which she agreed with him when he tackled her on her misdemeanours, but then calmly carried on regardless once she had driven out of the Victor Verster gates.

In the run-up to Mandela's as yet unannounced release, relationships in the Mandela family apparently improved. By December 1989, Mandela and Winnie were speaking to one another regularly. She and some of their children spent Christmas Day with him in the house outside Paarl.

In the previous months, when Winnie, the children and other family members had visited him, Mandela had been the understanding husband, caring father, proud grandfather and the involved family man. For hours on end he enquired about everyone's ups and downs. He revelled in the family's stories, asking particularly about the education of the children, and encouraged them all to study hard so that they could take their rightful place in society.

On the other hand, he also expressed concern about the family's morals and had confronted Zindzi about whether it was true that her three children all had different fathers – a disgrace to the family in his eyes. Time and again Mandela emphasised the role of the church in their lives and said that his immediate family and the broader family circle should also accept the community's moral values.

The Christmas Day visit was a convivial family gathering, but in truth it was merely a pleasant interlude in the deteriorating relationship between Nelson and Winnie Mandela.[8]

The troublesome question of how to handle Winnie had at least one good outcome: it strengthened the relationship between me and Mandela on a personal level. He could see that it was an embarrassment for me to talk to him about it and that our discussions on this matter were handled with the utmost privacy and confidentiality.

This experience brought home to me the realisation that this exceptional man was also just an ordinary, vulnerable person.

On an 'official' level we also learnt to understand each other better. Despite everything we had heard and believed about him over the years, he was not a communist at heart. He had certainly had flirtations with communism on an ideological level, but it was like a school boy who flirts with all and sundry yet in the end marries only one.

I gained great admiration for his nationalism, something that also inspires me. He spoke openly and unashamedly of his Xhosa traditions and was clearly proud of his roots. His love of his heritage and the fact that it was an integral part of his identity were conspicuous.

Perhaps most importantly, he was a man of his word. He held certain strong beliefs but, like any politician, could also come up with a trick or two to justify a comrade's untoward actions, for example. Not everyone can reconcile these two characteristics. Mandela could do it because he was not an opportunistic backbencher in party politics. He was a man of gravitas – this cannot be denied.

Hopefully, I made an impression on him as an Afrikaner who was similarly proud of his background and culture; we both hoped that all the things we valued as South Africans would live on in the new dispensation. Hopefully, he also realised that we had an understanding of black people's political aspirations, because we know what it is like to be trampled politically.

I always treated Mandela with the greatest respect and esteem – not only because he was my fellow man but because he was so much older than me. Indeed, it went beyond this: I treated him as the future president of the country because it was clear to everyone with a grain of intelligence that this was what he would soon become.

Nevertheless, from the government's corner, and especially from the viewpoint of minority groups, there were certain things he had to hear – issues I articulated calmly and respectfully. He evidently appreciated this.

CHAPTER 20

MANDELA'S POLITICAL TESTIMONY

From virtually the first day, Mandela made no secret of the fact that his objective for our secret talks was a meeting with the president. His dilemma was that the president had sent this young 'apartheid spy' to lead the discussion, apparently the only means of gaining access to PW Botha himself.

Presumably he decided to go along with the talks after all and to establish what advantages they would have for him and the ANC. In the meanwhile, however, time was marching on and he realised he was becoming increasingly vulnerable to rebellious elements in the ANC. He had to achieve his objective of reaching an understanding with the government about a peaceful negotiation process; a meeting with Botha was a prerequisite for this.

Mandela knew very well that a meeting with the president would boost his status as a politician who was not only popular but who could also achieve results. He did not want to walk out of jail empty-handed. An assurance that he would meet the president would give him something to show his people. He could then tell them: 'We must seize this chance with both hands.'

By the end of 1988 he became decidedly irritable on the issue. 'When can I see the president?' he asked, pressing me to answer. 'The matter is getting more urgent by the day.'

On another occasion he grew even more upset, saying we were not fulfilling our promise to him. He was feeling bitterly frustrated and deserted.

We realised we could not keep Mandela on a string any longer and still hope to retain our credibility. He could justifiably start doubting our motives. There was suspicion about, and resistance to, our secret talks in his inner circle; he sought a symbolic break-through to justify his belief in negotiation.

Botha, on the other hand, was in no hurry to meet the inter-national symbol of the struggle against apartheid. It had been five months since his serious stroke and his health was not always good. In addition, his position as the leader of the government had become increasingly uncertain after his resignation as leader of the National Party in February 1989.

Mandela had been promised a meeting with Botha and in the light of all of these factors it could no longer be postponed. In the last week of June 1989 I had a long and serious discussion with Botha in his office at the Union Buildings – the same office in which he had offered me the position at NIS ten years earlier. While on that occasion I had been too shaken to ask him anything, it was now my task to spell out what he simply had to do in the coun-try's best interests.

Botha's greatest fear was that the meeting would develop into an unpleasant and confrontational political argument, which was exactly the opposite of what we had been working so hard to achieve. 'If this whole thing goes awry, my people will always blame me for selling them out,' was Botha's abiding fear.

'On the contrary,' I reasoned, 'if you meet Mandela and the discussion goes well, it will immortalise you as the man who ini-tiated the peaceful revolution in South Africa and brought peace and prosperity to the country and all its people.

'If the meeting fails, you can say that you tried your best to walk the path of peace in South Africa. Whatever happens, you will come out of it the winner.'

Eventually he said, 'Very well, then. Arrange it for next week.'

Botha did not lay down clear conditions, but Mandela was to be informed that their meeting on Wednesday 5 July 1989 in Tuynhuys next to the Parliament buildings in Cape Town would be a social occasion to get to know each other – definitely not a platform for political debate.

Mandela was relieved to hear that the day he had looked forward to for so long was just around the corner. He was nevertheless wary of the Groot Krokodil.

'What kind of a man is he?' he asked me.

'He is a difficult but straight-talking and honest man,' I replied. 'With him one doesn't want to look for unnecessary trouble. Please keep this in mind.'

Somewhere along the line – in all the thousands of hours he spent in jail, or perhaps during the secret talks with the government team – Nelson Mandela had come to the realisation that the ANC would not be able to take power in South Africa by force of arms. At least, not in his lifetime.

There was only one alternative: to negotiate with the 'enemy'. To talk instead of shoot. But to conduct meaningful negotiations that would really make a difference, the highest authority of the other party would need to be involved. By 1988, this meant only one man: PW Botha.

With the help of his comrades Mandela began to draw up a political testimony that outlined the main political issues in the country at the time; provided a clear exposition of the ANC's standpoint on each; and suggested a way out of the current impasse. This document, which is provided as an appendix at the end of the book, also served as a petition to Botha in light of a possible personal meeting (hence the reference in the testimony to 'this meeting').

In the document, Mandela is at his resourceful best. His strategy is well considered and measured.

He begins by referring to the 'deepening political crisis in our country' and says that he considers it in the national interest for the ANC and the government to meet urgently 'to negotiate an effective political settlement'.

He goes on to say he is taking this step without conferring with the ANC because he is imprisoned and cannot consult with the ANC leadership in Lusaka, whose authority he accepts unreservedly. This is the only reason why he is acting on his own initiative; he earnestly hopes 'that the organisation will, in due course, endorse my actions'.

In his view, no prisoner, 'irrespective of his status and influence, can conduct negotiations of this nature from prison'. Because of this handicap, his role is of necessity limited to bringing the two opposing parties together to begin talks.

Mandela then proceeds to examine – one after another and probably on purpose – the three main themes we had already discussed in our secret talks. Although he says that he wants to promote negotiations between the ANC and the government, he cuts to the quick by saying: 'No self-respecting freedom fighter will take orders from the government on how to wage the freedom struggle against that same government, and on who his allies in the freedom struggle should be.'

White South Africans, he says, will simply have to accept the fact that there is no way that 'the ANC will suspend, to say nothing of abandoning the armed struggle, until the government shows its willingness to surrender the monopoly of political power'.

On what he calls the 'renunciation of violence', Mandela makes the point that the founding of Umkhonto weSizwe and the use of violence were a last resort 'to end that monopoly, and to forcibly bring home to the government that the oppressed people of this country were prepared to stand up and defend themselves'.

Despite all the progress the government team had made with the secret talks, Mandela claims that the government was doing 'nothing' to create a climate for political negotiations. On the contrary, he says: 'The truth is that the government is not yet ready for negotiation, and for the sharing of political power with blacks.'

On the influence of communists in the ANC, he repeats his view that the ANC will choose its own allies and will not accept instructions that come down to 'a betrayal of those who have suffered repression with us for so long'. According to Mandela the government had 'double standards', refusing to talk to South African Marxists but prepared to enter into agreements with Marxist states such as Angola, Mozambique and Zimbabwe. In his view, the government's stance on communism was all hot air.

Mandela maintains that the government is vehemently opposed to the idea of majority rule and that the rejection of political rights for black people means that 'the government has become the enemy of practically every black man'. He goes on to say that 'there will never be peace and stability in this country' until 'the principle [of majority rule] is fully applied'.

He accepts that the government and the ANC will have to reconcile two conflicting points of view: on the one hand the ANC's demand for majority rule in a unitary state, and on the other 'the insistence of whites on structural guarantees that majority rule will not mean domination of the white minority'.

To this Mandela adds a very important point of departure: 'Such reconciliation will be achieved only if both parties are willing to compromise.' He hopes that the government takes this opportunity without wasting too much time, because he believes that the 'overwhelming majority of South Africans, black and white, hope to see the ANC and the government working closely together to lay the foundations for a new era in our country'.

In the document, which Mandela calls a 'memorandum' in his autobiography,[1] he makes enough revolutionary noises to keep the masses, his power base, happy. At the same time he is tractable enough on the negotiation process to take the moral high ground should the government try to thwart the process.

We accepted Mandela's document, which he presented specifically as a 'non-paper' (a discussion paper without official status) in the same spirit, and reacted to it in writing with a contra-memorandum.[2] In our response we made it clear that Mandela was being far too liberal with the truth in claiming that he had made this move on his own without consulting the ANC. (During the last months before his release, regular consultation had taken place between him and the freed members of the Rivonia group. Telephone conversations, which were monitored by NIS, had also taken place, particularly between him and Thabo Mbeki in Lusaka. During these discussions, statements and declarations from both Mandela and the Lusaka leadership had been widely discussed.[3])

In my discussion with Mandela about the document I told him that we found the revolutionary rhetoric disappointing; it belied the good understanding that had been built up thus far in the course of our secret talks.

For the greater part of the document it was Mandela the freedom fighter talking, pandering to the militant rank and file in the ANC. There was also a second – short but positive – section dealing with the political settlement process, which provided constructive proposals. However, there were very few new thoughts on themes that had not already been debated almost ad nauseam. Mandela was told that for us to revisit these and embark upon extensive debates in long documents would not be worth a bean; this would merely encourage polarisation, suspicion and distrust.

We could, however, not neglect to point out various claims that were factually incorrect, such as the assertion that no political organisation had greater commitment to peaceful change than the ANC; that as far as the government was concerned black people had no cause to espouse or freedom rights to fight for and that white people had the sole right to political power; also that white people had so little regard for black people that they believed blacks could not think for themselves.

On the domineering role of the SACP in the ANC, we told Mandela that he was uninformed about the extent to which the SACP had tightened its grip on the ANC since 1964. It was almost laughable that he found it necessary to quote, of all sources, the US State Department which had published a report on the activities of the SACP in South Africa in January 1987.

Similarly, we rejected his standpoint on the government's resistance to majority rule. This was a calculated and malicious distortion of the situation.

Mandela was informed that especially towards the end of the document there was a positive approach, indicating the intention to place national above sectional interests. There were also encouraging points of agreement on some fundamental matters. The government fully accepted that white political dominance had to come to an end and was honest and sincere in its attempts to realise this through a peaceful negotiation process.

In my opinion, it was providential that Mandela's memorandum was never accorded official status. Both sides allowed it to die a natural death. Peaceful revolutions are brokered by reliable human interaction – not by bulky and controversial documents.

Nevertheless, he had compiled for posterity a political testimony that expressed his role as a peacemaker.

Mandela only gave us the document at the end of July 1989 but it had been sent several months earlier, without my knowledge, via Minister Kobie Coetsee to the president.[4] This makes the warm welcome that Mandela later received at Tuynhuys even more remarkable.

CHAPTER 21

A BRIDGE IS CROSSED

Nelson Mandela, like PW Botha, liked to dress smartly. On the big day neither he nor we would have wanted it any different.

A trim dark suit, white shirt and tie with a paisley and flower pattern were provided by Romens in Cape Town. Sitting beside me in the back seat of the state garage's silver BMW 735i, Mandela was a picture of elegant dignity.

He was one of the few people who, in an instant, could change from a dreary prison-issue overall to a neat three-piece suit and look stately and perfectly at ease in both. A desirable quality for a spy, I thought to myself, and remembered how after the first high treason trial in March 1961[1] he had gone underground and succeeded in evading the police for sixteen months.[2]

Only a practised eye would have noticed that a very ordinary-looking car accompanied us through the morning traffic and that another was on guard at the rear – no blaring sirens or blue lights for one of the world's best-known but most seldom seen people.

Mandela was visibly excited, but also fully focused. He was unusually quiet and not in the mood for talking. He was probably uncertain about what to expect, and worried about Botha, who was well known for his temper.

I tried to put him at ease by saying that we would make sure that his dignity was protected, but also warned him gently that a political altercation would get us nowhere.

Ironically, there was no trouble driving along a public road from Paarl to Cape Town. It was unlikely that anyone would rec-ognise him. The challenge would be to smuggle him past the ever-present protection units of the security police at Tuynhuys. After all, we could hardly smuggle him through the gate in a tied-up sack and then shake him out in front of the king as in the fairy tale!

As is often the case with the most difficult challenges, the solu-tion was reasonably simple. I nonchalantly informed the guard unit at Tuynhuys that I was bringing a guest from Africa to meet with the president at 10:00. It was a normal request that drew no attention at all; over the years I had, on many occasions, brought foreign political and intelligence leaders to Tuynhuys and the Union Buildings for confidential meetings.

We moved through the processes at Tuynhuys in very little time. At Ters Ehlers's office we joined the others – Minister Kobie Coetsee and General Willie Willemse, both of whom Mandela knew well.

While we were there I noticed that one of Mandela's shoelaces had become untied. He could no longer stoop easily – as was to be expected of a person who would turn 71 two weeks later. I quickly went down on my haunches and tied the laces.

By this time we had a very good personal relationship and it was a completely natural thing to do, but for a moment the irony did not escape me that the leading 'apartheid spy' was stooping to tie the shoelaces of the future president.

When we entered Botha's office the president walked towards us with a smile and extended his hand to Mandela. '*Hoe gaan dit, meneer die President?*' Mandela politely asked in Afrikaans.

He was reciprocally impressed by the warm manner in which Botha received him.

'From that very first moment, he completely disarmed me,'

Mandela later wrote in his autobiography. 'He was unfailingly courteous, deferential and friendly.'[3]

Before long the two began to talk about their health – PW assured Mandela that he had recovered well from his stroke – and then families on both sides were unpacked. They found an Eastern Cape connection in that Botha's father was born in Adelaidé and could speak Xhosa, and Mandela chatted about the Free State to which Botha, Coetsee and I all had strong links. Then our ages came up and Mandela mentioned that he was two years younger than the president.

'Then you should call me uncle,' quipped PW to the general entertainment of the rest of the group.

This was certainly not the kind of comment that Mandela would have expected from the man with the angry finger. The atmosphere was genial and relaxed.

Then the Anglo-Boer War came under discussion. Botha mentioned that his father had fought against the British for the duration of the war from 1899 to 1902; Mandela said diplomatically that he had the greatest regard for the Boers' struggle for independence against the mighty British empire.

Botha spoke with passion on the role that Afrikaners could play in Africa to help the continent and its people develop. According to him, there were key contributions that South Africans could make in the fields of education, transport, health, agriculture, employment, welfare and the advancement of Africa's enormous human potential.

By referring to meetings or contact with heads of state such as Félix Houphouët-Boigny of the Ivory Coast, Joaquim Chissano of Mozambique, Kenneth Kaunda of Zambia and Hastings Banda of Malawi, Botha sent a subtle message that the government also had friends in Africa. And, after Botha's glowing praise for Jonas

Savimbi, leader of the Unita rebels in Angola, Mandela did his best to find something positive to say about Savimbi.

Botha then spoke of a discussion he had had with President Kaunda, telling how the Zambian leader had said that if 'the people of southern Africa come to an agreement with the Afrikaners this would lead to far better conditions in the region'. However, Botha was adamant that there was too much interference from outsiders in South African affairs, saying: 'We must hold hands with one another and solve our problems without outside interference.'

On this Mandela agreed wholeheartedly with him: 'South Africa can be the powerhouse of Africa. Once we have overcome our problems there is no reason why we should not play a leading role. We have men who are well-equipped and once we solve our problems I have no doubt that South Africa will play a leading role.'

Botha referred to certain historical ironies, to which Mandela reacted by referring to a recent example: 'Well, I told the minister [Kobie Coetsee] just the other day that it is a contradiction that I should wish for the victory of the National Party in the coming election because I am against everything that the National Party stands for.'

Mandela immediately took the 'political gap' to expand on his well-meant and serious intentions about negotiations, but said he was well aware that no matters of great import would be discussed that day at Tuynhuys. Nevertheless he reiterated his now familiar viewpoint that the ANC had not wished to walk the path of violence, but that the refusal of previous NP prime ministers to meet with ANC leaders had left the organisation with no other choice.

He was very pleased with the discussions being held with the government team, and said the process was 'laying the foundation for fruitful negotiations'. He felt it was critical for opinions to be aired frankly, in confidence and in secrecy.

He contended, emotionally, that both the government and the ANC needed to stop insisting on conditions that neither side could meet before the negotiations could begin. He felt that the ANC's insistence that the organisation should first be unbanned, and the government's demand that the ANC had to renounce violence, were both stillborn.

'I have no doubt that when the country hears that we are busy with serious and fruitful talks, there will be an end to the violence,' declared Mandela. He added that the real negotiations should begin as soon as possible and that he was confident that the momentum of the process would make violence and bloodshed unnecessary.

On the matter of violence Botha was diplomatic, but he refused to budge from his well-worn standpoint. He insisted that 'violence can only lead to unrest and destruction and to dissatisfaction among young people'. He felt that unless the violence was halted, there could be no socio-political development in the country.

Botha did not see the renunciation of violence as a precondition for negotiations, but brought violence and negotiations into perspective in the following way: 'I think by exchanging ideas, by saying to each other 'let violence stop' and as I have often said in public, let us renounce violence as a means to achieve an end. Let us talk to each other, sit around a table, put ideas to one another and see to what extent the socio-economic development in South Africa can take place.'

Botha warned that everyone would have to exercise patience. He reiterated yet again that the role of the Afrikaners should be recognised and that they could make a unique contribution 'because the Afrikaner has no other soil to love'. He assured Mandela that the Afrikaners were 'ready to talk ... to participate in real discussions', and acknowledged that the government and the ANC both had a wise and experienced leadership; they should work together in the interests of everyone in the country.

Then the meeting almost derailed.

Mandela launched into a long monologue which came down to the assertion that no other organisation in the country could equal the ANC's historical record and commitment to peace.

I gasped. This was exactly the sort of chest thumping that would make a political opponent reach for his ammunition. But this time Botha somehow received the grace to keep his cool and, wisely, did not react.

He remarked that too many members of the ANC drifted around the world and listened to what South Africa's enemies said; these enemies merely threw mud at the country and did not behave as patriots should. The time had come for the ANC to re-evaluate its negative outlook on South Africa and not to allow the country's enemies to poison South Africans' good judgement of one another and of their country. He also thanked Mandela for honouring the confidentiality of the talks with the government team and for refraining from making public statements to seek cheap publicity.

Just as I cleared my throat to change the subject, Mandela – despite my advice not to do so – brought up the matter of the release of his old friend Walter Sisulu. He gave a long-winded explanation of Sisulu's exemplary leadership and asked that he be released to bring ANC members within the country, those outside the prisons, to order and restore stability.

He said he was sure Sisulu would play a responsible role and even linked this to his own credibility: 'This is also a way of judging whether you can attach any importance to anything I say in future.'

To our great relief, Botha reacted calmly to this and said he was pleased this point had been raised. He was being kept abreast of developments by the team and Mandela knew that in principle the decision to release Sisulu had already been taken. It was just 'a question of giving it the green light'. Mandela should discuss the matter further with me.

Mandela was delighted and told Botha that he had already spoken with Sisulu and would now make sure that he received the message.

Almost an hour had passed fruitfully. It was time to say goodbye.

With the permission of Mandela and PW, Ters Ehlers took the well-known photo in which Mandela, Botha and I featured, and which later caused such sensation.[4] Coetsee suggested the possibility of a short press statement, to which Mandela had no objection.

We descended the steps from Tuynhuys to the parking garage in good spirits and took the road back to Paarl.

As we pulled off, Table Mountain caught my eye; it stood above us, a bulwark of certainty, guarding the city below. 'Thank you, Father, that PW Botha was on a calm plateau today,' I said to myself.

It was a simple snippet of information that could be summed up in five words, but it was just too big and sensational to expect that no one would spill the beans. This was too much to ask – even for a disciplined man like PW Botha.

A day or two after the meeting with Mandela, Botha was on a hunting trip on a farm in the Northern Transvaal as a guest of Danie Hough, previously an administrator-general of South West Africa. Quite possibly there was a successful head shot or two on the hunt and a few glasses were raised in celebration.

That evening around the campfire Botha could no longer

remain silent about the big news. 'Gentlemen, I have something to tell you. Last week I met Nelson Mandela … received him in my office. We had a good discussion.'[5]

On the Monday morning after the hunting trip, at a meeting of the State Security Council (SSC), Botha circulated the photos Ters Ehlers had taken at the meeting. Eyes widened in amazement – for a range of different reasons.

The spiteful aggression directed towards me was almost tangible. If PW had not been there I would certainly have been tried in the SSC kangaroo court, found guilty and hanged from one of the beams at Tuynhuys!

For those in military circles who were still making plans to neutralise the 'Mandela factor' in politics, it must have been a considerable shock. Right before their eyes was proof that the supreme commander of the most powerful defence force in Africa had offered a hand of friendship to the world's most famous living 'terrorist'.

A thunderous silence reigned, especially among the members of the Cabinet, when they realised that a significant political and historic event had taken place without their knowledge and right under their noses. They probably felt correct procedure had not been followed, that their exclusion simply couldn't be justified.

On the other hand, it was totally justified: if the preparatory talks with Mandela had been made known too early, nothing would have come of the negotiation process that followed. A few members of the SSC – the minority, in all likelihood – were probably relieved that a symbolic breakthrough had been made in the impasse about the country's political future.

Anyone who had the slightest inkling of the importance of the meeting realised that regardless of what the future held, a bridge had been crossed. There was no turning back.

A few days after the meeting between PW and Mandela, with Mandela's permission Kobie Coetsee issued a short statement, compiled by NIS's Mike Louw, about the 'courtesy visit'.

The statement explained that no policy matters were discussed and that no negotiation took place, but Botha and Mandela had confirmed their support for 'peaceful development in South Africa'.[6] A report in *Business Day* was headlined 'Govt takes first step on long path to ANC talks'.[7]

This news caught the ANC and its struggle allies unawares. They bobbed around like corks on the open sea and made one contradictory statement after another.

At a news conference held at Winnie's house, Winnie Mandela and Frank Chikane, general secretary of the South African Council of Churches (SACC), dismissed the meeting as a political ploy to mislead the masses and the international community.

Tom Sebina, publicity secretary of the ANC, announced from Lusaka that the meeting at Tuynhuys should not be regarded as the beginning of the negotiation process. According to him it was a mere gimmick with an eye on the coming white election. Joe Modise, head of Umkhonto weSizwe, said the meeting should be denounced in the strongest possible terms and that violence was the only way the government would be forced to the negotiation table.[8]

Some reason did prevail, however. Bishop Desmond Tutu reacted positively and said that although the meeting was unexpected, it was an attempt to listen, at last, to the calls for negotiation.

Five days after the meeting with Botha, Winnie paid a visit to her husband at Victor Verster prison, during which he read her the riot act and stressed that there was no question of casting suspicion on the talks with the government team. The chain reaction that resulted saw others give their approval of the meeting and the talks. Chikane even praised Mandela on behalf of the SACC.

But the ANC comrades in London couldn't believe what they had heard and declared that Mandela had been outmanoeuvred and was selling the ANC down the river. They raised the possibility that it was all part of an exercise on PW's part to polish his ego and cover up his stroke.[9]

In London the South African Communist Party (SACP) expressed its dismay; it seemed apparent that the ANC was prepared to come to an agreement with the Boers and were excluding the SACP: 'This eagerness for power is seen by the SACP as a source of grave concern, primarily because they see it leading to a strongly repressive state.'

From a well-placed source in London there was the following comment: 'The impression seems to be that the ANC leadership, all in exile, have created a leader, Mandela, over whom they have no direct influence, and the talks between Botha and Mandela are a source of concern to them although they will not admit it.'

The cherry on top was the comment from another ANC member, also in London: 'Mandela may have been drugged or taken by force to the president's residence.'[10]

After the meeting between PW Botha and Nelson Mandela at Tuynhuys, the atmosphere that permeated the confidential discussions at the house in Victor Verster changed markedly. We both knew that it was now just a matter of time before Mandela would be released.

The discussions were more relaxed and easy-going as Mandela's nagging uncertainty about whether he would meet Botha was a thing of the past. In its place came a cautious optimism because the encounter had played out smoothly and amicably. He was visibly more relaxed and was clearly thinking about the future.

The genial tea-drinking in Tuynhuys, as could be expected, did not resolve all of the thorny issues in one fell swoop.

On the way back to Victor Verster prison Mandela was in a visibly upbeat mood and did not lack nerve. Not far from Paarl, he informed me in a tone very much akin to an instruction that I had to make sure that Walter Sisulu was released from jail as soon as possible.

This 'request' was not without a history. Prior to the meeting with Botha I asked Mandela to please not raise the issue of Sisulu's release because I knew it was a complicated and sensitive matter, one that troubled Botha too. Nevertheless, he had thrown my advice to the winds.

'I heard what the president said and it will be carried out,' I replied, 'but in light of what happened after previous releases, Sisulu cannot be released now. There are still many preparations and much convincing to be done.'[11]

Mandela was annoyed: 'You are a state official. You have to carry out the instructions of the president. Mr Botha and I expect this of you.'

I was by now equally annoyed: 'You are probably going to become the president of the country, but you are not in that position yet. The president has left it to me to handle this matter.

'Let me give you a good piece of advice for the future. You would do well, sir, not to appoint yes-men who make promises they know cannot be implemented.

'It is undesirable to release Sisulu in the current climate. I will not be intimidated about this. My opinion is that an orderly climate, such as the one in which you and I began our talks, is in the best interests of the negotiation process.'

Mandela listened to me quietly and did not react. On that memorable day we parted company on a less amicable note, but luckily it soon blew over.

The history behind the Sisulu issue was that by 1987 the government, particularly at the insistence of Kobie Coetsee and my colleague Mike Louw, decided to relieve the political pressure on the government somewhat by letting off some revolutionary steam. One way of accomplishing this was to release a few prominent political prisoners; this would also serve as a trial run for other possible releases.

In November 1987, Govan Mbeki, a member of the Rivonia group, was released – with a few PAC members – after serving 24 years' imprisonment on Robben Island. Mbeki, father of future president Thabo Mbeki, was a fiery, dyed-in-the-wool communist who wasted no time provoking emotions by making inflammatory speeches and statements. From the government's viewpoint – and much to our consternation at NIS – his release did not have the desired outcome; a banning order was eventually necessary to curtail his activities.

This was convenient ammunition for those in the SSC who were against the idea of releasing political prisoners, and Sisulu became the victim. He was to have been released in March 1989 – and Mandela was duly informed – but because of strong antagonism in the SSC these plans were put on the back burner. On instructions from Botha I had to tell Mandela that despite earlier undertakings, Sisulu's release had been postponed. Mandela was furious and accused me of breaking a promise. He had a point.

The unfortunate outcome of Mbeki's release strengthened Mandela's argument that Sisulu should be released as soon as possible, because he was convinced that Sisulu – 'He is generally a man of peace' – would have a tempering influence on the ANC's rank and file. He could also be a reliable channel of communication with the ANC exiles.

However, what complicated his release even further was the growing power struggle within the ruling party after its leader's stroke. At that stage, in NIS's opinion the leadership in the government was simply on too loose a footing to take high-risk decisions.

Eventually Sisulu, along with Ahmed Kathrada, Raymond Mhlaba, Andrew Mlangeni, Elias Motsoaledi, Wilton Mkwayi, Oscar Mpetha and Jeff Masemola, were released early on the morning of Sunday 15 October 1989 – not by PW Botha, but by the new president, FW de Klerk.

Although from time to time PW Botha reiterated his offer to release Mandela and attempts were made to solve the impasse about the ANC relinquishing the use of violence, they were not successful.

Eventually Mandela was released and the formal settlement process began *without* any definitive understanding having being reached about the use of violence. From a rigid ideological perspective this can probably be seen as a failure of the negotiation process, but I believe that the 'no-understanding' outcome was, in truth, the best outcome.

Nobody was able to comply with any undertaking in this regard – for example, that violence would not be used to reach political goals. To Mandela's credit he did not give any undertakings that he knew in his heart and soul he could not honour. Also, trying to mislead each other with tricks and gamesmanship during negotiations never works. The course of South Africa's formal negotiations during Codesa I and Codesa II are good examples of this.[12]

It is an error of judgement to believe that the issue of violence in revolutionary circumstances had to be resolved before settlement negotiations could begin. On the one hand, the government had to maintain law and order. On the other hand, the liberation movements justifiably regarded their terror tactics as their only weapon – losing it would rob them of all claims to, and means of, self-assertion.

In the course of the secret talks with Mandela, the foundation was laid for handling the question of violence in settlement politics. The answer lay not in solving this issue beforehand but in managing it, with mutual understanding and insight, throughout the negotiation process so that compromise and peace eventually triumphed over violence.

This removed the need for either side to go under *hardegat*, as PW Botha had feared on that day in 1986. The first seeds of the peaceful revolution that was destined to change the history of South Africa forever had been planted in secret.

I believe our biggest achievement in the 48 discussions that took place between May 1988 and December 1989 was the way in which we dealt with the question of violence.

CHAPTER 22

'HERE IS MY *KIERIE*'

Some years before he suffered a stroke in January 1989, rumours about PW Botha's deteriorating health did the rounds. Whether there was any truth to them is uncertain, but he deemed the rumours serious enough to speak publicly about them on several occasions.

At the NP congress in September 1985 in Port Elizabeth he joked about it, but a few months later he broached the topic again at an NP caucus meeting and said he planned to serve out his term 'on condition that he could count on the support and loyalty of the caucus'. He undertook to base any decision about his possible retirement primarily on his health.

The rumours persisted. At the 1987 Cape NP congress he raised the matter again, apparently feeling that some in the party wanted him to retire. His characteristic Botha-style message to them was: 'My entire political life is about the politics of fighting, and the harder you fight the less likely you are to get rid of me.'[1]

Nevertheless, there were strong indications that he wanted to scale down his duties. A month after the caucus meeting in January 1986 he asked a special cabinet committee[2] to advise him about possibly 'disconnecting' the presidency from the leadership of the ruling political party, clearly with his own position as president and leader of the National Party in mind. A few days later, according to his biographer, he wrote again to the committee about the matter.

Minister Chris Heunis, chairperson of the committee, understood the underlying reason for Botha's enquiry and wrote back: 'Based on our personal loyalty and regard for you as a person and the leader of our party, the answer to your question is thus an unequivocal confirmation that it is in the interest of South Africa and the National Party that you continue to fill this position.'[3]

The head of many a politician probably worked overtime to find out what these enquiries to the committee meant: 'Does PW want to retire but retain control?' 'Is he tired, or maybe sick?' 'Who will succeed him?' And, the most important question for every politician: 'How will this affect my position?'

In the months and years that followed, the names of various senior members of the Cabinet were bandied about in the media and elsewhere as potential successors. The merits of each were discussed and analysed: Chris Heunis, Gerrit Viljoen, FW de Klerk, Pik Botha and Barend du Plessis. A 'Club of 22' was even formed to promote Pik Botha's candidacy.

In June 1988 the government decided to put three controversial bills before Parliament that made provision for the stricter enforcement of the Group Areas Act, although they also allowed for so-called free settlement areas which would be racially mixed. It was the task of Ministers Heunis and De Klerk to 'sell' the idea of these laws to the coloured and Indian Houses of Parliament. While sensitive negotiations were underway to secure their acceptance, an extraordinary meeting of the NP caucus – strictly speaking, the prerogative of the leader of the NP – was arranged on the authority of De Klerk, as chairperson of the white Ministers' Council.

Botha was furious and refused to attend the meeting. A few days later he also walked out of a Cabinet meeting, of which he was the chairperson, following a heated clash over the same question between him on the one side, and Heunis and De Klerk on the other. Furthermore, Botha was unhappy about the agreement that had been reached with the coloured and Indian chambers.[4]

On 18 January 1989, Botha suffered the incident which, according to the official bulletin, was a 'mild stroke' but later proved to be far more serious. Less than two weeks after his collapse, while still on his sickbed, Botha wrote to the chairperson of the NP caucus and asked that the positions of president and the leader of the NP be separated (the 'disconnecting' he had enquired about three years earlier).

At the caucus meeting on 2 February, Botha's request was approved and FW de Klerk was elected as the new leader of the National Party. However, a month later the federal council and the caucus of the NP decided that the two positions should again be joined. Botha tried to stop this on technical grounds but his efforts were unsuccessful.

A prolonged leadership struggle ensued over who the real political head of state was. In the weeks and months that followed, the existence of two political power centres within the government led to fierce debates and clashes in the NP. One by one, Botha's most faithful supporters in the National Party and in the Afrikaans press turned against him.

The long knives were clearly being sharpened. No one had dared to take PW on while he was the leader of the pack, yet they suddenly found the courage to do so while he was down. In my opinion this was scandalous and cowardly.

It was during these months and against this background that the meeting between Botha and Mandela took place in July 1989. I was still seeing Botha regularly and reported to him, but it was clear that his days in politics were numbered. He was often surly and short-tempered – more so than previously – and he no longer had many friends.

The evening before the decisive Cabinet meeting of 14 August I was with him and Mrs Botha at Westbrooke. And who was there to provide him with advice while he grappled with his place in history? Boet Troskie, a film producer from Bloemfontein.

At the next day's extraordinary Cabinet meeting, Botha asked his ministers, one by one, for a decision on his position. Each of them indicated – some hesitantly, others more open-heartedly – that it was time for him to go.

According to the minutes of the meeting, for the most part Botha kept his emotions in check, but he was irked particularly by a remark from Minister Eli Louw who said: 'The leader PW Botha whom I knew prior to your stroke, is not the same man as the one after the attack.'

'I am healthy. I am healthy,' Botha snapped. 'Tell me, how many of you here have pills in your pockets?'[5]

Botha was forced to accept that his relationship with his ministers had broken down irreparably. That same evening, he announced his resignation on national TV.

The next day, the Cabinet appointed FW de Klerk, the leader of the National Party, as acting president. On 14 September he was formally elected president; six days later, he was duly inaugurated.

Shortly after his resignation I made a final appointment with Botha in Tuynhuys: to say farewell.

It was an emotional occasion in the same office where we had held hundreds of discussions and where, two months earlier, he had kept his appointment with history by receiving Nelson Mandela.

Botha had offered me an enormous opportunity in life and a very close bond had developed between us. Nonetheless, I was not blind to his faults.

I had seen this day coming. I had to say farewell to a great man who had tried to stay on the throne too long – a tragic story that had played itself out numerous times in the course of history.

He called Ters Ehlers into the office and walked to the umbrella stand where he always kept his walking stick. He said to Ehlers: 'I want you to be here. I am giving Dr Barnard my *kierie*, and I hope he understands the underlying meaning.'

'I think so, sir,' I responded, and took the walking stick. It was made of stinkwood; regular use had given it small, characteristic markings.

Just to make sure, Botha said: 'It means I relied on you when I needed someone.'

We are often remembered for our last deeds and actions. Unfortunately, to a large extent, this is also true of PW Botha. Mostly, it is his temper, his capriciousness and his tendency in his later years to offend his closest friends that we recall.

It would do him a great injustice to remember him only for these reasons – and to forget that his deteriorating health probably also played a significant role in this.

Botha had many admirable qualities. The fact that he was an outstanding administrator made it a pleasure to work with him and to give him feedback reports. The unique nature of an intelligence service – which meant that we were not subject to all manner of bureaucratic red tape – did, indeed, make it easier, but it was nevertheless impressive to see how efficiently he got things done. He was the right man at the right time for South Africa – administration and policy implementation had not been a strong point of his predecessor, Advocate John Vorster.

Botha was a doer who made things happen: roads, schools, houses and hospitals were built. Perhaps his limited patience helped him with this. Above all, he was driven by the desire to help people – to serve.

To the question whether he was the world's cleverest, most friendly and most tactful president with the most impressive oratorical prowess, my answer must, unfortunately, be no. However, it is not the wonderful speeches delivered by the head of state or his position at the top of the popularity stakes which make for a successful country.

In addition, Botha was both disciplined and orderly. For the hundreds of appointments I had with him, he was never late. Indeed, a few minutes before we were due to meet he would always ask his secretary: 'Is Dr Barnard here yet?'

The story is told of how in April 1982 he asked Minister Eli Louw what headway had been made with the construction of temporary facilities at Kopfontein on the border between Botswana and South Africa in preparation for Botha's planned meeting with President Kenneth Kaunda of Zambia. Louw carefully explained that because of the procedures that had to be followed with tenders, very little progress had been made.

Botha, who seldom cursed, cried out: 'Good God, colleague! When are you going to get it done? Leave it! General Malan, take over and arrange everything.'

Botha had an astute understanding of the nature and demands of power politics. He was not overly hasty to share or lose his political power, but he realised how critical it was to reconcile the political ideals of all of the population groups in the country. He did not shy away from the reality that Mandela was the centre of gravity in black politics.

PW Botha is often judged one-dimensionally, through a military prism, and seen as the instigator of the total onslaught policy, the man who built the SADF to formidable heights and thus had a militaristic attitude of 'let's shoot it right'. The truth, however, is firstly that Botha liked the SADF's ability to get things done quickly, without first completing heap of forms, and secondly because the SADF could form the shield behind which necessary political steps could be taken in relative peace.

He showed that he was receptive to new ideas. In the early years I often spoke to him about using what the Americans called soft power – diplomacy, discussions, sanctions, and so on – to solve conflict situations. While he was not academic or philosophical by nature, he was knowledgeable enough to recognise when an argument had merit. He was not blinded by ideology or dogma; instead, he was more inclined to reform, led by what was practical and just.

He is reviled for his hard-hitting action against revolutionaries and those who instigated unrest, but history has proved him correct in that it was necessary to create a milieu in South Africa in which the process of negotiation could be conducted reasonably peacefully.

It is probably true that the members of his Cabinet, with the exception of Alwyn Schlebusch, were too hesitant to oppose him – very few dared to do so when he took up his characteristic intimidating attitude about an issue. A priceless cartoon hung on the wall of his study at Westbrooke showing a typical Karoo koppie exploding skywards, captioned 'He erupts from time to time'. He had a quick and sometimes fiery temper but could appreciate jokes about this too.

You had to choose the right time and opportunity if you wanted to communicate something that was sensitive or potentially embarrassing. You do not pull a lion's whiskers while he is on the stage showing which rings of fire he can jump through; you wait until later when he is alone in his lair, relaxing while he eats his giraffe.

Botha could be crude and unreasonable, but the nickname Groot Krokodil does him injustice. While it was, perhaps, appropriate, it is doubtful whether little lizards, of which there were many, could have ruled South Africa in the stormy 1980s.

He had a weakness which is common among Afrikaners: failing to apologise when you insult or offend someone. He did try to make amends in other, subtler, ways, but I wonder how many people would have understood this.

Taking everything into account, PW will, one day, still be given his rightful and well-earned place in the history of South Africa.

THE BLOODY TAPE

After PW Botha's resignation from politics, he and his wife Elize settled down at their house at Wilderness in the southern Cape. He still took a lively interest in politics and events of the day. According to some, too lively.

Botha's biographer tells us that the ex-president listened to FW de Klerk's epoch-making speech on 2 February 1990 'without great enthusiasm' and he then let it be known that 'for him and the NP the sands of time had run out'. Two months later he informed the Wilderness branch of the NP that in reaction to the course taken by the current NP leadership he would not be renewing his membership of the Party that year.

A prominent photo of three men on the cover of *Die Volksblad* of 15 February 1990 attracted his attention: Nelson Mandela, Niël Barnard and PW Botha. It reminded the ex-president of the historic meeting between him and Mandela seven months earlier at Tuynhuys.[1] In media reports reference had been made to the fact that this meeting had paved the way for Mandela's eventual release and, by implication, also for the unbanning of the liberation movements and other steps De Klerk had announced on 2 February.

This was not what Botha wanted to be remembered for.

He then recalled the tape recording he and Ters Ehlers had made, without my knowledge, of the meeting with Mandela. With this he would be able to show, he reasoned, how strongly he had spoken to Mandela on, among other matters, the question of violence and that there had been no mention, for example, of the unbanning of the ANC.

These thoughts brought Botha to NIS.

A few days after the Mandela meeting at Tuynhuys, Ehlers had handed over the tape recording to me, which was the correct procedure in terms of civil service rules. I was uneasy about this because Mandela's approval had not been sought beforehand. Another worry was that the content could be misused for political purposes – which, in the light of Botha's later actions, was not unfounded. After consulting with my deputy, Mike Louw, and after he had also listened to the recording, I decided to have the tape burnt.

This was not the sort of news that Botha wanted to hear after 2 February 1990 and, after various telephone conversations and a great deal of correspondence had passed between us over a number of months, he turned to De Klerk. The upshot was that De Klerk asked me to go to Wilderness to see the ex-president and attempt to put the matter to rest.

I knew PW well and knew what to expect when I arrived on 12 November 1991 at Die Anker, which had been the Bothas' holiday home for years. I was received in a friendly manner, but also immediately warned that the discussion would be recorded and that Mrs Botha would be present as a witness.

Then the interrogation began.

Botha simply would not accept that the tape recording no longer existed, saying 'but it's my property'. I had to answer the same questions over and over again. He was not satisfied either with a copy of my notes of the meeting with Mandela which, according to him, did not give a true reflection of how firmly he had acted towards Mandela. He argued heatedly that he had had every right to make a recording of the meeting 'because Mandela was a prisoner'.

Botha gradually became more emotional and irrational: 'You people thought I was going to die … but I am just as healthy, if not even healthier.' I was then accused of no longer being his friend; that I should stop playing dumb; that he now distrusted me; that I had stabbed him in the back … and was informed that I had to stay for tea.[2]

I let him have his way. The longer he blustered and raged, the more I realised that it was the correct decision to destroy the tape. I shuddered at the thought of what he would probably have done with it and what the consequences could have been.[3]

At times I felt sorry for him and said to myself, 'Forgive him, for he does not know what he is doing.'[4]

A number of years before my father, once a proud and formidable man, also suffered a serious stroke. It was traumatic to experience what this had done to him. Many times we had to experience at close quarters the ups and downs he went through: emotional outbursts had never been in his nature.

When I left, Mrs Botha walked me to the car. She came to stand in front of me like a mother before her son, and looked deep into my eyes. She usually addressed me as 'doctor' but on that day she said, 'Niël, I am sorry. Please understand.'

I gave her a gentle hug and drove away.

It was certainly with premeditated intent that Botha had made a recording of our 'conversation' at Die Anker. Before the weekend he sent transcripts of the tape to *Rapport* and the *Sunday Times*, one of his old political enemies. They had a field day.[5]

A rare statement by NIS said that the recording of the meeting with Mandela had 'no crucial security relevance or value', despite the meeting's far-reaching historical and political significance. In our opinion, 'any further retention or utilisation of the tape could only lead to embarrassment and could serve no future purpose'. No transcription had been made of the tape despite the fact that it had been in the president's possession for a considerable length of time.[6]

Botha did not leave it at that. He asked the ombudsman Judge Piet van der Walt to investigate the matter. He found that it had been an error of judgement to destroy the tape before consulting Botha, that the recording had 'possible historical value' and that in the judge's opinion it was inappropriate for such a decision to be left legally to the discretion of the head of NIS.[7]

I respect the learned judge's finding and accept full responsibility for my decision. Nevertheless, I am still grateful that I had the power to make such a decision in the interest of the country. At the same time, the incident was the greatest humiliation of my life.

A few years later 'Tannie Elize' died of an unexpected heart attack. I attended the funeral service in the Wilderness and sat, as I usually did on such occasions, fairly far back in the church, on the aisle.

When the service was over, everyone waited for the family to leave the church first. PW also came past and greeted me warmly. 'I am pleased you came, doctor.'

Thereafter I phoned him regularly on his birthday on 12 January. In a strange way Mrs Botha had been instrumental, after all, in my reconciliation with her difficult husband.

CHAPTER 24

'IF THE BOERS WERE CLEVER ...'

'If the Boers were clever, they would release Mandela early next year, unban the ANC and set a date for elections that would be hard to meet ...'[1]

This remark in October 1989 by a certain Rashid in the Pamodzi Hotel – the unofficial headquarters of the ANC in Lusaka at the time – to a South African journalist shows that one should never underestimate one's opponent. Little did Rashid know that 'the Boers' were not so stupid after all and that the plans for this were already far advanced.

Even before his election as president on 14 September, it was clear that FW de Klerk would accelerate the pace of the reform his predecessor had initiated but which had since ground to a halt. A huge protest march, mainly against the state of emergency – the kind of illegal behaviour which before had time and again been nipped in the bud by the police with water cannons, rubber bullets and batons – was being planned for the day before in Cape Town.

However, after consulting with the security forces De Klerk decided to allow the march to go ahead subject to certain conditions. More than 30 000 people marched through Cape Town's streets peacefully and without any incident. In the following days similar marches were permitted in Johannesburg, Pretoria and Port Elizabeth. In October Walter Sisulu and seven other political prisoners were released.[2]

These steps sent a clear signal of a new, more relaxed management style. They were also in accordance with NIS's advice that symbolic steps would allow the politically overheated climate to cool down.

Even so, from the outset De Klerk and I did not have a good relationship. Within three days of his election as president, I handed in my resignation as the head of National Intelligence.

I believe that every head of state, because of the unique and close relationship he must have with the head of intelligence, must have the opportunity to appoint the person he regards as most suitable for the job. My bureaucratic ethic in this regard is not to wait to be asked to resign, but rather to resign and possibly be asked to stay on.

Secondly, from the beginning there was not the kind of rapport between us that is critical between people who have to work together so closely and in absolute mutual trust. I knew that when the shots of security establishment infighting rang out, De Klerk would not protect his head of intelligence.

It was clear that De Klerk did not feel at home in the State Security Council (SSC) and did not really want to make a contribution. His body language was that of a child who had been forced to go to church but would rather be playing outside.

Shortly after assuming his position he told me with some malicious joy: 'I shall restore government by Cabinet to its full glory.' What he was really saying was: 'You securocrats' days are numbered. I am going to clip your wings.' I had some sympathy for his stance, because I have never denied that the National Security Management System and the SSC had in reality established a semi-dictatorship aimed at maintaining security.

It was my conviction that this was what South Africa needed at the time to negotiate a peaceful settlement. De Klerk felt that the country did not – that, in fact, it undermined the process. He showed a lack of strategic insight and of the need for clear objectives, as was later to become evident during the constitutional negotiations at Codesa I and Codesa II.

Thirdly, on a personal level, I was resentful of how he and his political colleagues had attacked PW Botha when he was a sick man against the ropes. The manly way is to tackle an opponent on a level playing field, not when he is lying on the ground.

Despite the strained and formal relationship between us, De Klerk refused to accept my resignation. On his reasons for this I can only speculate.

He may have been afraid to let one of the roleplayers in the 'preliminary settlement' (particularly the talks in prison with Mandela) walk away, which could have been interpreted as a rejection of the peace process. Perhaps he did not like to make tough decisions because popularity was extremely important to him.

Whatever the case, I assured him that I would do my work with no less enthusiasm and diligence, would always accord him the necessary respect and would offer my advice as knowledgeably and objectively as possible.

It was conspicuous that from the outset De Klerk and Mandela had little affinity for each other. I was in Russia when they met for the first time, but soon afterwards I was present when Mandela, De Klerk and Minister Gerrit Viljoen met. There was very little evidence of any warmth between De Klerk and Mandela. They were clearly not kindred spirits. The one was relaxed and spoke with wisdom and authority. The other appeared uneasy, resorted to all kinds of showy talk and appeared to be worried about the new competitor in the popularity stakes.

Another trait of De Klerk that did not find favour with me is illustrated by the following. Despite my earnest requests not to make NIS responsible to a minister or a deputy but rather to let its head report directly to the head of state himself because it held clear advantages for the state, he disregarded my advice and placed NIS under the political control of a deputy minister. I suspected that he wanted to put distance between him and us while still enjoying the advantage of the secret and crucial information that we collected. This distance could benefit him: if anything cropped up that could embarrass him, he could turn away and say that he knew nothing about it.

I thought back with longing to the days of PW Botha, who would haul you over the coals privately if you messed up but in public defended you with his life.

By the second half of 1989, particularly after the departure of PW Botha, it was a foregone conclusion that Mandela would be released in the foreseeable future. The major consideration was *how* it should happen. Naturally the struggle organisations had to be unbanned. Mandela could not be a free man as long as the ANC was banned. The logic of this was unavoidable, but there was one problem: communism, the *rooi gevaar*.

The 'hawks' in the security establishment, represented in the SSC by certain leaders of the defence force and the police, had virtually devoted their lives to fighting communism. But now they were being asked not only to accept the legitimacy of the ANC, PAC and others, but also that of the South African Communist Party (SACP).

In the light of the decades-long propaganda campaign against the SACP, the resistance from policemen and soldiers was understandable. At the last SSC meeting before Mandela's release, Magnus Malan (Minister of Defence) and Adriaan Vlok (Minister of Law and Order) dug in their heels. Their reasoning was more or less that unbanning the SACP was as good as letting the devil loose in South Africa.

De Klerk, now chairman of the SSC, wavered back and forth.

I became agitated about the emotional reasoning and the inability to realise the implications of keeping the ban on the SACP in place while lifting it for the other organisations, so I entered the debate.

'Why would we want to drive the SACP underground again?' I asked. 'Communism has already disintegrated elsewhere in the world. Let the SACP take part in open democratic processes and shoot themselves in the foot. Then we can at least see all of them, who they are and what they do,' I argued.

'But more importantly: Mandela will never accept it. He will refuse to walk out of jail. What then? We will have no choice but to unban the SACP after all – with red faces.'

Fortunately, De Klerk appreciated the sense of this and it was decided to unban all the struggle organisations across the board.

Various meetings were held at Tuynhuys to discuss Mandela's release. At all costs it had to be a peaceful and orderly affair, unlike the chaotic return of Ayatollah Khomeini to Iran in February 1979. A measure of mass hysteria could be expected which the ANC's marshals would handle for the most part; while the security forces would be ready to step in if necessary.

After going through a stage of not receiving Winnie, by December 1989 Mandela was seeing her regularly again at the house at Victor Verster. Their conversations dealt mainly with political matters and his release; the expectation and excitement about this already hung heavily in the air.

Mandela told Winnie about his meeting with De Klerk on 14 December; she was wary of De Klerk and warned that he was not all that he appeared to be. Mandela disagreed with her and said he thought De Klerk was an honourable man. He mentioned that De Klerk was under great pressure on account of minority rights and warned that unless the ANC was well prepared, it would be caught unawares by De Klerk and the government in the negotiations that would necessarily follow his release.

Mandela again noted his concern about the ANC's support in the homelands and expressed his dissatisfaction that the ANC leadership owed him an answer about why Buthelezi was not permitted to see him.[3]

Later that same month, as a critical year in South Africa's history drew to a close, I paid my last official visit to Mandela. It was not only the end of the year but, in a sense, also the end of our discussions. In the new year there would be two shorter meetings, but they were completely different in content and mood.

The question of white fears about the future came under discussion again. The election two months earlier, in which the conservative right wing had made great strides, was still fresh in our memory.

Mandela listened to this patiently, perhaps with a touch of fear of what this could entail for him. White fear was a factor that had to be kept in mind, he said, and once again mentioned the possibility of an interim government in which white and black would have equal representation.

In the end nothing came of this, but in the years that followed at no stage did I ever, for example during the constitutional negotiations, try to hold Mandela to statements that he had made during our secret talks. Nor did I raise it when he later took a different stance on some issues from those he had adopted during our talks. The discussions were exploratory: to gain insight into each other's viewpoints, to look for commonalities, to prepare the ground for the seed that still had to be planted.

In January 1990 I visited Mandela briefly at Victor Verster to assure him that everything was on track for the opening of

Parliament in February where the unbanning of the liberation movements and his release would be announced. 'The speech will be written soon,' I told him.

A few weeks later, on 2 February 1990, in his speech to open Parliament, President De Klerk declared: 'The season of violence is over. The time for reconstruction and reconciliation has arrived.' He went on to claim that virtually all leaders in the country agreed that negotiations were the key to reconciliation, peace and a new, equitable dispensation.

De Klerk announced that the ban on the ANC, PAC, SACP and a number of subsidiary organisations had been lifted; that people who were serving prison sentences because they were members of these organisations would be freed; that restrictions on the media to report on the unrest due to state of emergency measures – which provisionally remained partially in force – were lifted; that the lifting of restrictions on certain organisations certainly did not mean that acts of terror and violence would be permitted under their banners; that the maintenance of law and order should not be placed in danger; and that peaceful protest should not become a breeding ground for lawlessness, violence and intimidation.

These steps were in accordance with the government's declared intention to normalise the political process in the country without endangering the maintenance of good order.

'The table is set for wise leaders to begin talking about a new dispensation and, through dialogue and discussion, to reach an agreement.' The agenda for these talks was open, and the government's overarching objectives included a new democratic constitution; universal franchise; no domination or suppression; equality before an independent judiciary; the protection of minorities; individual rights, including freedom of religion; and a sound economy based on private enterprise.

De Klerk thanked the security forces for their dedicated service to the country; their work had made it possible for reform to take place in a stable climate. 'Our country and all its people have been entangled for decades in conflict, tension and armed struggle. It is time that we free ourselves from the cycle of violence and broke through to peace and reconciliation. The silent majority of the population are looking forward to this with great longing. The youth deserve it.'[4]

De Klerk also announced that Mandela would be released within a few days.

It was a historic moment and a watershed in the history of South Africa.

When I visited Mandela a few days later for the last time in the house at Victor Verster, he had a restrained, even sombre, excitement about him. What he had looked forward to for so long was beginning to come true. By this time there was nothing more to say about the three key issues we had discussed so often and so intensely for almost twenty months.

The discussion was now about the arrangements for his release.

Initially Mandela wanted to be released in Soweto because that was where his last home was. His suggestion was that he be flown in secret to Johannesburg. However, it was simply too risky to attempt to control a vast crowd of highly excitable people in such a densely populated area. Mandela probably would have chosen to walk through the streets of Soweto to his old house in Vilakazi Street but the risks involved in this were just too great.

'There is so much steam in the kettle. Let us rather do it in phases,' I said and suggested that he be released in the Cape. I am not sure how the Grand Parade was decided on, but it was an excellent choice: the balcony of Cape Town's city hall was a dramatic and historic 'stage' and the Grand Parade itself could only accommodate a limited number of people.

Madiba consented. As I expected of him, because he always had a good sense of occasion, he made a brief speech about his appreciation for our talks, the role that the government team had played and the band of trust we had been able to establish.

I reacted in an appropriate manner and asked a final favour: 'Please ensure that your first few speeches are restrained. Please keep the crowds under control, because emotions are going to run high. We don't want to start shooting at each other again.'

When I drove through the gates of Victor Verster for the last time, my mind went back to the almost 50 meetings and discussions Mandela and I had. We had talked, and listened to each other, for more than 200 hours. In this time I had seen the rainbow of facets of his personality in action.

He was the courageous but shrewd politician who had embarked on the negotiations without consulting his party, then diplomatically persuaded them to put their faith in him. He was the somewhat anxious freedom fighter who assured everyone that he would not pawn the ideals of the struggle. The modest aspirant statesman who became older by the day and yearned for the recognition and opportunity that he knew awaited him if matters made headway quickly enough. The loyal team member who was at a loss to understand the rumours about his comrades' alleged corruption, smuggling and sexual harassment in the organisation that he had built up with so much love and devotion.

He was the wise old campaigner and Xhosa traditionalist, sincerely troubled by the behaviour of his fellow Xhosa in the Eastern Cape who did not promote the non-racial character of the ANC.

The concerned father and family man who was dismayed to learn about his wife's and some of his children's scandalous antics ...

He was all of these things and so much more – the remarkable and incomparable Madiba.

CHAPTER 25

FREE AT LAST

It was exactly how I wanted to experience this joyful and historic occasion. From behind the screens, one could say, together with my loved ones: Engela and the boys Nico (16), Hannes (13), Niela (7) and our trusty housekeeper, Salome Malipele, in our house in Waterkloof, Pretoria.

We watched as the television cameras panned the scene for some action – Madiba had still not made his appearance.

I could also have been there. During our last meeting, Mandela had asked: 'The day I walk out of Victor Verster's gates, you must be there with me. After all, we have walked this road together.'

I thanked him for his kind gesture, but turned the request down. 'Thank you very much. But it's your and Winnie's day. It's not my place. Furthermore, one of your comrades is bound to ask, 'What is the Boers' spy doing here?'

Not that I didn't have an answer for this, but I still believe that intelligence people should be behind the scenes. Recognition for good work must be sought at work, not in the public eye.

The TV reporter outside the prison's gate had by now discussed every possible nuance of the crowd's pent-up excitement and the rising temperature outside Paarl, but there was still no sign of Mandela. One of our greatest concerns about his release was coming true: Winnie was late, very late. A number of hours late.[1]

What a troublemaker! This was not the first time, nor would it be the last.

When Madiba and Winnie eventually made their appearance,

about three hours late, he was visibly let down, stony-faced. There was no sign of the characteristic broad smile that became so well loved. His wife had spoiled the occasion he had looked forward to for almost a quarter of a century. She was elated and shoved a balled fist into the air.

The cameras showed a rather battered placard of two pieces of brown cardboard held up by someone in the crowd: 'AFRICA' read the one, and on the other: 'FREEDOM IN OUR LIFETIME'.

The cameras followed the cavalcade to Cape Town. Later it looked as if the car transporting the Mandelas had taken a wrong turn, going off in another direction.

My heart skipped a beat. What was happening? The arrangements and the logistics for the event were a joint operation of the police and security forces and the ANC. Did the driver not know the road to Cape Town? Where was he off to?

Eventually we saw the Mandelas arrive at the Grand Parade, in the midst of a multitude, all jostling one another, each trying to get as close as possible to the black messiah who had descended. When Mandela eventually appeared on the city hall balcony, he seemed overwhelmed, even bewildered; he was probably still unsettled by Winnie's late arrival because he was never late.

When he had to deliver his speech, his glasses were nowhere to be found. Winnie came to the rescue with hers. The dignified Mandela looked comical peering out from behind the enormous frames, while Cyril Ramaphosa clung like a leech to the microphone and repeatedly appeared on the TV screen from every angle.

Mandela launched dramatically into a roll of honour of those to whom he wanted to pay homage. Then he changed to inflammatory rhetoric: 'Our struggle has reached a decisive moment. We call on our people to seize this moment so that the process towards democracy is rapid and uninterrupted. We have waited too long for our freedom. We can no longer wait. Now is the time to intensify the struggle on all fronts. [. . .] It is only through disciplined mass action that our victory can be assured.[2]

Conflicting emotions washed over me as I took in the moment. I felt contentment about our secret revolution – that we had helped to place the peaceful negotiation process on a secure footing thanks to the secret talks. I also felt embarrassment and disappointment that this unique, historic occasion of worldwide import had not unfolded smoothly and punctually. And I felt a large measure of gratitude that things had indeed gone very differently from how some of the 'hawks' in the security forces had hoped they would.

A report that they had drawn up in the secretariat of the State Security Council on Mandela's release came to my mind. Various options were outlined in the report.

One recommendation stated, among other things, that Mandela be released 'outside the Southern African region' and that, when released, he should be in 'relatively weak physical health so that he could not serve as leader for long'. A 'well-planned proactive psychological action programme should be conducted prior to, during and after the release'.[3] Whatever that meant.

What utter insanity!

Other bizarre ideas were put forward when the talks with Mandela became known. For example, there was a remark with sinister purport: 'You spent so much time together and surely drank coffee with him. Why then did it not occur to you to poison him?'

Others were of the opinion that I was a pathetic negotiator. Why, they asked, had I not been able to twist Mandela's arm until he supported apartheid? Why had we not threatened him with life imprisonment unless he renounce violence?

These questions clearly came from people who knew nothing about negotiation or how people's hearts and minds worked.

It was never our goal to force Mandela to make radical changes to what he believed and stood for. Not only would such attempts have been fruitless, but they would also have alienated him from his power base. And what purpose was there in reaching an understanding with someone who has little influence and no bearing on the essence of the political question at hand? All attempts to undermine his power and divide-and-rule plans would have the same end result. It would have been futile and very foolish to repeat the process used to create political puppets in the homelands.

The core objective of the secret talks was to gain reliable information about aspects of the political crisis in which the country was embroiled, as well as to show the other party in a credible manner that we were serious, trustworthy and reliable in our search for an understanding.

Another advantage of the discussions was that they prepared both Mandela and the ANC for the responsible and stabilising role they had to play. While in jail Mandela could not play such a role, but once released he could certainly do so.

The counter-question is: Suppose we had, one day, out of the blue, released him into a political vacuum – the ideal climate for attempting a radical and revolutionary takeover of the government by force. The SADF would undoubtedly have stepped in; full-scale civil war would have been our fate.

In my copy of his autobiography, Mandela wrote the following inscription: 'To my friend Dr Neil [*sic*] Barnard, Best wishes to one of those patriotic South Africans who strived tirelessly & without publicity to help lay the foundations of the new South Africa.'

I appreciated this a great deal, not only because it came from such an exceptional man but also because he recognised the qualities to which I aspire. It makes *Long Walk to Freedom* one of the most valuable and treasured books in my collection.

Thanks to NIS's excellent information on the liberation movements I knew from the outset that Mandela was, as the philosophers would put it, the Archimedean fulcrum of black people's struggle for freedom in South Africa.

I knew he would be a man of gravitas: no longer the young firebrand who wanted to take on the world and impress everyone, but someone in whom wisdom and insight, like good red wine, have matured. This is indeed how I experienced him.

He knew precisely what he wanted: political freedom for South Africa, built on democratic principles. His ultimate ideal was clear and logical, and he did not at any stage deviate from this leitmotif.

An initial hindrance was his adherence to bygone revolutionary figments of the imagination, and sometimes a stubborn refusal to accept the reality when it clashed with his own views. But is that not true of all of us?

That 'reality' was often put aside in debates does not, however, mean that it was not accepted in private. His later actions frequently showed that he had indeed come to accept certain realities – without necessarily admitting this to his opponents. Leaders must, after all, never be seen – in the eyes of their supporters – to have yielded to an opponent.

For me, the overwhelming truth of Mandela as a person was the easy grace with which he handled power. This is a gift given to few people – let alone world icons. Every day we see how people struggle to exercise power with restraint, be it political power, financial power, intellectual power or the power of beauty, popularity or pedigree.

This is Nelson Mandela's most valuable legacy to humanity: that he showed us how to handle our power with grace and modesty – however limited it may be.

For his entire life he was averse to arrogance and snobbishness, yet he was visibly proud of who he was. Because he remained a modest person despite his remarkable qualities, everyone could easily associate with him, even idolise him. But I am sure that from where he now tranquilly observes us, he would never want us to deify him.

He was a fallible person, but one of the very greatest in modern history.

I am immensely grateful to the Heavenly Father that I had the unique privilege, together with Mandela, of preparing the way for a political settlement in our fatherland, for which both he and I, two patriots, had endless love.

LONG WALK TO FREEDOM

THE AUTOBIOGRAPHY OF
NELSON MANDELA

To my friend Dr Neil Barnard,
Best wishes to one of those patriotic
South Africans who strived tirelessly
& without publicity to help lay
the foundations of the new South
Africa.
NMandela
4·2·98

LITTLE, BROWN AND COMPANY

NELSON MANDELA'S POLITICAL TESTIMONY, ADDRESSED TO PW BOTHA[1]

The deepening political crisis in our country has been a matter of grave concern to me for quite some time, and I now consider it necessary in the national interest, for the African National Congress and the Government to meet urgently to negotiate an effective political settlement.

At the outset I must point out that I make this move without consultation with the ANC. I am a loyal and disciplined member of the ANC. My political loyalty is owed primarily, if not exclusively, to this organisation and, in particular, to our Lusaka headquarters where the official leadership is stationed and from where our affairs are directed.

In the normal course of events, I would put my views to the organisation first, and if these views were accepted, the organisation would then decide on who were the best qualified members to handle the matter on its behalf and on exactly when to make the move. But in my current circumstances I cannot follow this course, and this is the only reason why I am acting on my own initiative in the hope that the organisation will, in due course, endorse my action.

I must stress that no prisoner, irrespective of his status or influence, can conduct negotiations of this nature from prison. In our special situation negotiation on political matters is literally a matter of life and death which requires to be handled by the organisation itself through its appointed representatives. The step I am taking should therefore not be seen as the beginning of actual negotiations between the Government and the ANC. My task is a very limited one, and that is to bring the country's two major political bodies to the negotiating table.

I must further point out that the question of my release from prison is not an issue, at least at this stage of the discussions and I am certainly not asking to be freed. But I do hope that the Government will as soon as possible, give me the opportunity from my present quarters to sound the views of my colleagues, inside and outside the country, on this move. Only if this initiative is formally endorsed by the ANC will it have any significance.

I will touch presently on some of the problems which seem to constitute an obstacle to a meeting between the ANC and the Government. But I must emphasize right at this stage that this step is not a response to the call by the Government on ANC leaders to declare whether or not they are nationalists, and to renounce the South African Communist Party before there can be negotiations. No self-respecting freedom fighter will take orders from the Government on how to wage the freedom struggle against that same Government, and on who his allies in the freedom struggle should be. To obey such instructions would be a violation of the long-standing and fruitful solidarity which distinguishes our liberation movement and a betrayal of those who have worked so closely and suffered so much with us for almost seventy years.

Far from responding to that call, my intervention is influenced by purely domestic issues, by the civil strife and ruin into which the country is now sliding. I am disturbed, as many other South Africans no doubt are by the spectre of a South Africa split into two hostile camps, blacks (the term 'blacks' is used in a broad sense to indicate all those who are not whites) on one side and whites on the other, slaughtering one another, by acute tensions which are building up dangerously in practically every sphere of our lives, a situation which, in turn, foreshadows more violent clashes in the days ahead. This is the crisis that has forced me to act.

I must add that the purpose of this discussion is not only to urge the Government to talk to the ANC, but it is also to acquaint you with the views current among blacks, especially those in the mass democratic movement. If I am unable to express these views frankly and freely, you will never know how the majority of South Africans think on the policy and actions of the Government; you will never know how to deal with their grievances and demands.

It is perhaps proper to remind you that the media here and abroad has given certain public figures in this country a rather negative image not only in regard to human rights questions, but also in respect of their prescriptive stance when dealing with black leaders generally. This impression is shared not only by the vast majority of blacks, but also by a substantial section of the whites. If I had allowed myself to be influenced by this impression, I would not even have thought of making this move. Nevertheless, I came here with an open mind, and the impression I will carry away from this meeting will be determined almost exclusively by the manner in which you respond to my proposal. It is in this spirit that I have undertaken this mission, and I sincerely hope that nothing will be done or said here which will force me to revise my views on this aspect.

Obstacles to Negotiation

I have already indicated that I propose to deal with some of the obstacles to a meeting between the Government and the ANC. The

Government gives several reasons why it will not negotiate with us. However, for purposes of this discussion, I will confine myself to only three main demands set by the Government as a precondition for negotiation, namely, that the ANC must first renounce violence, break with the SACP and abandon its demand for majority rule.

Renunciation of Violence

The position of the ANC on the question of violence is very simple. The organisation has no vested interest in violence. It abhors any action which may cause loss of life, destruction of property and misery to the people. It has worked long and patiently for a South Africa of common values, and for an undivided and peaceful non-racial state. But we consider the armed struggle a legitimate form of self-defence against a morally repugnant system of government, which will not allow even peaceful forms of protest.

It is more than ironical that it should be the Government which demands that we should renounce violence. The Government knows only too well that there is not a single political organisation in this country, inside and outside Parliament, which can even compare with the ANC in its total commitment to peaceful change.

Right from the early days of its history the organisation diligently sought peaceful solutions and, to that extent, it talked patiently to successive South African Governments, a policy we tried to follow in dealing with the present Government. Not only did the Government ignore our demands for a meeting, instead it took advantage of our commitment to a non-violent struggle, and unleashed the most violent form of racial oppression this country has ever seen. It stripped us of all basic human rights, outlawed our organisations and barred all channels of peaceful resistance. It met our just demands with force and, despite the grave problems facing the country, it continues to refuse to talk to us. There can only be one answer to this challenge: violent forms of struggle.

During the years oppressed people have fought for their birthright by peaceful means, where that was possible, and through force where peaceful channels were closed. The history of this country also confirms this vital lesson.

Africans as well as Afrikaners were, at one time or other, compelled to take up arms in defence of their freedom against British imperialism. The fact that both were finally defeated by superior arms and by the vast resources of that empire, does not negate this lesson.

But from what has happened in South Africa during the last 40 years, we must conclude that now that the roles are reversed, and the Afrikaner is no longer a freedom-fighter, but is in power, the entire lesson of history must be brushed aside. Not even a disciplined non-violent protest will now be tolerated. To the Government a black man has neither a cause to espouse nor freedom rights to defend. The whites must have the monopoly of political power, and of committing violence against innocent and defenceless people.

That situation was totally unacceptable to us and the formation of Umkhonto weSizwe was intended to end that monopoly, and to forcibly bring home to the Government that the oppressed people of this country were prepared to stand up and defend themselves.

It is significant to note that throughout the past four decades, and more especially over the last 26 years, the Government has met our demands with force only, and has done hardly anything to create a suitable climate for dialogue. On the contrary, the Government continues to govern with a heavy hand, and to incite whites against negotiation with the ANC. The publication of the booklet *Talking with the ANC ...* which completely distorts the history and policy of the ANC, the extremely offensive language used by Government spokesmen against freedom fighters, and the intimidation of whites who want to hear the views of the ANC at first hand, are all part of the Government's strategy to wreck meaningful dialogue.

It is perfectly clear on the facts that the refusal of the ANC to renounce violence is not the real problem facing the Government. The truth is that the Government is not yet ready for negotiation, and for the sharing of political power with blacks. It is still committed to white domination and, for that reason, it will only tolerate those blacks who are willing to serve on its apartheid structures. Its policy is to remove from the political scene blacks who refuse to conform, who reject white supremacy and its apartheid structures, and who insist on equal rights with whites.

This is the reason for the Government's refusal to talk to us, and for its demand that we disarm ourselves, while it continues to use violence against our people. This is the reason for its massive propaganda campaign to discredit the ANC, and present it to the public as a communist dominated organisation bent on murder and destruction. In this situation the reaction of the oppressed people is clearly predictable.

White South Africa must accept the plain fact that the ANC will not suspend, to say nothing of abandoning the armed struggle, until the Government shows its willingness to surrender the monopoly of political power, and to negotiate directly and in good faith with acknowledged black leaders. The renunciation of violence by either the Government or the ANC should not be a precondition to, but the result of negotiation.

Moreover, by ignoring credible black leaders, and imposing a succession of stillborn negotiation structures, the Government is not only squandering the country's precious resources, but it is in fact discrediting the negotiation process itself, and prolonging the civil strife.

The position of the ANC on the question of violence is, therefore, very clear. A Government which used violence against blacks many years before we took up arms, has no right whatsoever to call on us to lay down arms.

The South African Communist Party

I have already pointed out that no self-respecting freedom fighter will allow the Government to prescribe who his allies in the freedom struggle should be, and that to obey such instructions would be a betrayal of those who have suffered repression with us for so long. We equally reject the charge that the ANC is dominated by the SACP and we regard the accusation as part of the smearing campaign the Government is waging against us.

The accusation has, in effect, also been refuted by two totally independent sources. In January 1987 the American State Department published a report on the activities of the SACP in this country, which contrasts very sharply with the subjective picture the Government has tried to paint against us over the years. The essence of that report is that, although the influence of the SACP on the ANC is strong, it is unlikely that that Party will ever dominate the ANC.

The same point is made somewhat differently by Mr Ismail Omar, member of the President's Council, in his book *Reform in Crisis* published in 1988, in which he gives concrete examples of important issues of the day over which the ANC and the SACP have differed. He also points out that the ANC enjoys greater popular support than the SACP. He adds that despite the many years of combined struggle, the two remain distinct organisations with ideological and policy differences which preclude a merger of identity.

These observations go some way towards disproving the accusation. But since the allegation has become the focal point of Government propaganda against the ANC, I propose to use this opportunity to give you the correct information, in the hope that this will help you to see the matter in its proper perspective, and to evaluate your strategy afresh.

Cooperation between the ANC and SACP goes back to the early twenties and has always been, and still is, strictly limited to the struggle against racial oppression and for a just society. At no time has the organisation ever adopted or cooperated with communism itself.

Apart from the question of cooperation between the two organisations, members of the SACP have always been free to join the ANC. But once they do so, they become fully bound by the policy of the organisation set out in the Freedom Charter. As members of the ANC engaged in the anti-apartheid struggle, their Marxist ideology is not directly relevant. The SACP has throughout the years accepted the leading role of the ANC, a position which is respected by SACP members who join the ANC.

There is, of course, a firmly established tradition in the ANC in terms of which any attempt is resisted, from whatever quarter, which is intended to undermine cooperation between the two organisations. Even within the ranks of the ANC there have been, at one time or other, people – and some of them were highly respected and influential individuals – who were against this cooperation, and who wanted SACP members expelled from the organisation. Those who persisted in these activities were themselves ultimately expelled, or they broke away in despair.

In either case their departure ended their political careers, or they formed other political organisations which, in due course, crumbled into splinter groups. No dedicated ANC member will ever heed the call to break with the SACP. We regard such a demand as a purely divisive Government strategy. It is in fact a call on us to commit suicide. Which man of honour will ever desert a life-long friend at the insistence of a common opponent and still retain a measure of credibility among his people? Which opponent will ever trust such a treacherous freedom fighter? Yet this is what the Government is, in effect, asking us to do: To desert our faithful allies. We will not fall into that trap.

The Government also accuses us of being agents of the Soviet Union. The truth is that the ANC is non-aligned, and we welcome support from the East and the West, from the socialist and capitalist countries. The only difference, as we have explained on countless occasions before, is that the socialist countries supply us with weapons, which the West refuses to give us. We have no intention whatsoever of changing our stand on this question.

The Government's exaggerated hostility to the SACP, and its refusal to have any dealings with that party have a hollow ring. Such an attitude is not only out of step with the growing cooperation between the capitalist and socialist countries in different parts of the world, but it is also inconsistent with the policy of the Government itself when dealing with our neighbouring states.

Not only has South Africa concluded treaties with the Marxist states of Angola and Mozambique – quite rightly in our opinion – but she also wants to strengthen this with Marxist Zimbabwe. The Government will certainly find it difficult, if not altogether impossible, to reconcile its readiness to work with foreign Marxists for the peaceful resolution of mutual problems, with its uncompromising refusal to talk to South African Marxists.

The reason for this inconsistency is obvious. As I have already said, the Government is still too deeply committed to the principle of white domination and, despite lip-service to reform, it is deadly opposed to the sharing of political power with blacks, and the SACP is merely being used as a smokescreen to retain the monopoly of political power. The smearing campaign against the ANC also helps the Government to evade the real issue at stake, namely, the exclusion from political power of the black majority by a white minority, which is the source of all our troubles.

Concerning my own personal position, I have already informed you that I will not respond to the Government's demand that ANC members should state whether they are members of the SACP or not. But because much has been said by the media, as well as by Government leaders regarding my political beliefs, I propose to use this opportunity to put the record straight.

My political beliefs have been explained in the course of several political trials in which I was charged, in the policy documents of the ANC, and in my autobiography *The Struggle is My Life* which I wrote in prison in 1975. I stated in those trials and publications that I did not belong to any organisation apart from the ANC. In my address to the court which sentenced me to life imprisonment in June 1964 I said:

'Today I am attracted by the idea of a classless society, an attraction which springs in part from Marxist reading, and in part from my admiration of the structure and organisation of early African societies in this country. It is true, as I have already stated, that I have been influenced by Marxist thought. But this is also true of many of the leaders of the new independent states. Such widely different persons as Gandhi, Nehru, Nkrumah and Nasser all acknowledge this fact. We all accept the need for some form of socialism to enable our people to catch up with the advanced countries of the world, and to overcome their legacy of poverty.'

My views are still the same.

Equally important is the fact that many ANC leaders, who are labelled Communists by the Government, embrace nothing different from these beliefs. The term 'Communist' when used by the Government has a totally different meaning from the conventional one. Practically every freedom fighter who receives his military training or education in the socialist countries is to the Government a Communist. It would appear to be established Government policy that, as long as the National Party is in power in this country, there can be no black freedom struggle, and no black freedom fighter. Any black political organisation which, like us, fights for the liberation of its people through armed struggle, must invariably be dominated by the SACP.

This attitude is not only the result of Government propaganda, it is a logical consequence of white supremacy. After more than 300 years of racial indoctrination, the country's whites have developed such deep-seated contempt for blacks as to believe that we cannot think for ourselves, that we are incapable of fighting for political rights without incitement by some white agitator. In accusing the ANC of domination by the SACP, and in calling on ANC members to renounce the party, the Government is deliberately exploiting that contempt.

Majority Rule

The Government is equally vehement in condemning the principle of majority rule. The principle is rejected despite the fact that it is a pillar of democratic rule in many countries of the world. It is a principle which is fully accepted in the white politics of this country.

Only now that the stark reality has dawned that apartheid has failed, and that blacks will one day have an effective voice in Government, are we told by whites here, and by their Western friends that majority rule is a disaster to be avoided at all costs. Majority rule is acceptable to whites as long as it is considered within the context of white politics. If black political aspirations are to be accommodated, then some other formula must be found, provided that that formula does not raise blacks to a position of equality with whites.

Yet majority rule and internal peace are like the two sides of a single coin, and white South Africa simply has to accept that there will never be peace and stability in this country until the principle is fully applied. It is precisely because of its denial that the Government has become the enemy of practically every black man. It is that denial that has sparked off the current civil strife.

NEGOTIATED POLITICAL SETTLEMENT

By insisting on compliance with the abovementioned conditions before there can be talks, the Government clearly confirms that it wants no peace in this county but turmoil, no strong and independent ANC, but a weak and servile organisation playing a supportive role to white minority rule, not a non-aligned ANC but one which is a satellite of the West, and which is ready to serve the interests of capitalism. No worthy leaders of a freedom movement will ever submit to conditions which are essentially terms of surrender dictated by a victorious commander to a beaten enemy, and which are really intended to weaken the organisation and to humiliate its leadership.

The key to the whole situation is a negotiated settlement, and a meeting between the Government and the ANC will be the first major step towards lasting peace in the country, better relations with our neighbour states, admission to the Organisation of African Unity, re-admission to the United Nations and other world bodies, to international markets and improved international relations generally. An accord with the ANC, and the introduction of a non-racial society is the only way in which our rich and beautiful country will be saved from the stigma which repels the world.

Two central issues will have to be addressed at such a meeting; firstly, the demand for majority rule in a unitary state, secondly, the concern of white South Africa over this demand, as well as the insistence of whites on structural guarantees that majority rule will not mean domination of the white minority by blacks. The most crucial task which will face the Government and the ANC will be to reconcile these two positions. Such reconciliation will be achieved only if both parties are willing to compromise. The organisation will determine precisely how negotiations should be conducted. It may well be that this should be done at least in two stages. The first, where the organisation and the Government will work out together the preconditions for a proper climate for negotiations. Up to now both parties have simply been broadcasting their conditions for negotiation without putting them directly to each other. The second stage would be the actual negotiations themselves when the climate is ripe for doing so. Any other approach would entail the danger of an irresolvable stalemate.

Lastly, I must point out that the move I have taken provides you with the opportunity to overcome the current deadlock, and to normalise the country's political situation. I hope you will seize it without delay. I believe that the overwhelming majority of South Africans, black and white, hope to see the ANC and the Government working closely together to lay the foundations for a new era in our country, in which racial discrimination and prejudice, coercion and confrontation, death and destruction will be forgotten.

Nelson Mandela

ENDNOTES

CHAPTER 1

1. Louis le Grange was the Minister of Law and Order in PW Botha's Cabinet from 1982-1986.

CHAPTER 2

1. The Afrikaner Broederbond (AB) was a confidential political and cultural think tank for Afrikaner men. Membership was by invitation only. The AB was formed in 1918 to uplift Afrikaners economically and in other respects. It promoted the Afrikaans language and culture but was often criticised for creating jobs for pals.
2. The Ruiterwag was similar to the Afrikaner Broederbond but was aimed at Afrikaner men under the age of 35. It had branches across the country and a member of the Broederbond sat in on Ruiterwag meetings. I was a member of the Ruiterwag's executive with Dr Pieter Mulder, current leader of the Freedom Front Plus, and Roelf Meyer, later minister in the Cabinet of FW de Klerk.
3. *Rapport*, 18 November 1979; *Rand Daily Mail*, 15 November 1979. See also 'Nuwe Veiligheidshoof 'n puik akademikus', *Die Volksblad*, 14 November 1979.
4. *Beeld*, 4 June 1980.
5. *Financial Mail*, 6 June 1980.
6. She was the younger sister of Professor Gerhard Beukes, a well-known author and literary figure.
7. Under the commando system, white male citizens had to do national service for short periods over several years. It allowed young men to start their studies directly after school.
8. Barnard, LD. 1973. 'Moderne teoretiese benaderings van internasionale verhoudinge.' MA dissertation, University of the Orange Free State, Bloemfontein.
9. Barnard, LD. 1975. 'Die magsfaktor in internasionale verhoudinge.' PhD thesis, University of the Orange Free State, Bloemfontein.

CHAPTER 3

1. Literally, a hare.
2. The projects included bribery, the founding of *The Citizen* newspaper and a plan to buy the *Washington Star*. The scandal eventually claimed the scalps of Vorster, Mulder, Van den Bergh and Dr Eschel Rhoodie, the Secretary of Information. See also Rees, M & Day, C. 1980. *Muldergate*. Johannesburg: Macmillan and Rhoodie, E. 1983. *The Real Information Scandal*. Pretoria: Orbis.
3. The other members were Ministers PW Botha, Ben Schoeman, Hilgard Muller and SL Muller.
4. Government Notice 808 of 1969.
5. De Villiers, D & De Villiers, J. 1984. *PW*. Cape Town: Tafelberg, pp. 128-129.
6. It comprised bureaucratic heavyweights of the time Alec van Wyk and later Gert Rothmann of National Security, Generals Magnus Malan and later PW van der Westhuizen who represented the military, and Generals Mike Geldenhuys and Johann Coetzee of the police.
7. *Intellegere* 5. 1988. 'Geskiedkundige oorsig van die rasionalisering en koördinering van die Intelligensiegemeenskap gedurende die tydperk 1980 tot 1982'. (Historical overview of the rationalisation and co-ordination of the Intelligence community in the period 1980 to 1982) Pretoria, p. 12.

CHAPTER 4

1. *Intellegere 5*, pp. 13-14.
2. Crocker, CA. 1992. *High Noon in Southern Africa*. New York: WW Norton, p. 117.
3. Mr ID du Plessis represented the Department of Foreign Affairs.
4. See Jacobs, CJ. 2006. The forward defence strategy of the South African Defence Force, 1979-1989. *Joernaal vir Eietydse Geskiedenis* 31(3): 23-41. University of the Free State.
5. This should not be confused with so-called pre-emptive strikes in which the bases or hiding places of the liberation movements in neighbouring countries were attacked to avoid terrorist attacks in South Africa. I have always been a strong supporter of such preventive attacks if they are based on solid information and do not risk civilian lives.
6. *Intellegere 5*, pp. 16-18.
7. Letter by PW van der Westhuizen addressed to certain ministers and representatives of state departments who had reached the agreement on the division of functions at Simonstown, dated January 1981.

CHAPTER 5

1. Barnard, LD. 1983. Nasionale intelligensiewerk in internasionale verhoudinge. CR Swart lecture, no. 16/1983, presented on 2 September 1983 at the University of the Orange Free State, Bloemfontein.
2. Barnard, LD. 1990. Die intelligensiewerker. Lecture delivered on 22 August 1990 at a symposium at the National Intelligence Academy, Pretoria.
3. See, among others, Woodward, B. 2006. *State of Denial*. New York: Pocket Books.
4. For further information, see Chapter 7.
5. This included a psychological development centre where members and their families could be treated for stress and similar problems, and a service pastorate that attended to their spiritual wellbeing. Free medical services were introduced (and later curtailed); a crèche was opened; and sport and recreation also received attention, with new facilities being provided at Rietvlei.

CHAPTER 6

1. Numbers 13: 1-33.
2. Sun Tzu. 1971. *The Art of War*. Translated by Samuel B. Griffith. London: Oxford University Press.
3. Pullach is a symbol of the legendary German spymaster Reinhard Gehlen, who was active during the Second World War. For an insightful study on his life and modus operandi, see Gehlen, R. 1973. *Der Dienst: Erinnerungen 1942-1971*. Munich: Droemer. Recent research about the war on the German Eastern Front in Russia shows that Gehlen's information was often lacking.
4. I later wondered whether he had on purpose altered Shakespeare's 'All is not what it seems' in *As you like it*.
5. Teo, E. 1988. A Philosphy of Intelligence Work. *Intellegere* 9, Pretoria, p. 12.
6. Inscription on plaque given to the author by the Taiwanese government.
7. Barnard, LD. 1997. Presentation to the Truth and Reconciliation Commission, 14 July 1997.
8. Capture of Cuban 'Mata Hari' Led to Spy-Diplomats' Expulsion, 2012-10-09. https://cubaconfidential.wordpress.com/tag/jennifer-miles/. Accessed: 19 September 2014.
9. Casey was a prominent member. See Woodward, B. 1987. *Veil: The Secret Wars of the CIA, 1981-1987*. London: Headline, pp. 51-53, 61, 67, 80, 106 and

152-153. See also Waller, D. 2012. *Wild Bill Donovan*. New York: Free Press.

10. Weissman, SR. 2014. What really happened in Congo. *Foreign Affairs* 93(4): 14-24; also Devine, J. 2014. What really happened in Chile. *Foreign Affairs* 93(4): 26-35.

11. Tenet, G. 2007. *At the Center of the Storm: My Years at the CIA*. New York: Harper Collins, pp. 417-506.

12. Wolf, M. 1997. *Man without a Face*. New York: Public Affairs Books, pp. 311-313. See also Shubin, V. 2008. *ANC: A View from Moscow*. Johannesburg: Jacana.

13. Sun Tzu. *The Art of War*.

14. The author, Gert Rothmann and Mike Louw represented NIS. The Department of Foreign Affairs was represented by Les Manley and Dave Steward.

15. For further information, see Filatova, I & Davidson, A. 2013. *The Hidden Thread: Russia and South Africa in the Soviet Era*. Cape Town: Jonathan Ball, pp. 430-432.

16. Author's personal notes; minuted report no longer available.

17. The Anti-Apartheid Act of 1986 introduced wide-ranging sanctions and economic measures against South Africa. This Act resulted from a report from 1981 entitled 'The Report of the Study Commission on US Policy Toward Southern Africa', in *South Africa: Time Running Out*. Los Angeles: University of California Press, pp. 287-385. See also Papenfus, T. 2011. *Pik Botha en sy tyd*. Pretoria: Litera, pp. 363, 413.

18. *Die Burger*, 9 May 1988.

CHAPTER 7

1. Minister Chris Heunis signed the letter (dated 3 March 1989) as acting president in the absence of the president, PW Botha, who had suffered a stroke.

2. Letter from the president of South Africa, FW de Klerk, to the US president, George W Bush, dated 3 September 1990.

3. These were intelligence personnel, mostly spies, whose true identity and the nature of their work were not revealed to the host country.

4. In this context a debriefing is a comprehensive interview with someone under your control. It is a cordial interrogation during which the person is not threatened but realises all too well that he or she must provide the information the debriefer requires.

5. Additional information about this unmasking was provided by Mike Kennedy, at the time the deputy head of NIS's counter-espionage unit.

CHAPTER 8

1. In April 2014 Ball was awarded the Order of the Baobab (Silver) by President Jacob Zuma.

2. An important legislative restriction placed on NIS's work was that the service could not arrest or interrogate anyone.

3. From 'Die Namib-woestyn', translated into Afrikaans by Daniel Hugo, as featured in *Land van sonlig en van sterre*. Pretoria: Protea Boekhuis, 2004.

CHAPTER 9

1. His book *Serving Secretly: An Intelligence Chief on Record, Rhodesia into Zimbabwe 1964-1981* (published in 1987 by John Murray in London) provides an insightful view of intelligence activities in the former Rhodesia.

2. Wren, CS. 1990. Pretoria Journal; A Spy's Sorry Story: Espionage Wasn't Her Forte. *The New York Times*, 20 November 1990. http://www.nytimes.com/1990/11/20/world/pretoria-journal-a-spy-s-sorry-story-espionage-wasn-t-her-forte.html. Accessed: 10 September 2014. See also

Stiff, P. 2001. *Warfare by Other Means.* Alberton: Galago, pp. 351, 365.

3. Suleiman became head of Egypt's intelligence service in 1993 before being appointed as deputy president by President Hosni Mubarak in January 2011, a post he held for only two weeks until the outbreak of armed revolution in Egypt. This was part of the so-called Arab Spring, which began in Tunisia in December 2010.

4. Gevisser, M. 2007. *Thabo Mbeki: the Dream Deferred.* Johannesburg: Jonathan Ball, p. 370 ff.

5. Malan, M. 2006. *My lewe saam met die SA Weermag.* Pretoria: Protea Boekhuis.

6. Ellis, S. 2012. *External Mission: The ANC in Exile.* Johannesburg: Jonathan Ball, p. 230. See also Sisulu, E. 2002. *In Our Lifetime.* Claremont: David Philip, pp. 305-397.

CHAPTER 10

1. Barnard, LD. 1979. Staatkundige roeping. *Handhaaf.* September.

2. Beaufre, A. 1974. *Strategy for Tomorrow.* New York: Crane, Russak & Company; Aron, R. 1965. *The Century of Total War.* Boston: The Beacon Press; Alden, C. 1996. *Apartheid's Last Stand.* London: Macmillan Press, pp. 30-50.

3. *Intellegere* 6. 1988. Die kommissie van ondersoek na aangeleenthede betreffende die veiligheid van die staat. (The commission of enquiry into matters concerning the safety of the state). Pretoria.

4. Ellis, S. 2012. *External Mission: The ANC in Exile.* Johannesburg: Jonathan Ball, pp. 180-181.

5. Barnard, LD. 1997. Submission to the Truth and Reconciliation Commission, 14 July 1997.

6. In the late 1980s Heunis was entrusted with the key portfolio of constitutional development, in which he did excellent work. Nevertheless, the president did not include him in the secret talks with Mandela and the ANC, although he and Heunis were also personal friends. Botha probably felt – correctly, in my view – that Heunis's personality and style of communication were unsuitable for this particular task. (See also Ries, A & Dommisse, E. 1990. *Leierstryd.* Cape Town: Tafelberg, pp. 112-113.)

7. Malan, M. 2006. *My lewe saam met die SA Weermag.* Pretoria: Protea Boekhuis, pp. 207-211. See also Stiff, P. 2001. *Warfare by Other Means.* Alberton: Galago, pp. 75-91.

8. Malan, M. 2006. *My lewe saam met die SA Weermag,* pp. 212-215.

9. The journalist Brian Pottinger, who was critical of the NP government, admitted: 'South Africa, apart from the appallingly high routine levels of criminal violence […] enjoyed a certain visible tranquillity by the close of (PW) Botha's decade.' Pottinger, B. 1988. *The Imperial Presidency.* Johannesburg: Southern Book Publishers, p. 348.

10. Barnard, LD. 1997. Submission to the Truth and Reconciliation Commission, 14 July 1997.

11. The TRC found that while there was little evidence that a centrally controlled, cohesive and officially constituted 'third force' existed, there was indeed a network of security operators who at times took action with the collusion and/or knowledge of senior members of the security forces. http://www.justice.gov.za/trc/report/. Accessed: 22 October 2014.

12. This and other related questions from the period after 1990 are discussed in more detail in a forthcoming book.

CHAPTER 11

1. Fragment from *Die dieper reg.* Brink, AP.

2008. *Groot verseboek, deel 1.* Cape Town: Tafelberg, p. 135.

2. For an excellent exposition of the ANC's armed struggle, see Jeffery, A. 2009. *People's War: New Light on the Struggle for South Africa.* Johannesburg: Jonathan Ball.

3. Van der Merwe, J. 2010. *Trou tot die dood toe.* Dainfern: Praag, p. 402.

4. Giliomee, H. 2004. *Die Afrikaners: 'n biografie.* Cape Town: Tafelberg, pp. 561-566. See also the English version of this book published in 2003 as *The Afrikaners: Biography of a People* (Cape Town: Tafelberg).

5. The countrywide state of emergency was in force for four years and was only lifted on 7 June 1990, once the transformation process was underway.

6. Papenfus. *Pik Botha en sy tyd*, pp. 367-379.

7. Ries & Dommisse. *Leierstryd*, pp. 264-269.

8. See the exposition in Nye Jr, JS. 2004. *Soft Power.* New York: Public Affairs Books.

9. From Reflections on American Diplomacy. *Foreign Affairs*, October 1956, p. 43.

CHAPTER 12

1. NIS's code name for this project was 'Sagmoedige Neelsie' (Gentle Neelsie).

2. Mandela, N. 1994. *Long Walk to Freedom.* Johannesburg: Macdonald Purnell, p. 512.

3. Mandela was the 466th prisoner to arrive at Robben Island in 1964. The prison authorities used these two facts to compile a prisoner's unique number. Prisoners who had to serve more than two years' incarceration were also given a so-called board number (a reference to the Prison Board where long-term prisoners were registered).

Mandela's board number was 913. His prison number, 46664, enjoyed official priority. (Telephonic communication, General Willie Willemse, former Commissioner of Correctional Services, 12 September 2014.)

CHAPTER 13

1. Mandela, N. 2004. *Long Walk to Freedom*, pp. 510 and 511.

2. When the ANC's military wing Umkhonto weSizwe (MK) was founded in 1961, Mandela became its first commander.

3. Mandela, N. *Long Walk to Freedom*, pp. 510-511.

4. Mandela, N. *Long Walk to Freedom*, p. 578.

5. Secret report by a deep-cover NIS source.

6. Transcript of discussions.

7. Transcript of discussions.

8. See also Van Zyl Slabbert, F. 2006. *Duskant die geskiedenis.* Cape Town: Tafelberg and Jonathan Ball, pp. 156-157.

9. This was later revealed in books by Stephen Ellis (*External Mission*, Johannesburg, Jonathan Ball, 2012) and Paul Trewhela (*Inside Quatro*, Sunnyside, Jacana, 2010).

10. In September 1991 the ANC appointed the Skweyiya Commission of Inquiry with a limited scope to investigate torture and executions, mostly in Quatro. It published its report a year later. Early in 1993 then ANC president Nelson Mandela appointed the Motsuenyane Commission, which had a broader scope and powers. Its report was published in 1993.

11. Transcript of discussions.

12. Transcript of discussions.

13. Transcript of discussions.

14. Transcript of discussions.

CHAPTER 14

1. Telephonic interview with General Willie Willemse, former Commissioner of Correctional Services, 12 September 2014.
2. Mandela, N. *Long Walk*, p. 532.
3. Mandela, N. *Long Walk*, p. 520.
4. Brand, C & Jones, B. 2014. *Doing Life with Mandela*. Johannesburg: Jonathan Ball, pp. 193, 203, 204.
5. Sisulu, E. 2003. *Walter & Albertina Sisulu: In Our Lifetime*. Claremont: David Philip, p. 403.
6. Transcript of discussions.
7. www.sahistory.org.za. Accessed: 11 September 2014.
8. Transcript of discussions.
9. Transcript of discussions.
10. Needless to say, NIS also read Buthelezi's letters to Mandela.
11. Nelson Mandela to Mangosuthu Buthelezi, undated letter.

CHAPTER 15

1. Eight sets of talks were held in different parts of the world about Cuba's involvement in the conflict in Angola and about South West Africa in 1988 alone. In that year I was at home for a total of 56 days.
2. According to the American journalist Patti Waldmeir it can be compared to the peace process in Northern Ireland and the Middle East (*Anatomy of a Miracle: The End of Apartheid and the Birth of the New South Africa*, 1997, New York: WW Norton, p. 95). See also Theresa Papenfus's *Pik Botha en sy tyd* for an exposition of Botha's peace initiatives over two decades.
3. 'Mandela thanks Thatcher', *The Guardian*, 10 April 1989; 'The Mandela letter', *The Weekly Mail*, 14-20 April 1989.
4. Nelson Mandela to Sir Robin Renwick, 10 April 1989.

5. Letter to President PW Botha by Governor Michael Dukakis, 15 August 1988.
6. Letter to Governor Michael Dukakis by President PW Botha, 30 August 1988.
7. Savage, M. 2014. *Trekking Outward: A Chronology of Meetings between South Africans and the ANC in Exile, 1983-2000*. Department of Sociology, University of Cape Town. In many of the groups there was more than one source.
8. Due to Minister Chris Heunis's impatience with what he viewed as the lack of progress in talks with the ANC, he allowed two of his officials to make contact with the ANC with a view to setting up a met. However, it would not have made sense for the government to talk to the ANC from two sides. After Heunis and I had met, the two officials' security clearance was revoked so that they could not travel to Lusaka. This caused quite an uproar; for many years afterwards, they continued to launch attacks on NIS.
9. Reflections by Mike Louw, once in the author's possession but no longer available.
10. Transcript of discussions.

CHAPTER 16

1. Report by a deep-cover NIS source.
2. 'Report on Recent Plenary Session of the Central Committee of the SACP', January 1986.
3. See Kathrada, A. A self-effacing hero. In Asmal, K, Chidester, D & Wilmot, J. 2003. *Nelson Mandela: From Freedom to the Future*. Johannesburg: Jonathan Ball, pp. 444-446.
4. Transcript of discussions.
5. Scholtz, L & Scholtz, I. 2014. Nelson Mandela se houding teenoor die kommunisme. *Historia* 59(2): pp. 79-93.
6. Transcript of discussions.
7. Transcript of discussions.

CHAPTER 17

1. Prinsloo, D. 1997. *Stem uit die Wilderness: 'n biografie oor oud-pres. PW Botha*. Mossel Bay: Vaandel, pp. 362, 365-367.
2. Ries, A & Dommisse, E. *Leierstryd*, p. 79.
3. In August that year the president of the ANC, Oliver Tambo, also suffered a stroke. His health improved sufficiently for him to continue his work and in December 1990, after 30 years in exile, he returned to South Africa. The following year Nelson Mandela succeeded him as president of the ANC. Tambo died on 24 April 1993 in Johannesburg after another stroke.

CHAPTER 18

1. Transcript of discussions; recording no longer available.
2. Transcript of discussions.
3. Geldenhuys, J. 2007. *Dié wat gewen het*. Pretoria: Litera Publikasies, pp. 212-219. See also Malan, M. 2006. *My lewe saam met die SA Weermag*. Pretoria: Protea Boekhuis, pp. 302-306.
4. Transcript of discussions; recording no longer available.
5. Transcript of discussions.
6. In 1985 Mbeki became the ANC's Director of Information and Publicity and by 1989 he was head of the party's Department of Foreign Affairs.
7. Transcript of discussions.
8. Transcript of discussions.
9. Esterhuyse, W. 2012. *Eindstryd*. Cape Town: Tafelberg, pp. 195-202.
10. Resolution of the State Security Council, 5 July 1988.
11. Resolution of the State Security Council, 15 August 1989.
12. Spaarwater, M. 2012. *A Spook's Progress*. Cape Town: Zebra Press, pp. 176-179

CHAPTER 19

1. As the talks between the government team and Mandela progressed, the two of us met more frequently. Towards the end there were more one-on-one meetings than team discussions.
2. Gilbey, E. 1994. *The Lady: The Life and Times of Winnie Mandela*. London: Vintage, p. 145.
3. Transcript of discussions; recording no longer available.
4. Transcript of discussions.
5. Transcript of discussions.
6. Intercepted note of Winnie Mandela to Nelson Mandela; author's personal documentation.
7. The attorney Ismail Ayob, who visited Mandela on 9 October 1989.
8. While Mandela was in prison, Winnie had an affair with an attorney 27 years her junior. Details about the affair were made public in September 1992 when excerpts from a letter Winnie had written to her lover were published in the *Sunday Times*. During their divorce proceedings Mandela testified that after his release from prison his wife never entered his bedroom once while he was awake. In his words, he was 'the loneliest man on earth'. In March 1996 their marriage of 38 years was officially annulled. See http://www.independent.co.uk/voices/comment/like-many-others-i-have-appropriated-mandela-as-my-own-8987147.html.

CHAPTER 20

1. Mandela, N. *Long Walk*, p. 535.
2. Untitled document from the government team to Nelson Mandela, dated 3 August 1989.
3. Funnily enough, during this discussion Mbeki called Mandela 'Uncle Nelson' and, on occasion, even 'Oom Nel'.
4. Prinsloo, D. *Stem uit die Wilderness*, p.

285. See also O'Malley, P. 2007. *Shades of Difference*. Johannesburg: Penguin, p. 302.

CHAPTER 21

1. Mandela was one of 156 people who were charged with high treason and plotting to overthrow the government in December 1956. After a trial of more than four years, none of the accused were found guilty.
2. Mandela spent about five months of this time elsewhere in Africa, visiting twelve countries in an effort to garner support for Umkhonto weSizwe (MK), of which he was the first commander in chief. In Morocco and Ethiopia he received training in guerrilla warfare. His ability to evade the South African Police earned him the nickname 'Black Pimpernel'. He was eventually arrested near Howick on 5 August 1962.
3. Mandela, N. *Long Walk to Freedom,* p. 539.
4. The photo first appeared in *Die Volksblad* of 15 February 1990, shortly after Mandela's release. Botha, who had written political reports for the newspaper as a correspondent in 1935/36, gave this provincial newspaper a world scoop.
5. A Cabinet member who was present informed me about this telephonically the following day.
6. This was another example of Louw's resourcefulness and his way with words. With this formulation he cleverly by-passed the impasse about renouncing violence, stating that both leaders had committed themselves to finding a way to peace.
7. *Business Day*, 14 July 1989.
8. Transcript of discussions.
9. Transcript of discussions.
10. Reports received from deep-cover sources in London.
11. This referred specifically to the State Security Council.
12. This topic will be discussed in greater detail in a forthcoming book.

CHAPTER 22

1. Prinsloo, D. *Stem uit die Wilderness*, pp. 339, 425.
2. Botha established this committee, chaired by Minister Heunis, to look into how black political aspirations could be channelled (Prinsloo, p. 208).
3. Prinsloo, D. *Stem uit die Wilderness*, p. 338. It is unclear exactly what Heunis meant by 'this position', but there is no doubt about what he was saying between the lines!
4. Heunis, J. *Die binnekring*, pp. 122-124.
5. De Klerk, FW. 1998. *Die laaste trek – 'n nuwe begin*. Cape Town: Human & Rousseau, p. 164.

CHAPTER 23

1. Prinsloo, D. *Stem uit die Wilderness*, pp. 426, 430.
2. Potgieter, D. 2007. *Totale Aanslag: Apartheid se vuil truuks onthul*. Cape Town: Zebra Press, pp. 145-157.
3. The historian Hermann Giliomee suggests that it was 'perhaps wise' to have destroyed the tape, considering how Botha had used a recording of the confidential conversation between him and the former leader of the opposition, Dr Frederik Van Zyl Slabbert (*Die Laaste Afrikanerleiers*, p. 289).
4. A few weeks later I received a letter from Alex van Breda, NP politician and chief whip of the NP caucus, in which he wrote (translated): 'This is no longer the PW Botha whom we knew and respected … I am extremely saddened about the way Mr Botha treated you … Thank you for remaining respectful and polite in those

humiliating circumstances ...' (A van Breda to LD Barnard, 5 December 1991).

5. 'Bande: PW bars los', *Rapport*, 24 November 1991; 'Now PW demands inquiry into fate of that tape of Mandela', *Sunday Times*, 24 November 1991; 'More *krokodil* tears from PW', *Sowetan*, 25 November 1991.

6. 'PW/Mandela-band was só irrelevant ...', *Beeld*, 19 November 1991; 'Why NIS destroyed tape', *Business Day*, 19 November 1991.

7. Prinsloo, D. *Stem uit die Wilderness*, p. 434.

CHAPTER 24

1. Report by a deep-cover NIS source.
2. Ahmed Kathrada, Raymond Mhlaba, Andrew Mlangeni, Elias Motsoaledi, Wilton Mkwayi, Oscar Mpetha and Jeff Masemola.
3. Transcript of conversation; recording no longer available.
4. Debates of Parliament, Second Session, Ninth Parliament: 2 February to 22 June 1990; col. 1-18. See http://www.fwdeklerk.org/index.php/en/home-eng/2-english/general/85-his-

torically-significant-speech for the full speech.

CHAPTER 25

1. Years later, it came to light that Winnie had refused to fly from Johannesburg to Cape Town in the same chartered aeroplane as Murphy Morobe. Morobe was the publicity secretary of the Mass Democratic Movement (MDM) and it had earlier been his task to distance the MDM from Winnie and her controversial 'soccer club'. A second plane had to be chartered for Winnie – which took four hours to fly to the Cape. (Green, P. 'Waiting for Mandela'. *Mail & Guardian*. 12 February 2010. Accessed: 24 September 2014.)
2. Mandela, N. *Long Walk*, p. 510.
3. Report of the secretariat of the State Security Council.

APPENDIX

1. Dated March 1989. A copy of this document is in the possession of the author.

INDEX